THE HOBBIT
AND
PHILOSOPHY

The Blackwell Philosophy and Pop Culture Series

Series Editor: William Irwin

THE HOBBIT
AND
PHILOSOPHY

FOR WHEN YOU'VE LOST YOUR DWARVES, YOUR WIZARD, AND YOUR WAY

Edited by Gregory Bassham
and Eric Bronson

WILEY

John Wiley & Sons, Inc.

Library of Congress Cataloging-in-Publication Data:

> *The Hobbit* and philosophy : for when you've lost your dwarves, your wizard, and your way / edited by Gregory Bassham and Eric Bronson.
>> pages cm.—(The Blackwell philosophy and pop culture series)
>> Includes bibliographical references and index.
>> ISBN 978-0-470-40514-7 (pbk.); ISBN 978-1-118-22019-1 (ebk);
>> ISBN 978-1-118-23389-4 (ebk); ISBN 978-1-118-25855-2 (ebk)
>> 1. Tolkien, J. R. R. (John Ronald Reuel), 1892-1973. Hobbit. 2. Tolkien, J. R. R. (John Ronald Reuel), 1892-1973—Philosophy. 3. Fantasy fiction, English—History and criticism. 4. Middle Earth (Imaginary place) 5. Philosophy in literature. I. Bassham, Gregory, 1959- editor of compilation. II. Bronson, Eric, 1971- editor of compilation.
> PR6039.O32H6365 2012
> 823'.912—dc23

2012007299

For our halflings, Dylan, Asher, and Max

A vanimar, nai tielyar nauvar laiquë arë laurië

CONTENTS

ACKNOWLEDGMENTS

Thag You Very Buch

In putting together this book, we have been blessed by good luck far exceeding the usual allowance. Our warm appreciation to our long-suffering contributors for their patience in bearing with two grim-voiced and grim-faced editors; to Connie Santisteban, Hope Breeman, and the other good folks at Wiley who shepherded the book to publication; and to copyeditor Judith Antonelli for covering our tracks through the deep, dark forest. As with most of our previous collaborations, this fellowship began with a beer- and pipeweed-fueled council with series editor, Bill Irwin. We are especially grateful to Bill for encouraging our adventure in coediting not one, but two, popular culture books on Tolkien and philosophy. Two large flagons of thanks go out to Madeline and Lyndsey Karp and Greg's students in his Faith, Fantasy, and Philosophy course at King's College.

But our greatest debt is to our fairy wives, Aryn and Mia, and to our own hobbits—Dylan, Asher, and Max, to whom this book is dedicated. There are few earthly joys that can match reading Tolkien's tales of Middle-earth to one's children and seeing that spark kindle from mind to mind, like the beacons of Gondor.

INTRODUCTION

Never Laugh at Live Philosophers

Gregory Bassham and Eric Bronson

In a hole in the ground there lived a man who passed a quiet, uneventful life in a community that greatly prized convention and respectability. One day, however, he left his hole and journeyed off into the Blue. His adventure, though frightening and at times painful, changed him forever. His eyes were opened, and he matured in mind and character. When he returned to his hole, his neighbors regarded him as "cracked" because they couldn't accept that there is more to life than order and predictable routine. Although he lost his reputation, he never regretted going on the adventure that enabled him to discover his true self and to experience an exciting new world.

If this sounds familiar, it should. It's Plato's (ca. 428–348 BCE) "The Allegory of the Cave," possibly the most famous there-and-back-again story ever told. Plato's tale isn't about hobbits or wizards, of course. It's a parable about a man,

1

shackled since birth in an underground prison, who ventures forth and discovers that the world is far larger, richer, and more beautiful than he had imagined. Plato hoped that the readers would learn a few lessons from the allegory, such as these: Be adventurous. Get out of your comfort zone. Admit your limitations and be open to new ideas and higher truths. Only by confronting challenges and taking risks can we grow and discover what we are capable of becoming. These lessons are essentially the same ones that J. R. R. Tolkien teaches in *The Hobbit*.

The Hobbit, one of the best-loved children's books of all time and the enchanting prequel to *The Lord of the Rings*, raises a host of deep questions to ponder. Are adventures simply "nasty, disturbing, uncomfortable things" that "make you late for dinner," or can they be exciting and potentially life changing? Should food and cheer and song be valued above hoarded gold? Was life better in preindustrial times when there was "less noise and more green"? Can we trust people "as kind as summer" to use powerful technologies responsibly, or should these technologies be carefully regulated or destroyed, lest they fall into the hands of the goblins and servants of the Necromancer?

What duties do friends have to one another? Should mercy be extended even to those who deserve to die? Was the Arkenstone really Bilbo's to give? How should Smaug's treasure have been distributed? Did Thorin leave his "beautiful golden harp" at Bag-End when he headed out into the Wild? If so, how much could we get for that on eBay? From the happy halls of Elrond's Last Homely House to Gollum's "slimy island of rock," great philosophical questions are posed for old fans and new readers.

Tolkien—all praise to his wine and ale!—was an Oxford professor of medieval English, not a professional philosopher. But as recent books such as Peter Kreeft's *The Philosophy of Tolkien*, Patrick Curry's *Defending Middle-Earth*, and our own The Lord of the Rings *and Philosophy* make clear, Tolkien was a profoundly learned scholar who reflected deeply on the big questions. The story goes that while laboriously grading exams one fine summer day, the Oxford professor came across a blank piece of paper. After losing himself in thought for some time, Tolkien allegedly picked up his pen and wrote his famous opening, "In a hole in the ground there lived a hobbit."

Peter Jackson—may the hair on his toes never fall out!—returns to the director's chair for *The Hobbit* (2012), after taking home an Academy Award for his stellar direction of the three *Lord of the Rings* films (2001–2003). Hobbits may be small, but Jackson and New Line Cinema are going big, stretching the story into two movies, bringing back much of the cast from *The Lord of the Rings* films, and filming in 3D. After a dark and conflict-filled decade, fans of Middle-earth can finally watch Jackson's latest installment of the greatest fantasy epic of our time.

In this book, our merry band of philosophers shares Tolkien's enthusiasm for philosophical questions of "immense antiquity," but we also keep our "detachable party hoods" close at hand. Above all, this is a book written *for* Tolkien fans *by* Tolkien fans. Like other volumes in the Blackwell Philosophy and Pop Culture Series, it seeks to use popular culture as a hook to teach and popularize the ideas of the great thinkers.

Some of the chapters explore the philosophy of *The Hobbit*—the key values and big-picture assumptions that provide the moral and conceptual backdrop of the story—and others use themes from the book to illustrate various philosophical ideas. In this way, we hope to both explore some of the deeper questions in *The Hobbit* and also teach some powerful philosophical ideas.

Much like hobbits, our authors "have a fund of wisdom and wise sayings that men have mostly never heard of or forgotten long ago." So pack your pipe with your best Old Toby and bring out that special bottle of Old Winyards you've been saving. It's going to be quite an adventure.

PART ONE

DISCOVER YOUR INNER TOOK

THE ADVENTUROUS HOBBIT

Gregory Bassham

The gem cannot be polished without friction, nor
man perfected without trials.

—Confucius

The Hobbit is a tale of adventure. It is also a story of personal
growth. At the beginning of the tale, Bilbo is a conventional,
unadventurous, comfort-loving hobbit. As the story pro-
gresses, he grows in courage, wisdom, and self-confidence. *The
Hobbit* is similar in this respect to *The Lord of the Rings*. Both
are tales, J. R. R. Tolkien informs us, of the ennoblement of
the humble.[1] Both are stories of ordinary persons—small in the
eyes of the "wise" and powerful—who accomplish great things
and achieve heroic stature by accepting challenges, enduring
hardships, and drawing on unsuspected strengths of character
and will.

What's the connection between an adventurous spirit and personal growth? How can challenge and risk—a willingness to leave our own safe and comfy hobbit-holes—make us stronger, happier, and more confident individuals? Let's see what Bilbo and the great thinkers can teach us about growth and human potential.

A Hobbit's Progress

Hobbits in general are not an adventurous folk—quite the opposite. Hobbits "love peace and quiet and good tilled earth"; have never been warlike or fought among themselves; take great delight in the simple pleasures of eating, drinking, smoking, and partying; rarely travel; and consider "queer" any hobbit who has adventures or does anything out of the ordinary.[2]

Bilbo is an unusual hobbit in this regard. His mother, the famous Belladonna Took, belonged to a clan, the Tooks, who were not only rich but also notorious for their love of adventure. One of Bilbo's uncles, Isengar, was rumored to have "gone to sea" in his youth, and another uncle, Hildifons, "went off on a journey and never returned."[3] Bilbo's remote ancestor, Bandobras "Bullroarer" Took, was famous in hobbit lore for knocking a goblin king's head off with a club. The head rolled down a rabbit hole, and thus Bullroarer simultaneously won the Battle of Green Fields and invented the game of golf.[4]

In contrast, the Bagginses, Bilbo's father's side of the family, were thoroughly respectable hobbits who never did anything unexpected or adventurous. The conflict between these two parts of Bilbo's makeup is frequently played out in *The Hobbit*.

Gandalf noticed Bilbo's adventurous Tookish side when he visited the Shire in 2941, twenty years before the events described in *The Hobbit*. The young Bilbo impressed Gandalf with his "eagerness and his bright eyes, and his love of tales, and his questions about the wide world."[5] When Gandalf returned to the Shire two decades later, he found that Bilbo "was getting rather greedy and fat," but he was pleased to hear that Bilbo was still regarded as "queer" for doing odd things like going off for days by himself and talking with dwarves.[6] When Bilbo says good morning to Gandalf and dismisses adventures as "nasty disturbing uncomfortable things" that "make you late for dinner," Gandalf realizes that the Baggins side of Bilbo's personality is winning out.[7]

Bilbo's inner Took is rekindled, however, by the dwarves' treasure song and Gloin's slighting reference to him as "that little fellow bobbing and puffing on the mat."[8] Bilbo reluctantly agrees to join the dwarves' quest and finds himself in an adventure that proves to also be a quest for his own true self. Quite early in his perilous journey, Bilbo realizes that "adventures are not all pony-rides in May-sunshine."[9] He is constantly fearful and dependent and often thinks regretfully of his cozy hobbit-hole with the kettle just beginning to sing.

On several occasions he is saved by sheer luck. Gradually, however, his confidence and courage grow. Alone and unaided, he is able to outwit Gollum, escape from the goblins' cave, and free his companions from both the Mirkwood spiders and the Elvenking's fortress. When the Company arrives at the Lonely Mountain, it is Bilbo who discovers how to open the secret door, and only he has the courage to walk down the dark tunnel to face the terror of the dragon. "Already," we are told, "he was a very different hobbit from the one that had run out without a pocket-handkerchief from Bag-End long ago."[10]

His decision to continue walking down the tunnel when he hears the dragon's rumblings "was the bravest thing he ever did."[11] When Bilbo returns with a beautiful two-handled cup he stole from the dragon's hoard, he is acknowledged as "the real leader" in the dwarves' quest.[12] Later, when Bilbo risks his life and unselfishly gives up the Arkenstone in an effort to prevent a fratricidal war over dragon-gold, the Elvenking praises him as "more worthy to wear the armour of elf-princes than many that have looked more comely in it" and later lauds him as "Bilbo the Magnificent."[13]

After the Battle of Five Armies, the dying Thorin Oakenshield recognizes Bilbo's growth in moral stature, remarking that there "is more in you of good than you know, child of the kindly West. Some courage and some wisdom, blended in measure."[14] And when Bilbo recites a bittersweet homecoming poem upon his return to the Shire, Gandalf exclaims, "My dear Bilbo! Something is the matter with you! You are not the hobbit that you were."[15]

In short, *The Hobbit* is an adventure tale in which an ordinary and distinctly nonheroic person is morally ennobled by confronting and overcoming challenges and dangers. But how is such a transformation possible? Let's consider what some of the world's great philosophers have said about the linkage between challenge and personal growth.

Bilbo's Growth in Wisdom

Men shall learn wisdom, by affliction schooled.

—Aeschylus

Humans can grow in various respects: physically, emotionally, spiritually, artistically, and so forth. Merry and Pippin grew physically—they became several inches taller—after drinking the Ent-draughts in Fangorn Forest. But in Bilbo's case we're talking about moral and intellectual growth. In traditional philosophical terms, Bilbo grows in both *wisdom* and *virtue* as a result of his adventures. The term "philosophy" derives from Greek roots meaning "the love of wisdom." So to help us get our bearings, let's start by asking: What is wisdom?

Not all philosophical and religious traditions conceive of wisdom in the same way. A Zen Buddhist's definition of wisdom won't be the same as that offered by a Hindu or a

Southern Baptist. But we needn't be stymied by specific theo-retical disagreements. Nearly all philosophical and religious traditions agree that wisdom, whatever it is precisely, con-sists of deep insight about living.[16] A wise person understands what's important in life, keeps lesser things in proper perspec-tive, and understands what's needed in order to live well and to cope with the problems of life.[17] Wisdom comes in degrees. Gandalf is wiser than Elrond, and Elrond is wiser than Bard. But however, exactly, we define wisdom, it's clear that Bilbo is wiser at the end of *The Hobbit* than he was at the beginning. How did this occur?

Philosophers have noted two important ways in which challenging experiences can make us wiser: they can *deepen our self-understanding* and they can *broaden our experiences*. With Bilbo, we can see both factors at work.

The first step toward becoming wise, Socrates (ca. 470–399 BCE) said, is to realize how little you know. "Know thyself" was his mantra. Socrates saw that people tend to have inflated views of themselves. They tend to be overconfident and imagine that they know more than they do or that they are better in some way than they really are. People who think they're already wise and good won't be motivated to pursue wisdom and goodness. So the first and most important step toward becoming wise, Socrates declared, is to engage in fearless self-examination.

We should constantly be asking ourselves the following: Do I really know this, or do I only think I do? Could I be wrong? Could I be guilty of wishful thinking? Am I living the life I want to live? Am I walking the walk I talk? What are my true talents and abilities? How can I live most meaningfully and authentically? Only in this way can we root out our self-deceptions, discover our true potential, and discern where our greatest talents and opportunities lie.

Philosophers and religious thinkers have long pointed out how one particular kind of challenging experience, pain and suffering, can deepen one's self-understanding. Pain, said

C. S. Lewis (1898–1963), can curb our pride, teach us patience, steel us against adversity, teach us not to take life's blessings for granted, and remind us that we were "made for another world."[18] Pain, he noted, is God's "megaphone to rouse a deaf world."[19] God's attitude to humans, said the Roman philosopher Seneca (ca. 4 BCE–65 CE), is that of a stern but loving father: "'Let them be harassed by toil and sorrow and losses . . . that they may acquire true strength.' . . . God hardens and exercises those he approves and loves."[20]

In *The Hobbit* we see Bilbo slowly growing in self-understanding. As the story opens, he reacts to Thorin's forebodings of danger by shrieking like "an engine coming out of a tunnel" and "kneeling on the hearth-rug, shaking like a jelly that was melting."[21] On his journey to the Lonely Mountain, he encounters many dangers and suffers greatly through cold, hunger, sleeplessness, fear, and fatigue. Slowly, he grows in self-confidence and discovers hidden strengths, including an unsuspected talent for leadership.

Bilbo achieves a deeper understanding of the conflicting sides of his makeup and realizes that he wants more out of life than simply comfort, good pipe-weed, a well-stocked cellar, and six meals a day. At the same time, he doesn't develop a swollen head and get delusions of grandeur. After all his adventures and heroic deeds, he stills thinks of himself—and gratefully so—as "only quite a little fellow in a wide world after all."[22]

There is another way in which Bilbo becomes wiser: his eyes are opened by travel and a wider range of experience. Philosopher Tom Morris points out that taking a philosophy class can be like an Outward Bound experience for the mind. Students of philosophy find themselves on an intellectual adventure in which the great philosophers serve as native guides: mapmakers of the spirit who can broaden their horizons, guide them to exciting vistas, enlarge their imaginations, warn them of potential pitfalls, and teach them essential existential survival skills.[23] Many writers have noted that travel and adventure can also have paradigm-shifting, life-altering consequences.

The hobbits of the Shire are insular and provincial; they know and care little about the wider world of Middle-earth. Bilbo, though more adventurous than most hobbits, initially shares many of the limited and confining views of his fellows.[24] Like his hobbit friends and neighbors, he places great value on respectability, routine, comfort, and the simple bodily pleasures of eating, drinking, and smoking.

In the course of his adventures, Bilbo comes to realize that there are weightier concerns and higher values in life. He experiences heroism, self-sacrifice, ancient wisdom, and great beauty. Like the crew of the starship *Enterprise*, he encounters "new worlds and new civilizations," sees wondrous new sights, and meets peoples with very different value systems and ways of life. When he returns to the Shire, he is able to see it with new eyes and is better able to appreciate both its limitations and its unique charms.

When all is said and done, he finds that he has "lost the neighbours' respect" but has gained much of greater value.[25] By the final pages of *The Hobbit*, we find the contented and cosmopolitan Bilbo "writing poetry and visiting the elves."[26] Truly, he is not the hobbit that he was. His adventures have made him wiser.

Bilbo's Growth in Virtue

Too often, comfort gets in the way of inner reckonings.

—Lance Armstrong

Bilbo doesn't just grow intellectually, however; he also becomes a more virtuous, or ethical, person. Through his adventures he becomes more courageous, more resourceful, hardier, less dependent, and more self-controlled. His decisions to spare Gollum's life and to replace the keys on the belt of the slumbering elf-guard suggest that he has become more compassionate.[27] His choice to give up the precious Arkenstone in an attempt to broker peace, his refusal to take more than two small chests of treasure home with him (all of which he later gives away), and his donation of the priceless *mithril* coat to the museum at Michel Delving indicate that the "rather greedy" Bilbo has grown more generous and less materialistic.[28] Philosophers have noted two ways in which challenging adventures can promote moral development, one quick and one gradual.

Sometimes big moral transformations can occur rapidly, even instantly. These major ethical changes often take place when something shocking or traumatic occurs in our lives. A loved one dies, we're involved in a nearly fatal accident, or we wake up in the gutter—and we reevaluate our lives and make up our minds to change. In many cases, as the American philosopher William James (1842–1910) noted in his classic, *The Varieties of Religious Experience*, such transformations have a religious impetus. On Christmas Eve, Ebenezer Scrooge was a grumpy and mean-spirited old miser; on Christmas Day he was the soul of generosity and good cheer. But sudden and radical ethical changes need not be religiously motivated.

Rapid ethical makeovers are rare in Tolkien's writings, but there are some notable examples. Pippin undergoes one after his terrifying encounter with Sauron when he foolishly peers into the Seeing Stone of Orthanc.[29] Prior to this experience and Gandalf's stern rebuke, he is thoughtless and immature, constantly exposing the Fellowship to danger through his carelessness. Afterward, he is radically changed. He offers his service to Denethor, serves in Gondor's Tower Guard, saves Faramir's life, slays a troll at the Battle of the Morannon, plays a key role in the scouring of the Shire, and later serves for fifty years as Thain of the Shire.

Thorin's deathbed conversion and reconciliation with Bilbo is another example of a Scroogelike sudden transformation (foreshadowing Boromir's repentant death in *The Fellowship of the Ring*). Throughout *The Hobbit* Thorin is depicted as proud, greedy, and pompous. After he gains possession of the treasure, Thorin's pride and greed swell, and he nearly provokes a senseless war among the Free Peoples, who should be united. By nature, dwarves "are a calculating folk with a great idea of the value of money."[30] Moreover, Thorin is suffering from "dragonsickness," a corrupting possessiveness that afflicts all who touch a treasure that a dragon has long brooded over.[31] But even Thorin, as he lies dying, realizes "it would be a merrier world . . . if more of us valued food and cheer and song above hoarded gold."[32]

Sudden moral transformations can occur, but they are rare and often don't last for very long. A more common and sustainable path to moral growth is through *habit* and *training*. Virtue, as Aristotle (384–322 BCE) noted, is a habit, an ingrained pattern of moral response. A person is truly courageous, for example, only if he or she has a fixed tendency or disposition to act boldly in support of important values, even at great personal risk.[33] Throughout human history, character building through habit formation has been the standard method of moral education.

Athletics provides a model of how this works. Suppose you want to become a world-class long-distance runner. There's no way to achieve it except through pain, sweat, and fierce determination. Great runners have great work habits. They're not born with the habits of perseverance, commitment, self-discipline, and resiliency—they work hard to achieve them. That's why the physician-philosopher George Sheehan speaks of running as "a path to maturity, a growth process."[34] We pursue excellence by forming good habits and testing our limits.

Aristotle's great insight was to see that ethical development usually occurs the same way. To develop the virtue of self-discipline, it's not enough to desire to be self-disciplined. We need to work at it, to develop good habits. As legendary basketball coach Rick Pitino says, "Good habits create organization and discipline in our lives. . . . They become the rock, the standard of behavior that we must stick with so that we don't go off track."[35]

We can see this process of ethical habit formation in *The Hobbit*. Bilbo's moral development takes place gradually, as he learns new things, finds himself tested, increases in self-confidence, and develops virtuous habits. As Bilbo becomes accustomed to being cold, hungry, and wet, he complains less and becomes tougher. As his comrades' spirits sag and his own remarkable good luck continues, he becomes more encouraging and hopeful—even quoting the Roman philosopher Seneca's famous saying "Where there's life there's hope" before Seneca existed![36]

As Bilbo repeatedly responds bravely and effectively in dangerous situations, his confidence grows and he develops the habit of acting courageously. As he finds himself willy-nilly forced to take the initiative, he becomes more comfortable in a leadership role and develops the habit of effective servant leadership. As he returns to the Shire, and "Eyes that fire and sword have seen/And horror in the halls of stone/Look at last on meadows green/And trees and hills they long have known," he learns true thankfulness for simple blessings.[37]

Bilbo's adventures changed him, and these changes, as we learn in *The Lord of the Rings*, were permanent. In *The Fellowship of the Ring*, there is a deeply moving scene in which Bilbo, in extreme old age, volunteers to attempt to destroy the Ring of Power. At Rivendell, where Bilbo has retired, Elrond calls a Council to determine what to do with the Ring. The Council decides that the Ring must be carried into the heart of Mordor and cast into the fires of Mount Doom, where it was forged. When Elrond notes that such an apparent suicide mission "may be attempted by the weak with as much hope as the strong," Bilbo speaks up:

> Very well, very well, Master Elrond. . . . Say no more! It is plain enough what you are pointing at. Bilbo the silly hobbit started this affair, and Bilbo had better finish it,

or himself. I was very comfortable here, and getting on with my book. . . . It is a frightful nuisance. When ought I to start?

When Boromir, the mighty warrior from Gondor, heard this, he "looked in surprise at Bilbo, but the laughter died on his lips when he saw that all the others regarded the old hobbit with grave respect. Only Gloin smiled, but his smile came from old memories."[38]

In the end, Bilbo chose the path less traveled, the Tookish path, and this indeed made all the difference—to Bilbo and to all of Middle-earth. His fellow hobbits may have thought him mad, but Bilbo, to the end of his days, which were "very happy" and "extraordinarily long," would have agreed with Theodore Roosevelt:

> Far better is it to dare mighty things, to win glorious triumphs, even though checkered by failure, than to rank with those poor spirits who neither enjoy much nor suffer much, because they live in the gray twilight that knows not victory nor defeat. . . . The highest form of success . . . comes not to the man who desires mere easy peace, but to the man who does not shrink from danger, from hardship or from bitter toil, and who out of these wins the splendid ultimate triumph.[39]

The Road goes ever on and on, so grab your favorite walking stick and head out for adventure. And don't sweat it if you leave your pocket handkerchiefs at home.

NOTES

1. Humphrey Carpenter, ed., *The Letters of J. R. R. Tolkien* (Boston: Houghton Mifflin, 1981), 235, 237.

2. J. R. R. Tolkien, *The Lord of the Rings: The Fellowship of the Ring* (New York: Del Rey/Ballantine Books, 2001), 1, 6; J. R. R. Tolkien, *The Hobbit: or, There and Back Again* (New York: Del Rey/Ballantine Books, 2001), 302, 304.

3. J. R. R. Tolkien, *The Lord of the Rings: The Return of the King* (New York: Del Rey/ Ballantine Books, 2001), 424.

4. Tolkien, *The Hobbit*, 18.

5. J. R. R. Tolkien, "The Quest of Erebor," in *Unfinished Tales of Númenor and Middle-Earth*, ed. Christopher Tolkien (Boston: Houghton Mifflin, 1980), 323.

6. Ibid.

7. Tolkien, *The Hobbit*, 4.

8. Ibid., 18.

9. Ibid., 33.

10. Ibid., 214.

11. Ibid., 215.

12. Ibid., 221.

13. Ibid., 273, 295.

14. Ibid., 290.

15. Ibid., 302.

16. Tom Morris, *Philosophy for Dummies* (Foster City, CA: IDG Books, 1999), 35.

17. Robert Nozick, *The Examined Life: Philosophical Meditations* (New York: Simon & Schuster, 1989), 267.

18. C. S. Lewis, *Mere Christianity* (San Francisco: HarperCollins, 2001), 137.

19. C. S. Lewis, *The Problem of Pain* (San Francisco: HarperCollins, 2001), 91.

20. Moses Hadas, trans., *The Stoic Philosophy of Seneca: Essays and Letters* (New York: Doubleday, 1958), 30, 38.

21. Tolkien, *The Hobbit*, 17. The train whistle is one of many deliberate anachronisms in *The Hobbit*. For others, see Tom Shippey, *The Road to Middle-Earth*, rev. ed. (Boston: Houghton Mifflin, 2003), 65–70.

22. Tolkien, *The Hobbit*, 305.

23. Morris, *Philosophy for Dummies*, 22.

24. Tolkien says that among hobbits "only about one per mil" had any real spark of adventure. Carpenter, *Letters*, 365.

25. Tolkien, *The Hobbit*, 2.

26. Ibid., 304.

27. Ibid., 87, 180.

28. Tolkien, *The Fellowship of the Ring*, 235. Compare with Tolkien, *The Hobbit*, 304, where it states that "his gold and silver was largely spent on presents, both useful and extravagant." In Tolkien, *The Return of the King*, 287, however, we're told that Bilbo still had some of Smaug's gold eighteen years after he left Bag-End; Tolkien, *The Fellowship of the Ring*, 15. Gandalf notes that the coat's "worth was greater than the value of the whole Shire and everything in it." Ibid., 357; Tolkien, "The Quest of Erebor," 323.

29. J. R. R. Tolkien, *The Lord of the Rings: The Two Towers* (New York: Del Rey/Ballantine Books, 2001), 218–19.

30. Tolkien, *The Hobbit*, 213.

31. Ibid., 305.

32. Ibid., 290.

33. Tom Morris, *If Harry Potter Ran General Electric: Leadership Wisdom from the World of the Wizards* (New York: Doubleday, 2006), 36.

34. George A. Sheehan, *This Running Life* (New York: Simon & Schuster, 1980), 244.

35. Rick Pitino with Bill Reynolds, *Success Is a Choice: Ten Steps to Overachieving in Business and Life* (New York: Broadway Books, 1997), 98.

36. Hadas, *The Stoic Philosophy of Seneca*, 203. An earlier version of the maxim appears in Cicero. See E. O. Winstedt, trans., Cicero: *Letters to Atticus*, vol. 2 (London: William Heinemann, 1928), 229 ("a sick man is said to have hope, so long as he has breath"). Seneca ascribed the dictum to an unnamed person from Rhodes and condemns it as unmanly. Bilbo attributes the saying to his father, Bungo, and Sam says it was a common saying of his father, the Gaffer (Tolkien, *The Two Towers*, 348). The maxim may ultimately be traced to Euripides's saying that "life hath always hope." Euripides, *The Trojan Women*, trans. Gilbert Murray, in Whitney J. Oates and Eugene O'Neill Jr., eds., *The Complete Greek Drama*, vol. 1 (New York: Random House, 1938), 984. A similar saying is found in Jewish tradition: "For a man who is counted among the living, there is still hope; remember, a live dog is better than a dead lion" (Ecclesiastes 9:4).

37. Tolkien, *The Hobbit*, 302. Tolkien must have felt much the same when, as a young British army officer in World War I, he returned from the killing fields of the Somme in November 1916 to recover from trench fever.

38. Tolkien, *The Fellowship of the Ring*, 302.

39. Tolkien, *The Hobbit*, 304; Theodore Roosevelt, "The Strenuous Life," speech delivered at the Hamilton Club, Chicago, April 10, 1899, History Tools, http://historytools.org/sources/strenuous.html.

"THE ROAD GOES EVER
ON AND ON"

A Hobbit's Tao

Michael C. Brannigan

Embody to the fullest what has no end and wander
where there is no trail. Hold on to all you have
received from Heaven but do not think you
have gotten anything. *Be empty, that is all.*

—Chuang-tzu[1]

Throughout his journey, a voice inside Bilbo yearns for home, for the solace and safety of the familiar. Bilbo also discovers that one finds home by leaving it. So too, Taoist (pronounced "dow-ist") sages remind us that we find our true dwelling in the journey itself. Is this not echoed in *The Lord of the Rings*' message that "not all those who wander are lost"?

Bilbo's apparently conflicting yearnings for security and adventure resonate well with Western readers and moviegoers.

The struggle to reconcile such dualities in ourselves has helped to spawn a wealth of popular psychology and self-help industries. But the ancient Chinese Taoists were a couple of thousand years ahead of us on this one. According to these early Eastern philosophers, such disparate yearnings don't need to be reconciled. They aren't even contradictory.

The Fellowship of the Tao

The Tao is the fundamental principle of reality, the origin of the universe, and the indescribable way of nature, life, and death that pulsates throughout existence. Change and stability coexist all through reality. We see the Tao at work in Bilbo the adventurer, who welcomes and embraces change, and in Bilbo the homebody, who yearns for security.

One way to think of the Tao is to consider early Chinese cosmology, which views the universe as a drama in which two primordial forces, yin and yang, interact with each other. The Tao is the supreme principle that gives birth to yin and yang. *Yin*, literally the "dark side of the mountain," is the force of darkness, receptivity, and femininity. *Yang*, literally the "light side of the mountain," is the force of light, activity, and masculinity. Yin and yang complement each other in an eternal balance.[2]

Bilbo's adventure especially reveals these literal meanings. As our wayfarers journey toward, up, and then finally down into the bowels of the Lonely Mountain, the forces of light and darkness regularly interweave, somewhat like the trolls who, composed from the mountain darkness, revert to their origin once they face light. And just as the dark side of the mountain sooner or later becomes the light side, yin eventually transforms into yang. The Tao represents this universal dance of light and dark.

A valley, being free from the mountain's excess of darkness and light, nicely captures the harmony of yin and yang. The good Elrond lives in the "fair valley of Rivendell." And when our pilgrims discover the valley, they "hear the voice of hurrying water in a rocky bed at the bottom; the scent of trees was in the air; and there was a light on the valley-side across the water."[3] When we look inward, the forces of yin and yang should be treasured and allowed to operate without hindrance. In the classic Taoist text, the *Tao Te Ching*, we are encouraged to approach the Tao "Not by decree/But by spontaneity."[4]

Unfortunately, we tend to ignore the Tao within us and treasure other things instead. In so doing, we steer away from our true nature, which is to be in harmony with the Tao. Hobbits are prone to value reputation and conventionality; goblins are obsessed with machinery, especially the technologies of war; dwarves are fixed on acquiring gold, silver, and gems; Smaug hoards for the sake of hoarding; Gollum (and even Bilbo, momentarily) is bewitched not only by possessing the ring but just by the *idea* of possessing the ring.

In his letters, Tolkien claims that such desires represent our fall from innocence and grace, a central theme in his writings. As he puts it, our fall begins when we desire in ways that "become possessive, clinging to the things made as 'its own.'"[5] We hear echoes of Gollum's "my precious" and know full well the pervasive lust for gold in "dwarvish hearts."

In contrast, the power of the Tao within us (the Chinese *te*, pronounced somewhat like "duh"), is the power not of invisibility but of living according to our original and true nature. Like his fellow hobbits, Bilbo presumes that his nature is to simply live in his hobbit-hole, which "means comfort," and his voice of reason utters, "Don't be a fool, Bilbo Baggins . . . thinking of dragons and all that outlandish nonsense at your age!"[6] Yet after his unexpected visit from dwarves, he hears another voice inside him:

> Then something Tookish woke up inside him, and he wished to go and see the great mountains, and hear the pine-trees and the waterfalls, and explore the caves, and wear a sword instead of a walking stick.[7]

The Hobbit is ultimately a parable of Bilbo's awakening to his true nature as a Took as well as a Baggins, as an adventurer and a risk taker as well as a seeker of comfort and familiarity.

Hobbits belong to the human race and represent an original innocence, loving the simple life: partying, eating, drinking, laughing, and being in touch with what life is really all about—companionship, comfort, and contentment.[8] (I reread *The Hobbit* while in Wales, and there is nothing like good Welsh ale to simplify complexity.) Tolkien writes that hobbits are "more in touch with 'nature' (the soil and other living things, plants and animals), and abnormally, for humans, free from ambition or greed of wealth."[9]

Like Taoist sages, the Little Folk live uncomplicated lives in close touch with nature. Their rustic, well-ordered lives, embodying a natural simplicity, allow for spontaneity. And spontaneity enables *te*, the power of the Tao, to surface within them so that they can be true to their nature. This is in contrast to the Big Folk, whose lives are more encumbered, who are therefore much less simple and spontaneous, and whose bigness depicts complexity, excess, and oversized ambition. The Big Folk represent the fall from grace decried by Tolkien, the fall from our natural path.

Another Taoist concept, *wu-wei* (pronounced "woo way"), refers to acting naturally, without force. It means yielding to, rather than resisting, the natural flow of things and is reflected in the idea of government without governing. The Taoist sage "rules through not-ruling." So also the hobbit Shire has no official government.[10] In describing to his son Christopher his own leaning toward anarchy, Tolkien writes the following:

> The most improper job of any man, even saints (who at any rate were at least unwilling to take it on), is bossing other men. Not one in a million is fit for it, and least of all those who seek the opportunity.[11]

The ultimate principle of Tao, then, is our true and original nature. Taoism teaches that we ought to pursue our own Tao, our own journey, in a way that is consistent with this ultimate principle. *The Hobbit* reveals characters whose ways are troubling and downright harmful. When Thorin stubbornly insists on hoarding the entire lot of gold, silver, and gems, what makes his way questionable? His greed is clearly not the path of the Tao, so it hinders him from being true to his nature.

Consider Smaug. If Smaug's disposition is to possess treasure and relish its possession, is he cultivating the Tao? Certainly not, for his disposition is one thing; his true nature is another. His disposition is such that it suppresses *te*, the power of the Tao. The genuine nature of all living things is to act in accord with the Tao.

We need to delve more deeply here. What does it really mean to act in harmony with the Tao? Why are certain paths, like Thorin's, and certain dispositions, like Smaug's, inauthentic and not worth pursuing?

Another Way of Thinking of the Way:
Seven Taoist Masters

Let's consider *The Hobbit* in light of one of my favorite Taoist stories, *Seven Taoist Masters*. Written around 1500 during the Ming Dynasty (1368–1644), the story highlights the journeys of the Taoist sage Wang Ch'ung-yang and his seven disciples in their quest for self-discovery and cultivation of the Tao.

In one episode, Wang encounters two beggars named Gold-Is-Heavy and Empty-Mind, whom he takes home and feeds. Unknown to him, the beggars are Taoist sages in disguise who became immortals after cultivating the Tao. Wang is impressed by their simplicity and detachment from material objects and worldly matters. After seeing to their needs, Wang follows the beggars across a mysterious bridge and up steep mountain passages until they finally reach a crystal-clear lake. There Empty-Mind hands Wang seven lotus flowers and instructs him to care for them tenderly, for they are the spirits of seven souls destined to be his disciples.[12]

Gold-Is-Heavy

The name of this Taoist immortal, Gold-Is-Heavy, is patently relevant to our tale. When Bilbo encounters Smaug, the dragon tries to cast the hobbit under his spell by planting doubts about the mission to retrieve the gold:

> I don't know if it has occurred to you that, even if you could steal the gold bit by bit—a matter of a hundred years or so—you could not get it very far? Not much use on the mountain-side? Not much use in the forest? Bless me! *Had you never thought of the catch?* A fourteenth share, I suppose, or something like it, those were the terms, eh? But what about delivery? What about cartage? What about armed guards and tolls?[13]

Bilbo had not anticipated such practical concerns. He and his companions had thought only of seizing the treasure, not transporting it. So on a purely literal level, gold, once acquired, is indeed a heavy burden.

But as philosophers let's dig deeper. The catch is onerous in another way. As Thorin and his dwarf companions discover, the desire for gold can easily be transformed into a consuming and weighty lust. From the start, Thorin is intent on recapturing what he considers to be his rightful heritage. Seizing the gold has been his clear mission; as he tells Bilbo and Gandalf, "we have never forgotten our stolen treasure."[14] However, he is so driven by his desire to recapture his treasure that his desire in turn overtakes him. But let's not be too hard on Thorin. Even the narrator admits he is "decent enough . . . *if you don't expect too much.*"[15]

Thorin's ensnarement under the weight of desire clearly surfaces in his exchange with the dragon-slayer, Bard. Despite Bard's pleas to distribute the gold fairly, and in compensation for the loss of life caused primarily by Thorin's unquenchable quest to seize the treasure, Thorin is unflinching in coveting the gold. Bilbo is troubled by Thorin's demeanor:

> He did not reckon with the power that gold has upon which a dragon has long brooded, nor with dwarvish hearts. Long hours in the past days Thorin had spent in the treasury, and the lust of it was heavy on him. Though he had hunted chiefly for the Arkenstone, yet he had an eye for many another wonderful thing that was lying there, about which was wound old memories of the labours and the sorrows of his race.[16]

Thorin is not the only character in *The Hobbit* oppressed by the desire for gold. Even though the Wood-elves are basically good people, their king, ever greedy to acquire more silver and white gems, has a special weakness for treasure. And when the treasure's guardian in the Lonely Mountain is slain, men, elves, and dwarves grow increasingly bewitched to seize the gold, culminating in the terrible Battle of Five Armies.

Even hobbits are not free from the weight of desire. With the buzz of Bilbo's demise, hobbits, particularly the Sackville-Bagginses, are eager to auction off his property. Greed has a way of clouding even kind souls. And in the opening chapter of *The Fellowship of the Ring*, gossip of Bilbo's hidden treasure again seizes the hobbits' hearts.

Goblins, or orcs, are "cruel, wicked, and bad-hearted." Although they are not obsessed with gold, their treasure lies in machinery. They delight in creating effective instruments, particularly technologies that destroy:

> They make no beautiful things, but they make many clever ones. . . . It is not unlikely that they invented

some of the machines that have since troubled the world, especially the ingenious devices for killing large numbers of people at once, for wheels and engines and explosions always delighted them.[17]

Goblins create their machines and have slaves do their work for them. Yet they are enslaved by their own creations, just as the desire for gold enslaves us.

In a letter to his youngest son, Christopher, who was serving with the British Royal Air Force in South Africa during World War II, Tolkien gives an interesting critique of machinery in the context of war:

> There is the tragedy and despair of all machinery laid bare. Unlike art, which is content to create a new secondary world in the mind, it attempts to *actualize desire*, and so to create power in this World; and that cannot really be done with any real satisfaction. Labour-saving machinery only creates endless and worse labour. And in addition to this fundamental disability of a creature, is added the Fall, which makes our devices not only fail of their desire but turn to new and horrible evil. So we come inevitably from Daedalus and Icarus to the Giant Bomber. It is not an advance in wisdom![18]

For the Taoist, the real problem lies not with the machines themselves but with their seductive power over us, with our willing surrender to efficiency even if it means sacrificing nature and humanity.

So gold is indeed heavy. The desire for wealth and power is oppressive. Stooped under the weight of our desires, we lose sight of our original nature, our Tao. From a Taoist viewpoint, however, we can free ourselves from this weight. Attachment to gold leads to obsession, and obsession leads to enslavement. Therefore, the key lies in being free from attachment. The secret consists of detachment.

Empty-Mind

Empty-Mind, Gold-Is-Heavy's fellow sage, represents detachment. According to my father-in-law, Carl Wilhelm, the meaning of detachment is really quite simple: "There's nothing to it!"

Consider the dwarves. They are hindered by their ambitions, which, though noble in principle (restoring justice), overpower them in deed. They become so obsessed with the goal that they in turn become attached, and thus enslaved, to it. Attachment to an idea may well be the worst form of attachment. An idea does not breathe; living creatures do. Yet Taoists (along with Buddhists, Hindus, poets, artists, mystics, and numerous philosophers) caution us against assigning more reality to an idea, an image, or a symbol than to reality itself. The Zen poet warns us against "mistaking the finger that points to the moon for the moon."

Empty-Mind's name does not mean mindlessness or idiocy but refers instead to what Taoists (and Buddhists) call a mirror mind, a state of mind and heart that reflects what is presented to it but is not attached to what is reflected.[19] Thus, we ought to cultivate a state of mind and heart that is like a clear mirror. This is the meaning of this chapter's opening quote by Chuang-tzu (369–286 BCE). Like a clear mirror, the empty mind reflects but does not evaluate or judge what comes into it. It is ever attentive. It does not privilege one point of view over any other.

Beorn provides an oasis of solace, a rollicking feast, and rest for the pilgrims before they set out on the most difficult part of their journey. The skin-changer represents Empty-Mind. True to his dual bear-human nature, he lives in harmony with all living things. He thrives on honey and has no concern with gold, jewels, and other so-called treasures. He offers his guests some critically important advice before they set out across Mirkwood Forest, warning them, as does Gandalf, not to stray from the path.

"Path" is both literal and figurative. They should not stray from the path through the dark forest, but they should also not stray from their original natures, their personal paths. The enchanted stream of forgetfulness can dim the memory of their true path. All this is sound advice from one who has managed to keep to his own path by maintaining an empty mind, clear as a mirror.

The fact that Beorn is a skin-changer is particularly instructive. When we acquire dispositions (like Thorin's enslavement to revenge, Beorn's occasional surrender to his hot temper, and Smaug's obsession with acquisition), we suppress our true nature in accord with the Tao. In a sense, we change our skin. We present an inauthentic face to others and to ourselves. We also pay a price: concealing and suppressing our original skin or, as Zen Buddhists call it, "our original face before we were born."

Bilbo remains throughout the tale a hobbit of pure heart. He personifies the empty mind, not only because of his natural simplicity and childlike innocence but also because he deliberately chooses to remain detached from the desire for gold. Even though a spark of desire flickers in his heart when they come upon the treasure, and an enchantment entices him into keeping the Arkenstone, in the spirit of *wu-wei* he lets go of his desire for the treasure and avoids the bewitchment experienced by the dwarves. He would, in fact, trade it all for a foamy pint in the Green Dragon!

After disappearing from his neighbors at his 111th birthday party, ready to reassume his role as wayfarer, Bilbo is not quite ready to give up the ring. It requires a bit of urging on Gandalf's part to convince him, and the wizard warns him, "It [the ring] has got far too much hold on you. Let it go! And then you can go yourself, and be free."[20] Bilbo struggles and finally empties his mind of desire to possess that which is not his to keep, although even he once thought of it as precious.

Our Taoist tale ends where it began: on a path, along a way, a never-ending road as Bilbo sings to himself:

The Road goes ever on and on
Down from the door where it began.
Now far ahead the Road has gone,
And I must follow, if I can,
Pursuing it with eager feet,
Until it joins some larger way
Where many paths and errands meet.
And whither then? I cannot say.[21]

A Taoist sage couldn't come up with better words, although words, mind you, are never enough.

NOTES

1. Burton Watson, trans., *Chuang Tzu: Basic Writings* (New York: Columbia University Press, 1964), 94–95 (emphasis added).

2. Jennifer L. McMahon and B. Steve Csaki, "Talking Trees and Walking Mountains: Buddhist and Taoist Themes in *The Lord of the Rings*," in The Lord of the Rings *and Philosophy: One Book to Rule Them All*, ed. Gregory Bassham and Eric Bronson (Chicago: Open Court, 2003), 188–91.

3. J. R. R. Tolkien, *The Hobbit: or, There and Back Again* (New York: Del Rey/Ballantine Books, 2001), 47.

4. Ellen M. Chen, trans., *The Tao Te Ching: A New Translation with Commentary* (New York: Paragon House, 1989), 175.

5. Humphrey Carpenter, ed., *The Letters of J. R. R. Tolkien* (Boston: Houghton Mifflin, 1981), 145.

6. Tolkien, *The Hobbit*, 28.

7. Ibid., 15–16.

8. The hobbits' innocence and simplicity are nicely paralleled with Taoist ideas in Greg Harvey, "Tao Te Ching," in *The Origins of Tolkien's Middle-Earth for Dummies* (Hoboken, NJ: John Wiley & Sons, 2003), 112.

9. Carpenter, *Letters*, 158.

10. Tolkien's dislike of government is discussed in Peter J. Kreeft, *The Philosophy of Tolkien: The Worldview Behind* The Lord of the Rings (San Francisco: Ignatius Press, 2005), 163.

11. Carpenter, *Letters*, 64.

12. Eva Wong, trans., *Seven Taoist Masters: A Folk Tale of China* (Boston: Shambhala Press, 1990), 5.

13. Tolkien, *The Hobbit*, 225 (emphasis added).

14. Ibid., 25.

15. Ibid., 213 (emphasis added).

16. Ibid., 265.

17. Ibid., 62.

18. Carpenter, *Letters*, 87–88.

19. In ancient China, the mirror not only reflected what was in front of it, it also "miraculously" produced fire and had the power to reveal the hidden (for example, invisible demons) as well as to protect the reflected one from evil spirits. Thus, a mirror had power over invisibility.

20. J. R. R. Tolkien, *The Lord of the Rings: The Fellowship of the Ring* (New York: Del Rey/Ballantine Books, 2001), 36.

21. Ibid., 38.

BIG HAIRY FEET

A Hobbit's Guide to Enlightenment

Eric Bronson

Never trust a thought that didn't come by walking.
—Friedrich Nietzsche

Hobbits are good walkers. They're built that way, really.

In his prologue to *The Lord of the Rings,* Tolkien notes that from the earliest times, hobbits "seldom wore shoes, since their feet had tough leathery soles and were clad in a thick curling hair, much like the hair of their heads, which was commonly brown."[1]

Such feet are made for walking, and Bilbo especially liked a good hike in the country. In the hall near his walking sticks hung a large map "of the Country Round with all his favourite walks marked on it in red ink."[2] Bilbo is self-assured. Throughout his adventures, he never forgets who he is and where he is from. Perhaps that's one reason the diminutive hobbit holds such appeal for us humans today.

In his groundbreaking work "The Consequences of Modernity," sociologist Anthony Giddens argues that "Modernity 'dis-places' . . . place becomes phantasmagoric. Yet this is a double-layered, or ambivalent, experience rather than simply a loss of community."[3] I like Giddens, and not just because he uses words like "phantasmagoric" without a trace of irony.

His point is that in the modern age we've become very good at negotiating our way through "abstract systems." We buy clothing on credit cards, keep up with distant friends on Facebook, and easily rent cars to embark on long drives down unfamiliar highways, confident that organizational systems will see us through without a hitch. But as Giddens explains, "With the development of abstract systems, trust in impersonal principles, as well as in anonymous others, becomes indispensable to social existence."[4] Something is always lost and gained with each new technological advance. The moment your GPS friend Tom-Tom gives you wrong directions, you realize that he never really was a friend to begin with, no matter which accent you chose for him to speak with.

Western philosophers since Russian novelist Fyodor Dostoyevsky have pointed out this ambivalence of place confronting the modern person. Famous thinkers have proposed different solutions for this modern dilemma. Friedrich Nietzsche (1844–1900) found hope in art, Simone de Beauvoir (1908–1986) delineated an ethics of ambiguity, and contemporary philosopher Jürgen Habermas has called for authentic communication with others.

Tolkien, however, was ever suspicious of modern solutions to modern problems.[5] For the Oxford professor who confronted the horrors of World War I, place still mattered. And if his fellow countrymen were feeling disconnected, they didn't need to read a whole lot of philosophy books to ease their existential angst. What they needed most was to go outside and take a walk.

In both Western and Eastern philosophical traditions, walking holds a central place. The search for truth begins with one's feet. "There is nothing like looking, if you want to find something," Thorin explains to his fellow dwarves. "You certainly usually find something if you look, but it is not always quite the something you were after."[6]

"Not So Hasty"

In *The Spell of the Sensuous*, philosopher, anthropologist, and sleight-of-hand magician David Abram discusses oral cultures and their symbiotic relationship to their natural environment. He argues that the natural world is calling out to us, but we're often in too much of a hurry to notice. Walks take on more importance as we lose our connection to the land.

In 1981, Zen poet Gary Snyder was riding in a pickup truck through the Australian outback. His companion, a Pintupi elder, was telling a story about mythological creatures at a mountain they were passing. Immediately, the elder launched into another story. Snyder was befuddled. "I couldn't keep up," he confessed. "I realized after about half an hour of this that these were tales meant to be told while *walking*, and that I was experiencing a speeded-up version of what might be leisurely told over several days of foot travel."[7]

People and places are intimately connected, as Tolkien profoundly grasped. "I wisely started with a map, and made the story fit," he said of *The Lord of the Rings*.[8] People who understand their connection to their place are often better grounded and feel less disconnected. But connections to one's immediate environment are rarely established in an instant. Such relationships take time and often involve years of walking through one's immediate neighborhood.

In *The Lord of the Rings*, it is Treebeard the Ent who teaches Pippin and Merry to slow down and not be so hasty. "Real names tell you the story of things," Treebeard instructs the young hobbits, knowing they won't understand his Old Entish. "It is a lovely language, but it takes a very long time to say anything in it, because we do not say anything in it, unless it is worth taking time to say, and listen to." Treebeard won't even begin to listen to the hobbits' story until he walks seventy thousand entstrides and drains "one long, slow draught" of something resembling Entwash.[9]

Good conversation, like a good walk, takes time. Speed walkers and fast talkers too often get muddled in their thoughts. Tolkien himself was a slow walker who sometimes irritated his speedier companions by pausing to observe flowers and trees. "He's a great man," C. S. Lewis, author of *The Chronicles of Narnia*, once said of Tolkien, "but not our sort of walker. He doesn't seem able to walk and talk at the same time. He dawdles and then stops completely when he has something interesting to say." Lewis's mistake was that he walked too fast; he was one of the "ruthless walkers," as Tolkien called them.[10] Treebeard would have been most displeased.

Walks can be transformative once one learns how to take it slow. In September 1931, while *The Hobbit* was still in early draft form, Tolkien took another walk with Lewis and Lewis's friend, Shakespeare scholar Hugo Dyson.[11] They strolled down Oxford's Addison Walk along the River Cherwell near Magdalen College. Discussions of the relation of myths and facts lasted until three o'clock in the morning. After Tolkien left for home, Lewis continued walking with Dyson until four o'clock, and shortly thereafter he experienced a life-changing religious conversion.[12] Perhaps he also learned something important about slowing down his walk.

Religious transformations are not uncommon in the history of great walks. Whether it's Moses hiking up Mount Sinai or modern-day Muslims walking slow circles around the Kaaba in Mecca, most if not all of the major world religions feature walks of quiet contemplation. As Geoff Nicholson, the author of *The Lost Art of Walking*, wryly observes, "I don't know much about gods, but it seems that they like their believers to do a lot of walking."[13]

Walk for a Cure

Walking can help to save a life, we are told. Nearly all of us, at one time or another, have either walked for a cause or sponsored friends or coworkers who have, in order to make a difference in the world. Only a goblin who lives without sunlight would seriously object to giving one's time or money to a good cause. But Nicholson brings up an important point. The connection between charity and walking is a bit strained, when you really think about it. "It suggests that walking is some eccentric and out-of-the-ordinary activity, so rare that people would only do it for money, even if the money was going to a good cause."[14]

Walking, however, does indeed save lives. It saved Thorin's life when Smaug first attacked the mountain that was filled with the dwarves' hand-carved jewels and toys. Only a select few escaped the fury of Smaug by sneaking out the secret side door. But there was another group of dwarves who didn't need a magical map to lead them out of the treasure hoard. The dwarves with Thorin were already away from the gold and silver when the dragon attack began.

"I was," as Thorin explains, "a fine adventurous lad in those days, always wandering about, and it saved my life that day."[15] What saved Thorin's life was not the walking itself but how it led him out of the same greedy traps that snared most of his smaller-minded friends (and would later do Thorin in when he chose to sit on his gold on the Lonely Mountain rather than walk out like Bilbo).

French philosopher Michel de Montaigne (1533–1592) also chose to walk away from his gold and silver. On the wall of his study, Montaigne wrote the following:

> In the year of Christ 1571, at the age of thirty-eight, on the last day of February, his birthday, Michel de Montaigne, long weary of the servitude of the court and of public employments, while still entire, retired

to the bosom of the learned virgins, where in calm and freedom from all cares he will spend what little remains of his life, now more than half run out.[16]

Granted, retiring "to the bosom of the learned virgins" (the Muses) doesn't exactly bring to mind St. Francis of Assisi striking out to live a life of poverty, but there is something transformative about the decision to walk away from the rat race. Inherent in such a change is the belief that the day-to-day life of household responsibilities is often emotionally insufficient and sometimes morally bankrupt. Instead of working for the courts, Montaigne chose to walk away and meditate in his tower.

But it is not enough to walk away from your uninspiring job if all you can do is lie on your couch watching *Two and a Half Men* reruns. Although Montaigne claimed, "My walk is quick and firm," his thoughts still occasionally returned to the same petty problems he was stuck on before his change.[17] As any philosopher knows, the mind takes at least as much exercise and training as the body does. Montaigne understood it at last:

> When I dance, I dance; when I sleep, I sleep; yes, and when I walk alone in a beautiful orchard, if my thoughts have been concerned with extraneous incidents for some part of the time, for some other part I lead them back again to the walk, to the orchard, to the sweetness of this solitude, and to myself.[18]

Walk This Way

Henry David Thoreau (1817–1862) was another would-be sourpuss who, in the end, was saved by walking. The same man who cut out on his own "to live deliberately" firmly believed that his physical and mental health would quickly deteriorate if he didn't "spend a day at least—and it is commonly more than that—sauntering through the woods and over the hills and fields absolutely free from all worldly engagements." But like

Montaigne before him, Thoreau also knew the importance of staying mentally vigilant while one walks.

He wrote, "I am alarmed when it happens that I have walked a mile into the woods bodily, without getting there in spirit. In my afternoon walk I would fain forget all my morning occupations and my obligations to Society. But it sometimes happens that I cannot easily shake off the village." It's the age-old problem. Walking can help you to leave behind your more mundane, less urgent responsibilities. But the more philosophical dilemma is always what you take with you in your head. As Thoreau asks, "What business have I in the woods, if I am thinking of something out of the woods?"[19]

The idea is to link your thoughts to your immediate surroundings. English critic William Hazlitt (1778–1830) became acquainted with Romantic poetry by walking with Samuel Coleridge (1772–1834) and William Wordsworth (1770–1850). He discovered that the walking paths preferred by each poet directly influenced their writing styles. Wordsworth was more lyrical, Coleridge more dramatic. Not coincidentally, so was their walking.

Hazlitt wrote, "Coleridge has told me that he himself liked to compose in walking over uneven ground, or breaking through straggling branches of a copse-wood; whereas Wordsworth always wrote (if he could) walking up and down a straight gravel-walk, or in some spot where the continuity of his verse met with no collateral interruption."[20]

Taken in this sense, walking is not simply an escape from harmful thinking; it can also be the beginning of reconnecting with yourself. In *The Lord of the Rings*, it is no coincidence that the expert walker, appropriately named Strider, is also the future king of men. "But I may say that I know all the lands between the Shire and the Misty Mountains, for I have wandered over them for many years. I am older than I look," he tells Frodo Baggins.[21] Such wandering helps Strider to build his strength before finally living up to his true identity.

But such walking must come with thoughtful actions, as Strider firmly explains to Pippin. "It would take more than a few days, or weeks, or years of wandering in the Wild to make you look like Strider. . . . And you would die first, unless you are made of sterner stuff than you look to be."[22]

In *The Hobbit*, Tolkien's wisest characters are walkers who turn their backs on the unnaturally dull things of the world. Think of Beorn, who loves good stories but grows sleepy when the dwarves go on about their treasures. "They spoke most of gold and silver and jewels and the making of things by smith-craft, and Beorn did not appear to care for such things: there were no things of gold or silver in his hall, and few save the knives were made of metal at all."[23] While the dwarves (and the hobbit) slept, Beorn shape-shifted into his bear outfit (excellent walking gear, by any standard) and walked "over the river and right back up the mountains—from which you can guess that he could travel quickly, in bear's shape at any rate."[24]

For most *Hobbit* fans, though, the sharpest image of the philosopher-walker has always been Gandalf. Gandalf is Gandalf only because of his walking stick. As Tom Shippey points out, Tolkien believed the Icelandic definition of *gandr* was in fact a wand or staff.[25] Time after time, Gandalf saves the day through vigilant walking. How does one walk vigilantly? The wizard says it better than even Montaigne or Thoreau:

> "Where did you go to, if I may ask?" said Thorin to
> Gandalf as they rode along.
> "To look ahead," said he.
> "And what brought you back in the nick of time?"
> "Looking behind," said he.
> "Exactly!" said Thorin; "but could you be more plain?"[26]

Hobbits have a few advantages over men and dwarves that include fine ale and pipe-weed. But an even more useful skill is the ability to move in silence. Tolkien tells us that "hobbits can move quietly in woods, absolutely quietly."[27] Bilbo takes a particular pride in his silence, and well he should. His silence aboveground and his sense of direction underground save himself and his friends from more than one predicament. It's an ordinary sort of magic, Tolkien notes, but in the annals of Eastern philosophy, such silent walking is quite rare and can signal the highest level of happiness.[28]

Mind Your Steps

"Good travelers leave no tracks," we read in the ancient *Tao Te Ching*.[29] When Taoists speak of traveling along the path (the Tao) there is usually something more going on than literal walking. For example, the famous Taoist Chuang-tzu (369–286 BCE) wrote frequently about the wandering life. But his wandering entailed rigorously developing virtues like "vacuity, tranquility, mellowness, quietness, and taking no action."[30]

These are virtues meant for governing people, not walking away from one's worldly obligations. "When a person retires with these virtues and roams at leisure, all the scholars in the rivers and seas and hills and forests will admire him. If one assumes office with them to pacify the world, his achievements will be great and his fame will be prominent, and the empire will become unified."[31]

Taoists generally believe that it takes many years to learn and practice such virtues, but hobbits come by them naturally. Although Tolkien's own knowledge of Taoism was negligible, his hobbits have something of the spirit. Tolkien might be describing any number of Taoist sages when he observes that "Mr. Baggins was not quite so prosy as he liked to believe, also . . . he was very fond of flowers."[32]

Walking into the woods as Bilbo does is a well-trodden theme in many Eastern philosophies besides Taoism. In Hindu mythology, the philosopher-king Rama, banished from his father's kingdom, must trade his fancy clothes for leaf and bark before walking into the woods. Duty, justice, and courage are only a few of the essential virtues he develops while walking through the enchanted forests of India.

In a similar fashion, Siddhartha Gautama (560–480 BCE) left his father's palace to walk with wandering ascetics before meditating under a tree, reaching enlightenment, and becoming the Buddha. As the first monks began spreading the word, the Buddha only reluctantly allowed them to hole up and take refuge during the rainy season. At all other times they were expected to hit the road on foot.

Many Buddhist schools today still preach the philosophical importance of hoofing it. Some of the more extreme Tibetan Buddhists, for example, will on occasion travel thousands of miles on foot, practicing prostrations (falling to the ground and stretching outward) with each step. Such enormous feats of strength and patience often culminate with a religious festival.[33] The prostrations are means of reminding yourself after every step that you are doing something important. It helps to break petty thoughts before they begin to take over your unsuspecting mind.

In Southeast Asia, the Theravada schools of Buddhism also emphasize the more philosophical side of walking. Walking meditations are ways of gaining insight into your inner thoughts and radically increasing your powers of concentration in the everyday world. In the ancient Pāli texts, a poem credited to Buddha is translated thus:

> The open air provides a life
> That aides the homeless bhikku's [monk's] strife,
> Easy to get, and leaves his mind
> Alert as a deer, so he shall find
> Stiffness and torpor brought to halt.
> Under the star-bejewelled vault
> The moon and sun furnish his light,
> And concentration his delight.
> The joy seclusion's savour gives
> He shall discover soon who lives

In open air; and that is why
The wise prefer the open sky.[34]

Many of today's leading Zen Buddhists also advocate walking meditations. The idea is to pay attention to each step forward, each bend of the knee, and the sound that is made by one's feet.

Thich Nhat Hanh is a Vietnamese Buddhist monk who founded the Plum Village Buddhist retreat in southern France. During the Vietnam War, Martin Luther King Jr. nominated Hanh for the Nobel Peace Prize, boldly claiming, "His ideas for peace, if applied, would build a monument to ecumenism, to world brotherhood, to humanity." Hanh's ideas for peace involve using Buddhist meditation techniques to engage in the world by helping the needy.

Obviously, the world is a lot more complicated than that, as Hanh recognizes. He therefore argues that one should begin with small steps—literally. In his book, *Peace Is Every Step*, Hanh discusses the importance of walking meditation. "While we practice walking meditation, we do not try to arrive anywhere," he writes. "We only make peaceful, happy steps. If we keep thinking of the future, of what we want to realize, we will lose ourselves."[35]

Losing ourselves, as we have seen, is one of the great dangers of living in the modern world. Thoreau saw the dangers and worried about whether future generations of city slickers would be mentally strong enough to confront it. "I have met with but one or two persons in the course of my life who understood the art of Walking, that is, of taking walks," he wrote.[36]

As Tolkien notes, there were many ways over the Misty Mountains. "But most of the paths were cheats and deceptions and led nowhere or to bad ends; and most of the passes were infested by evil things." Thanks to Gandalf, however, Bilbo and the dwarves "took the right road to the right pass."[37]

This is easier said than done, of course. It takes concentration, courage, and discipline to know the right paths to take in life. We would do well to heed Tolkien's call and slow ourselves down. As philosopher-comedian Stephen Wright reminds us, "Anywhere is walking distance, if you've got the time."

NOTES

1. J. R. R. Tolkien, "Prologue," in *The Lord of the Rings: The Fellowship of the Ring* (New York: Del Rey/Ballantine Books, 2001), 1–2.

2. J. R. R. Tolkien, *The Hobbit: or, There and Back Again* (New York: Del Rey/Ballantine Books, 2001), 21. Before Bilbo set off for Rivendell, he went to the hall and "chose his favorite stick from the stand." Tolkien, *The Fellowship of the Ring*, 37.

3. Anthony Giddens, "The Consequences of Modernity," in *Contemporary Sociological Theory*, ed. Craig Calhoun, Joseph Gertels, James Moody, Steven Pfaff, and Indermohan Virk (Malden, MA: Blackwell, 2002), 251.

4. Ibid., 245.

5. Joe Kraus, "Tolkien, Modernism, and the Importance of Tradition," in The Lord of the Rings *and Philosophy*, ed. Gregory Bassham and Eric Bronson (Chicago: Open Court, 2003), 137–49.

6. Tolkien, *The Hobbit*, 58.

7. Quoted in David Abram, *The Spell of the Sensuous* (New York: Vintage, 1996), 173.

8. This point is discussed in some depth in Tom Shippey, *The Road to Middle-Earth* (Boston: Houghton Mifflin, 2003), 96–104.

9. J. R. R. Tolkien, *The Lord of the Rings: The Two Towers* (New York: Del Rey/Ballantine Books, 2001), 66.

10. Quoted in George Sayer, "Recollections of J. R. R. Tolkien," in *Tolkien: A Celebration*, ed. Joseph Pearce (San Francisco: Ignatius Press, 1999), 4.

11. Dyson, a fellow Inkling (member of a literary discussion group) of Tolkien's, had a genius for apt Shakespearean quotations. Often, when the beer was flowing freely at Inkling gatherings, he excused himself to go to the lavatory by quoting *Macbeth* (Act 2, Scene 3): "Let's briefly put on manly readiness, and meet i' th' hall together." Quoted in A. N. Wilson, *C. S. Lewis: A Biography* (New York: W. W. Norton, 1990), 192.

12. C. S. Lewis to Arthur Greeves, September 22, 1931, in *The Collected Letters of C. S. Lewis*, ed. Walter Hooper (San Francisco: HarperSanFrancisco, 2004), 1:969–70.

13. Geoff Nicholson, *The Lost Art of Walking* (New York: Riverhead, 2008), 172.

14. Ibid., 13.

15. Tolkien, *The Hobbit*, 24.

16. Michel de Montaigne, "Introduction," in *The Complete Essays of Montaigne*, trans. Donald Frame (Stanford, CA: Stanford University Press, 1976), ix.

17. Montaigne, "Of Experience," in *The Complete Essays of Montaigne*, 848.

18. Ibid., 850.

19. Henry David Thoreau, "Walking," with study text by Margaret M. Brulatour, 1999, American Transcendentalism Web, http://www.vcu.edu/engweb/transcendentalism/authors/thoreau/walking/.

20. William Hazlitt, "My First Acquaintance with Poets," in *William Hazlitt: Selected Writings* (Middlesex, UK: Penguin, 1970), 60.

21. Tolkien, *The Fellowship of the Ring*, 187.

22. Ibid., 194.

23. Tolkien, *The Hobbit*, 126.

24. Ibid., 131.

25. Shippey, *The Road to Middle-Earth*, 97.

26. Tolkien, *The Hobbit*, 43.

27. Ibid., 34.

28. Ibid., 2.

29. Lao-tzu, *Tao Te Ching*, trans. Stephen Adiss and Stanley Lombardo (Indianapolis, IN: Hackett, 1993), verse 27.

30. Burton Watson, trans., *Chuang Tzu: Basic Writings* (New York: Columbia University Press, 1964), 208.

31. Wing-Tsit Chan, ed. and trans., "The Chuang Tzu," in *A Source Book in Chinese Philosophy* (Princeton, NJ: Princeton University Press, 1963), 209.

32. Tolkien, *The Hobbit*, 5. For more on Taoism, see the chapter by Michael C. Brannigan, "The Road Goes Ever On and On": A Hobbit's Tao," in this book.

33. Director Werner Herzog captures some of these prostrations on film in his engaging documentary, *Wheel of Time*, 2003.

34. Bhadantācariya Buddhaghosa, *The Path of Purification*, trans. Bhikkhu Ñānamoli (Kandy, Sri Lanka: Buddhist Publication Society), 2:63.

35. Thich Nhat Hanh, *Peace Is Every Step* (New York: Bantam Books, 1992), 37.

36. Thoreau, "Walking."

37. Tolkien, *The Hobbit*, 55.

BILBO BAGGINS
The Cosmopolitan Hobbit

Dennis Knepp

Cosmopolitan. It's more than a magazine. It's more than a martini. It's a word with an ancient Greek pedigree, and it's an inspiring philosophical idea. A cosmopolitan is a citizen of the world who recognizes that other people live in different ways and wishes good for all of them. In short, a cosmopolitan strives to love all peoples.

A *provincial*, in contrast, fears everyone who lives differently. Shire hobbits are provincials who consider even the hobbits who live across the Brandywine a little queer.[1] But Bilbo learns to become a cosmopolitan by becoming comfortable around dwarves and marveling at elves. And his transformation encourages the reader to take the same journey.

Hobbits in Kansas

Although most of the peoples of Middle-earth already existed
in Norse mythology, hobbits are entirely Tolkien's creation.
Tolkien scholar Tom Shippey explains that they are anach-
ronistic creatures who engage in modern activities despite
their ancient setting.[2] They smoke tobacco and eat potatoes,
both of which are imports from the New World and not
found in medieval England. They enjoy bourgeois creature
comforts such as mantel clocks, teapots, daily postal service,
brass buttons, and fancy waistcoats. They use modern gram-
mar rather than the archaic dialects of other Middle-earth
speakers.

Simply put, hobbits are a representation of rural, late
Victorian Englishness. In addition, they are provincials who
fear the differences of others and who like it when other hobbits are reliably predictable. They don't like weirdos, never go
on adventures for fear of missing a meal, and are highly set in
their traditional ways.

I can identify with hobbits. Like nearly everyone else
growing up in Wichita, Kansas, I was a provincial who feared
foreigners, liked predictable conversations, scorned weirdos,
and mocked the people of our town who lived on the other
side of the Arkansas River.[3] (Our shopping mall was Towne
East, whereas *theirs* was Towne West. What a funny name for
a mall!)

Bilbo remains a modern person throughout *The Hobbit*, and
this enables the reader to identify with him. But by the end
he is no longer a provincial: he has seen the world, eaten foreign food, heard foreign languages, lived with strange people,
encountered exotic dangers, and lived to tell about it. Bilbo
becomes a cosmopolitan hobbit who recognizes that other
people have valid ways of living, and he wishes good for all of
them. In so doing, Bilbo steps into a particularly philosophical
way of living in the world.

An Ancient New Way to Live in the World

Some of the earliest recorded cosmopolitans were ancient Greek thinkers like Socrates (ca. 470–399 BCE) and the notorious Cynic philosopher Diogenes of Sinope (412–323 BCE).[4] Just like today, in the ancient world it was natural for ordinary people to feel a kinship toward family and extended relations. It is normal to identify with your tribe.

In addition, ancient peoples were under increasing pressure to identify with something larger, like the Persian Empire or the Hellenized world. The ancient Athenians encouraged patriotic citizenship in their city and surrounding farmland—a political unit the Greeks called the *polis*.[5] Philosophers took this progression to its logical conclusion and declared an affinity with everyone. To be a citizen of the *cosmos*—the entire universe—is to be a *cosmopolitan*.

Today, too, we find a natural affinity for family and tribe, a patriotic push to identify with one's country, and philosophers advocating something larger. One example of the latter is Kwame Appiah, author of *Cosmopolitanism: Ethics in a World of Strangers*.[6] His life reads like a minilecture in cosmopolitanism.

According to his online biography, "Kwame Anthony Akroma-Ampim Kusi Appiah was born in London (where his Ghanaian father was a law student) but moved as an infant to Ghana, where he grew up."[7] His father was an accomplished lawyer and politician in Ghana. His mother's family is English, but his mother lived in Ghana, where she was active socially and philanthropically. Appiah earned a PhD in philosophy at Cambridge University in England, and he is currently a professor of philosophy at Princeton University. He writes eloquent books about topics from African proverbs to developing experiments in ethics.

Appiah's discussion of cosmopolitanism reminds me of Bilbo's journey. Bilbo learns to be less provincial and more accepting of the big wide world than other hobbits do. Bilbo travels, gets involved in things larger than his home, and learns to tolerate and celebrate the differences of others. In particular, Bilbo learns that we have obligations to others beyond simply family and neighbors and that we should value cultural differences. Appiah notes the following:

> There are two strands that intertwine in the notion of cosmopolitanism. One is the idea that we have obligations to others, obligations that stretch beyond those to whom we are related by the ties of kith and kin, or even the more formal ties of a shared citizenship. The other is that we take seriously the value not just of human life but of particular human lives, which means taking an interest in the practices and beliefs that lend them significance. People are different, the cosmopolitan knows, and there is much to learn from our differences. . . . Whatever our obligations are to others (or theirs to us) they often have the right to go their own way. As we'll see, there will be times when these two ideals—universal concern and respect for legitimate difference—clash. There's a sense in which cosmopolitanism is the name not of the solution but of the challenge.[8]

I particularly like that Appiah acknowledges the *challenge* of having an obligation to others and valuing their differences. Before looking at two deeper philosophical issues, let's look at Bilbo's challenges.

Dwarves as the "Other"

Bilbo learns to accept the dwarves and Gandalf, although acceptance does not mean agreement. He disagrees with the dwarves about all sorts of vital matters, but what is important is that they manage to work together. Bilbo may be pursuing the dragon's hoard on a lark, the dwarves may be restoring honor for their king, and Gandalf may have a more cosmic rationale for the adventure. It doesn't matter that they each have different reasons for going on the quest, as long as they are all going through the experience together. They learn to respect one another's idiosyncrasies through familiarity, cohabitation, and shared meals.

At just over four feet in height, dwarves are shorter than humans but taller than hobbits. Dwarves are also stockier and heavier than hobbits. Living and working in mountain mines has made them strong and stubborn, enduring in labor and hardship, proud in battle, and resistant to pain. Male dwarves wear long beards tucked into their belts, which hold their functional cloaks around their waists. They create wonders in metalwork, masonry, and stone carving. They sing stories of the lost gold and treasures of long-forgotten dwarf kings. They appreciate the natural beauty of a cave as well as palaces built by hard labor.[9]

The dwarves' hard life of toil underground is reflected in their "taciturn language."[10] Using a minimum of pleasantries in their conversation, dwarves do not waste time on small talk. They have work to do, and would you kindly get out of the way? Consider Bilbo's first encounter with a dwarf when he opens his door expecting to meet Gandalf and instead finds "a dwarf with a blue beard tucked into a golden belt, and very bright eyes under his dark-green hood. As soon as the door was opened, he pushed inside, just as if he had been expected. He hung his hooded cloak on the nearest peg, and 'Dwalin at your service!' he said with a low bow."[11]

Dwalin the dwarf doesn't wait around. He comes into the hobbit-hole and makes himself at home. He isn't trying to be rude, but Bilbo's uncomfortable reaction provides great comedy for this early scene. Soon a dozen more dwarves trample Bilbo's hospitality.

Even the dwarves' names reflect their life of labor: Dwalin, Balin, Fili, Kili, Dori, Nori, Ori, Oin, Gloin, Bifur, Bofur, Bombur, and Thorin. It's as though dwarves do not want to waste time with more than two-syllable names. You'll never meet a dwarf named Giambattista Vico.

These invaders, who eat all of his food and dirty all of his dishes, understandably put off Bilbo ("Confusticate and bebother these dwarves!").[12] And the dwarves are understandably unimpressed by this comfortable well-fed squire who Gandalf claims could burglarize for them on their adventure. Gloin harrumphs, "He looks more like a grocer than a burglar!"[13]

But with Gandalf's encouragement, they all go, anyway. And that makes all the difference. Bilbo never once tries to convince the dwarves to shave off those ridiculous beards and move out of the mountains, and the dwarves never try to get Bilbo to wear a gold belt and carry an ax. Even though they argue frequently over the merits of popping into barrels ("This is a mad idea!"), stealing from Smaug ("After that of course the dwarves begged his pardon"), and the giving of gifts for peace ("What have you to say, you descendant of rats?"), they learn to live together for the duration.[14] They become used to each other.

By the end of their adventures, the dwarves respect Bilbo the burglar, and Bilbo honors the dwarves' traditions and forms of beauty. The dwarves did not talk Bilbo into enjoying dwarfish art and traditions. No one convinced him. Rather, it is enough that together they achieved their quest and survived trolls, stone giants, goblins, wargs, Wood-elves, giant spiders, vampire bats, and a dragon. We often believe that those who have endured much with us are those who really know us. They have *compassion*—literally, "shared suffering."

Consider what happens when Bilbo leaves on his return journey:

> Then the dwarves bowed low before their Gate, but words stuck in their throats. "Good-bye and good luck, wherever you fare!" said Balin at last. "If ever you visit us again, when our halls are made fair once more, then the feast shall indeed be splendid!"

"If ever you are passing my way," said Bilbo, "don't wait to knock! Tea is at four; but any of you are welcome at any time!"[15]

This exchange highlights just how much they've come to respect and enjoy each other's company. It also illustrates how different they are even in their own dialects. The dwarves' language is archaic and heroic: we shall feast in our splendid hall! In contrast, Bilbo is a modern Englishman inviting them over for tea at precisely four o'clock. Differences in approach don't matter as long as both are hospitable. Despite their differences, they each want to continue the friendship by eating together.

As Appiah notes, living around other traditions makes you far more accepting and tolerant of them than any philosophical argument would. As a professional philosopher, he is not discouraging conversation across traditions. But the value of those conversations will not be in persuading others, but rather in bringing people together. Appiah expands the concept of conversation to mean any interactive encounter with another culture (eating ethnic food, watching foreign films, and so forth) rather than simply a debate between contestants who keep score. He writes, "Conversation doesn't have to lead to consensus about anything, especially not values; it's enough that it helps people get used to one another."[16] In three hundred pages of adventure, Bilbo gets used to the dwarves. It's fine that they have different ideas, traditions, and ways of living. All that matters is that they can survive the adventure together.

Everyone Wants a *Mithril* Coat

The tension between dwarves and elves is legendary. I think the problem can partly be traced to fundamental differences in the way they live. Dwarves are tough creatures who work with their hands and live under mountains. Elves are magical creatures who love to sing silly songs that mock dwarf beards. Dwarves are blue-collar and earthy, whereas elves are spiritually refined immortals. It's easy to see why they don't get along.

Even though the elves taunt Bilbo and the dwarves, Elrond's Last Homely House provides much-needed rest and recuperation. Among the trolls' plunder, the adventurers find two swords. Elrond can read the ancient runes and informs them, "They are old swords, very old swords of the High Elves of the West, my kin. They were made in Gondolin for the Goblin-wars."[17] One is Orcrist, the Goblin-cleaver; the other is Glamdring, Foe-hammer. Elrond also helps the adventurers read the moon-letters on their map, providing an essential clue to the secret entrance to the Lonely Mountain and Smaug's lair. Although the moon-letters are dwarvish inventions and the runes are about dwarvish events, it takes the elf Elrond to discover and read them.

Much later, among Smaug's dragon-hoard, Thorin finds "a small coat of mail, wrought for some young elf-prince long ago. It was of silver-steel, which the elves call *mithril*, and with it went a belt of pearls and crystals."[18] In a magnificent gesture, Thorin gives the coat to Bilbo, who suspects that he looks "rather absurd" and imagines that the provincial hobbits back home would probably laugh at his elvish costume. But the coat of *mithril* is not only extremely valuable, it's also light and strong—Bilbo wears it in the Battle of Five Armies, and it saves Frodo's life several times in *The Lord of the Rings*.

The swords and the *mithril* coat are good examples of what Appiah calls, without disapproval, "cultural contamination."[19] Cultural purists are mistaken in their desire to keep out foreign elements. Everyone absorbs elements from other cultures and makes them his or her own. The potatoes and pipe-weed so enjoyed by Tolkien's contemporary Englishmen (and hobbits!) are both native to the New World and were imported. Trade and migration have cross-fertilized and hybridized every culture. Even provincials in Kansas drink German beer, eat Italian pizza, and watch movies filmed in New Zealand.

So it is with Bilbo and the dwarves. Despite the history of distrust between dwarves and elves, Thorin and company are more than happy to carry elfish swords into battle and use Elrond's knowledge to read their own map. Despite feeling rather silly, Bilbo is happy to wear a coat of strong yet light-weight *mithril* that protects him from harm. When it makes sense to do so, smart people use good stuff from other cultures, no matter how foreign they may seem.

Learning from Other Cultures

The improbable friendship of Gimli the dwarf and Legolas the elf in *The Lord of the Rings* is Tolkien's most documented example of cross-cultural understanding and tolerance. In contrast, Smaug and the goblins are striking examples of the limitations of tolerance and peaceful coexistence. Why do they differ?

Explaining their differences requires looking more deeply into the philosophy of cosmopolitanism. Appiah discusses two basic cosmopolitan principles: *fallibilism* and *pluralism*.[20]

Fallibilism is basically a fancy word for humility. It is accepting that you might be wrong and not even know it. It's being open to learning from others.

Pluralism is accepting that in many areas of life there may be more than one right answer. In arithmetic there is only one right answer. But in living a life, raising children, studying for a test, or cooking food, there may be more than one right way.

Legolas the elf and Gimli the dwarf accept that their beliefs are fallible: they realize that they could be wrong about impor-tant things and that there may be something to learn from the other guy. That is why Legolas accepts Gimli's invitation to explore the Glittering Caves of Aglarond—he realizes that he might learn something from his dwarf friend about beauty.[21] Similarly, Gimli accompanies Legolas into gloomy and mem-ory-filled Fangorn Forest.

The two friends also accept pluralism: they realize that dwarves and elves live in very different ways, and that's okay. That is why Galadriel, the beautiful co-ruler of Lothlórien, can impress Gimli. Gimli accepts that elves have a different and equally viable way of life, and this allows him to be open to that life.

In my own life I often meet members of the Church of Jesus Christ of Latter-Day Saints (known as Mormons). I will never become a Mormon. But I accept that their different way of life is equally valid (pluralism); and for all I know, they could be right about the ultimate questions about how to live, and I could be wrong (fallibilism).[22] I don't agree with them—if I did, I would become a Mormon! But my wife and I enjoy taking our kids to see their nativity artwork at Christmastime. Pluralism and fallibilism don't require complete agreement—just acceptance, tolerance, and perhaps even appreciation.

Goblins, in contrast, reject pluralism and fallibilism. Goblins, later called orcs, are cruel, black-blooded, fanged creatures armed with whips and scimitars. Their squat bodies sport steel armor, and their long arms carry poisoned daggers and arrows. Living underground, they prefer darkness and avoid sunlight when they can.[23] Goblins believe that they have the only correct way to live and that there is nothing to learn from others. They live in fear and wish to impose this fear on everyone.

Smaug the dragon has absolutely no humility ("I kill where I wish and none dare resist").[24] He thinks there is nothing he could learn from hobbits or dwarves. The lives of others are not interesting or valuable.

Smaug and the goblins are countercosmopolitans who are completely intolerant of others. Appiah uses contemporary Muslim extremists as his example of countercosmopolitans, people who believe that they have the one correct way to live and that other cultures are unfortunate products of human corruption.[25] Muslim extremists may allow some tolerance for variation on unimportant matters (such as what kind of cloth a woman uses for a headscarf), but they are completely intoler-ant about many important matters (such as the demand that a woman should wear a headscarf).

Furthermore, they do not hesitate to use violence to impose their views on others—just like Smaug and the goblins. Provincial hobbits (like provincial Kansans) fear others, but they can still be peaceful. Countercosmopolitan goblins (like all extremists) typically add violence to their hatred.

Can We Really Live Like Bilbo?

Philosophers Pauline Kleingeld and Eric Brown note that there are many different versions of cosmopolitanism. For example, some political cosmopolitans argue for a world gov-ernment. Other cosmopolitans, such as Princeton philosopher Peter Singer, claim that all sentient beings belong to a single community of moral equals and that duties to strangers can be just as morally compelling as duties to family members, neigh-bors, and compatriots.[26]

Bilbo is clearly not a cosmopolitan in either of these senses. Bilbo is what Kleingeld and Brown call a "moderate moral and cultural cosmopolitan."[27] That is, he recognizes that although local ties and allegiances are important, all the Free Peoples of Middle-earth—elves, dwarves, humans, hobbits, and so forth—belong to a single community, and cultural diversity should be appreciated and encouraged. Let's think for a moment about the value of cultural diversity.

Consider cooking breakfast—a hobbit favorite. I could eat pancakes with butter and maple syrup with a side of bacon and a cup of hot coffee with milk. But that's what my parents ate, so perhaps that is too provincial. To be a cosmopoli-tan, I should accept that other people have equally appetizing breakfasts, and I should try them. Maybe I should make a full English breakfast with fried eggs, sausages, baked beans (a recent hugely popular import from the United States), and toast with marmalade served with hot tea and milk. Perhaps I should go online and learn about a traditional breakfast in southern India, Singapore, or Argentina. How can I decide what to eat for breakfast?

It's impossible to imagine a hobbit missing breakfast while fretting about the variety of equally good things to eat. And it seems that Tolkien himself celebrates the rustic and tradition-bound ways of hobbits. He never mocks them as ignorant provincials. Hobbits are rightfully happy in their small lives. They confidently cook meals, brew beer, and build holes in the ground without worrying about how others do it. They are set in their ways and reject most innovations and mechanizations, but rightfully so. Sam and Merry are happy conventional hobbits who end up happily married and celebrated. By contrast, after his return home, Bilbo "had lost his reputation" and "was no longer quite respectable."[28]

Still, Bilbo's adventure was necessary, for it led to the discovery of the Ring, and that led to the downfall of the Lord of the Rings and the return of the King. Ultimately, that fact outweighs the cost. Bilbo's disreputable cosmopolitanism saves Middle-earth.

A moment of difficulty in deciding on breakfast is a small price to pay for being a participatory citizen in our growing, expanding, increasingly interconnected and wired world. Appiah writes, "Depending on the circumstances, conversations across boundaries can be delightful, or just vexing: what they mainly are, though, is inevitable."[29] The elf Gildor says to Frodo, "The wide world is all about you: you can fence yourself in, but you cannot forever fence it out."[30] You can't hide from the influences of the outside world. And claiming that one culture is the absolute best really puts you into the same camp as some of the worst tyrants of human history.[31]

I say *vive la différence*. It's not enough to be good just to your friends and family. To live together, we must all learn kindness to strangers.[32]

NOTES

1. J. R. R. Tolkien, *The Lord of the Rings: The Fellowship of the Ring* (New York: Del Rey/Ballantine Books, 2001), 23.

2. Tom Shippey, *J. R. R. Tolkien: Author of the Century* (Boston: Houghton Mifflin, 2001), 5–11.

3. It is pronounced as it is spelled. We mocked anyone who called it the Arkansaw River.

4. Diogenes considered himself a citizen of the world and spurned local customs and mores, such as rules against having sex in public. He lived in a barrel on the beach, disdaining "unnatural" things such as houses and preferring to live "naturally," as the animals do. I suppose nobody ever asked him why he thought barrels were natural.

5. *Polis* gives us words like "politics" and "politician."

6. Kwame Anthony Appiah, *Cosmopolitanism: Ethics in a World of Strangers* (New York: W. W. Norton, 2006).

7. "Kwame Anthony Appiah," http://www.appiah.net.

8. Appiah, *Cosmopolitanism*, xv.

9. David Day, *Guide to Tolkien's World: A Bestiary* (San Diego: Thunder Bay Press, 1979), 60–75.

10. Shippey, *J. R. R. Tolkien*, 70–71.

11. J. R. R. Tolkien, *The Hobbit: or, There and Back Again* (New York: Del Rey/Ballantine Books, 2001), 7.

12. Ibid., 11.

13. Ibid., 18.

14. Ibid., 179, 220, 277.

15. Ibid., 294.

16. Appiah, *Cosmopolitanism*, 85.

17. Tolkien, *The Hobbit*, 52.

18. Ibid., 240.

19. Appiah, *Cosmopolitanism*, 101.

20. Ibid., 144.

21. J. R. R. Tolkien, *The Two Towers* (New York: Del Rey/Ballantine Books, 2001), 166.

22. For example, Mormons do not drink coffee, whereas I drink at least three cups a day. I accept that these are different ways of living and acknowledge that the Mormons may be right, given the negative health effects of drinking so much coffee.

23. Day, *Guide to Tolkien's World*, 198–203.

24. Tolkien, *The Hobbit*, 226.

25. Appiah, *Cosmopolitanism*, 137–40.

26. Peter Singer, *One World: The Ethics of Globalization* (New Haven, CT: Yale University Press, 2002).

27. Pauline Kleingeld and Eric Brown, "Cosmopolitanism," *Stanford Encyclopedia of Philosophy*, Stanford University, http://www.plato.stanford.edu/entries/cosmopolitanism/.

28. Tolkien, *The Hobbit*, 303, 304.

29. Appiah, *Cosmopolitanism*, xxi.

30. Tolkien, *The Fellowship of the Ring*, 93.

31. Appiah, *Cosmopolitanism*, xvi, notes that both Adolf Hitler and Joseph Stalin were vocal opponents of cosmopolitanism.

32. "Kindness to Strangers" is the title of the last chapter of Appiah's *Cosmopolitanism: Ethics in a World of Strangers*. I thank Dean Rachel Anderson and Librarian Carolyn Riddle of Big Bend Community College, my lovely wife, Jennifer McCarthy, and editors Eric Bronson and Greg Bassham.

PART TWO

THE GOOD, THE BAD, AND THE SLIMY

THE GLORY OF BILBO BAGGINS

Charles Taliaferro and Craig Lindahl-Urben

In Western poetry and history, a great deal of blood has been shed over glory. *The Iliad*, the *Aeneid*, *Beowulf*, and other great Western epics and sagas locate the source of glory (fame, honor, reputation) in the heroic killing of an enemy or, as in *Beowulf*, in defeating a monster, its mother, and then a dragon. From Homeric poetry through much of subsequent history and literature, the concept of glory has been refined, but it has often retained some of its bloody pedigree.

Plato (ca. 428–348 BCE) and other early philosophers were keenly aware of the glory tradition, and they sought to challenge it by introducing an alternative: the love of beauty. In opposition to the Homeric and Spartan ideal of glory through violence, Plato conceived of life as more of a journey or quest. The journey, for Plato, had as its destination the good, the true, and the beautiful. In Plato's *Apology*, Socrates (ca. 470–399 BCE) chastised the citizens of Athens: "Are you not ashamed of heaping up the greatest amount of money and honour and reputation, and caring so little about wisdom and truth and the greatest improvement of the soul, which you never regard or heed at all?"[1] Although Plato and many philosophers after him recognized the good of heroism and the martial virtues, they were suspicious of a glory that required aristocratic violence. The Roman orator and philosopher Cicero (106–43 BCE), for example, once wrote, "We ought to beware of the passion for glory."[2]

In this chapter, we locate J. R. R. Tolkien in this Platonic tradition. In Middle-earth, there are ample opportunities for glory in the classical tradition, but Tolkien also warns us about the seductive danger of pursuing glory for its own sake. *The Hobbit* is particularly brilliant in offering an alternative for those who seek glory first and foremost. Tolkien entreats us to take seriously the good of domestic beauty and the simple delights of home and hearth.

Before looking for domestic beauty in Tolkien's works, though, let's consider more closely the glory tradition in both the classical heroic tradition and in Tolkien's Middle-earth.

Glory in the West and Middle-Earth

At its inception, glory (*kleos*, in Greek) had a crude physical dimension: it involved the public physical display of the spoils of battle achieved through heroic action. The glory of victory was a matter not simply of bloodlust but of disciplined action, and it was not necessarily limited to individual honor, for the glory achieved could flow to the hero's family, tribe, city, or empire. The great early Christian thinker St. Augustine (354–430 CE) wrote the following about classical heroes:

> They were passionately devoted to glory; it was for this that they desired to live, for this they did not hesitate to die. This unbounded passion for glory, above all else, checked their other appetites. They felt it would be

shameful for their country to be enslaved, but glorious for her to have dominion and empire; and so they set their hearts first on making her free, then on making her sovereign.[3]

The heroic acquisition of glory in achieving such power was in proportion to the prestige of the enemy that was killed and despoiled. In *The Iliad*, this is the kind of glory that Achilles and Hector seek when they face each other outside the walls of Troy.[4] When Hector kills Achilles's best friend and then Achilles slays Hector, Achilles gains glory, both for the vengeance of the death of his friend and because of the greatness of Hector, the most noble prince of Troy and its greatest warrior.

The ideal of the glorious hero has not been confined to literature; world history itself has been influenced by the quest for Homeric glory. Alexander the Great (356–323 BCE) was entranced by what he saw as the manly virtues of glory in *The Iliad* and sought to model himself on Achilles. According to the historian Plutarch (ca. 46–120 CE), Alexander kept a copy of *The Iliad* with him throughout his military campaigns, even sleeping with it under his pillow! Alexander's pursuit of glory became a model for Julius Caesar (100–44 BCE) as he sought to identify the glory of Rome with the glory of his own person. This ancient pursuit of glory may also be seen as fueling modern imperial ambitions in the great European powers of France, Spain, Great Britain, and Germany's Third Reich.

With the rise of Christianity, the concept of glory shifted from earthly battlefields and imperial power to the idea that God deserves the ultimate glory and fealty. Christians saw the pagan pursuit of glory as sinful and vain. Augustine wrote the following:

> This "lust for domination" brings great evils to vex and exhausts the whole human race. Rome was conquered by this lust when she triumphed over the conquest of Alba, and to the popular acclaim of her crime she gave the name of "glory," since "the sinner," as the Bible says,

"is praised in the desires of his soul, and the man whose deeds are wicked is congratulated."[5]

For Augustine and other early Christians, glory and praise was due first and foremost to God. Glorifying God for His gifts and perfections was not only good in itself, it also helped to keep in check human vanity and violent ambition. Given that many early Christians embraced complete pacifism, there was also a real opportunity for the concept of glory to be cut loose from its pagan past. However, as Tolkien noted, it wasn't easy for Christians to let go of classical glory.

In 1936, Tolkien delivered a lecture to the British Academy titled "Beowulf: The Monsters and the Critics." The Old English heroic epic *Beowulf* (composed between the eighth and eleventh centuries) has all sorts of Christian elements. But Tolkien pointed out that these elements were largely decorative. Underneath these Christian references there was a very lively, pre-Christian heroic tradition of glory, the earning of praise through violence. The hero of the tale, Beowulf, is more akin to the classical heroes than to the nonviolent Jesus of the New Testament, who urges his followers to love their enemies and turn the other cheek. Whereas Jesus preached compassion, forgiveness, and humility, Beowulf's focus was much more on the thrill of victory and the achievement of glorious renown.

In Tolkien's Middle-earth, there is certainly a place for heroism on the field of battle. In *The Hobbit*, Thorin's foray into the Battle of Five Armies fits squarely into the classical heroic tradition:

> Suddenly there was a great shout, and from the Gate came a trumpet call. They had forgotten Thorin! . . . Out leapt the King under the Mountain, and his companions followed him. Hood and cloak were gone; they were in shining armour, and red light leapt from their eyes. In the gloom the great dwarf gleamed like gold in a dying fire.[6]

Even though Thorin dies in the battle, he achieves glory for the ultimate vanquishing of his enemies and the successful achievement of his heroic quest. Thorin succeeds in winning great glory especially because of the massive overwhelming power he must confront; for as Cicero observed, "The greater the difficulty, the greater the glory."[7]

Such opportunities for classic glory are even more evident in *The Return of the King* when Tolkien describes what appears to be Aragorn's last stand. In perhaps his greatest moment, Aragorn organizes his forces before the Black Gate of Mordor. Tolkien offers this breathtaking portrait of Aragorn just after the gate is swung open and the Men of the West are confronted by hostile forces many times their number:

> Little time was left to Aragorn for the ordering of his battle. Upon the one hill he stood with Gandalf, and there fair and desperate was raised the banner of the Tree and Stars. Upon the other hill hard by stood the banners of Rohan and Dol Amroth, White Horse and Silver Swan. And about each hill a ring was made facing all ways, bristling with spear and sword. But in the front toward Mordor, where the first bitter assault would come, there stood the sons of Elrond on the left with the Dúnedain about them, and on the right the Prince Imrahil with the men of Dol Amroth tall and fair, and picked men of the Tower Guard.[8]

This array of warriors, with their proud names and battle insignia, are set for their moment of glory. The fact that victory seems impossible makes their heroism even more resplendent: Aragorn and his people will, if necessary, be true to the death.

In *The Hobbit*, Bilbo himself seems to gain glory through brave fighting. Bilbo courageously attacks and overcomes monstrous spiders in order to liberate his friends; he successfully frees his friends (again) after they are imprisoned in the underground halls of the Elvenking; he stands up to a deadly dragon;

he uses his wit and skill to outfox the treacherous Gollum; and at great personal risk he compels a proud king to agree to surrender part of his heritage, even though this costs Bilbo a fortune.

Despite all these elements of classical glory in his works of fantasy, Tolkien in fact offers us a critique of that tradition.

Beauty First! Then Glory!

As we noted at the beginning of the chapter, Plato was skeptical of the pursuit of heroic glory for its own sake. This was probably in part because of his experiences in the Peloponnesian War (431–404 BCE), a life-and-death struggle between Athens and Sparta. The war was unimaginable in its brutality, leaving tens of thousands dead from violence, disease, and starvation. Initially defended by Athenian statesmen in the name of imperial dominion and immortal glory, the conflict almost led to the annihilation of Athens and the suicide of Greek civilization.

In place of glory, Plato urged the pursuit of beauty, truth, and goodness, which he saw as naturally life enhancing and the source of the best creativity. By taking pleasure in goodness, we are better able to pursue justice, Plato argued. In the *Symposium*, Plato paid tribute to the power of glory, but he insisted that true creativity and productivity was to be found in taking pleasure in the beautiful. He likened the love of the beautiful to procreation in contrast to the love of battle.

Neither Socrates nor Plato taught strict nonviolence. In his discussion of the ideal state in *The Republic*, Plato clearly acknowledged the need for public order and armed defense. What is missing, however, is the kind of pride in glory that propelled Athens into its disastrous conflict with Sparta. In fact, at the end of *The Republic*, Plato recommended a quiet life devoted to virtue and wisdom rather than the pursuit of power and martial glory.[9] As we have seen, *The Hobbit* and Tolkien's other works of fantasy do have a place for classical glory, but proper glory is defined and deepened by a fundamentally

Platonic (and Christian) identification of glory with virtue, including the virtues of humility, kindness, sociability, and unselfishness.

When Thorin asks Gandalf about taking a particularly dangerous route to his lost kingdom, Gandalf counsels against this:

> "That would be no good," said the wizard, "not without a mighty Warrior, even a Hero. I tried to find one; but warriors are busy fighting one another in distant lands, and in this neighbourhood heroes are scarce, or simply not to be found. Swords in these parts are mostly blunt, and axes are used for trees, and shields as cradles or dish-covers."[10]

Bilbo is chosen to join Thorin and Company not as a fierce warrior but as a burglar, a comparatively comic role. Hence, Bilbo can't be expected to achieve glory in the classical martial tradition, for as Cicero wrote, "The military costume which adorns almost all our statues is a further proof of our passion for glory in war."[11] Aside from Pippin's brief stint as a member of the Tower of the Guard of Gondor and the hobbits' scouring of the Shire, the only time hobbits wear military costumes in Tolkien's works is when Frodo and Sam don ridiculously oversized orc helmets and armor as disguises in Mordor.

The Hobbit does not begin the way that Thorin might introduce himself, with aristocratic titles and songs of ancient lineage. We do not open the book to read of the wrath of Thorin the way we learn of the wrath of Achilles in the opening lines of *The Iliad*. Rather, at the beginning of Tolkien's book we learn that hobbits are plain, quiet folks who never have any adventures or do anything unexpected. They love teapots, pipes, mushrooms, beer, well-tended fields, and cozy burrowlike homes. On first meeting Bilbo, one of the dwarves describes him as looking "more like a grocer than a burglar!"[12]

Tolkien's dwarves, elves, and humans are drawn by the lure of glory and renown. Dwarves seem especially fond of their reputation in fashioning weapons, goblets, harps, and all manner of precious things. At the beginning of *The Hobbit*, as the dwarves sing at the unexpected party in Bag-End, Bilbo is moved by their praise for objects of desire:

> As they sang the hobbit felt the love of beautiful things made by hands and by cunning and by magic moving through him, a fierce and a jealous love, the desire of the hearts of dwarves. Then something Tookish woke up inside him, and he wished to go and see the great mountains, and hear the pine-trees and the waterfalls, and explore the caves, and wear a sword instead of a walking stick. He looked out of the window. . . . He thought of the jewels of the dwarves shining in dark caverns.[13]

So Bilbo is certainly capable of being enchanted by the glories that may be won with a sword and treasure, and the awe and glory of wealth comes over him when he encounters Smaug's stolen wealth:

> Bilbo had heard tell and sing of dragon-hoards before, but the splendour, the lust, the glory of such a treasure had never yet come home to him. His heart was filled and pierced with enchantment and the desire of dwarves; he gazed motionless, almost forgetting the frightful guardian, at the gold beyond price and count.[14]

But while Bilbo feels the appeal of glory, he is not seduced by it. Bilbo's ultimate immunity to the allure of glory and worldly celebrity is apparent in his response to Dain's lament that Bilbo will not get a generous share of the riches. Bilbo's reply is humble. He also seems to imply that great wealth is by its nature unsafe, as it tends to excite violence:

> "Very kind of you," said Bilbo. "But really it is a relief to me. How on earth should I have got all that treasure home without war and murder all along the way, I don't

know. And I don't know what I should have done with it when I got home. I am sure it is better in your hands."

In the end he would only take two small chests, one filled with silver, and the other with gold, such as one strong pony could carry. "That will be quite as much as I can manage," said he.[15]

When Bilbo bids farewell to the dwarves who survived the great battle, he doesn't offer the farewell of a mighty warrior who risked all to create an alliance that won the day. The dwarves speak of a great feast they would offer Bilbo on his return, but Bilbo's response is disarmingly ordinary and nonheroic:

> Then the dwarves bowed low before their Gate, but words stuck in their throats. "Good-bye and good luck, wherever you fare!" said Balin at last. "If ever you visit us again, when our halls are made fair once more, then the feast shall indeed be splendid."
>
> "If ever you are passing my way," said Bilbo, "don't wait to knock! Tea is at four; but any of you are welcome at any time!"[16]

Bilbo thereby resists the kinds of temptations that haunted the Master of Lake-town, Thorin, Smaug, and others with a lust for worldly goods and celebrity.

The stirring bravery of Aragorn is certainly equal to the best in the classical litany of heroes, but note that his great stand before the gates of Mordor was to create a distraction so that two brave but humble hobbits (with a little unintended help from Gollum) could deal the decisive blow to the enemy by destroying the Ring of Power. Bilbo may have seemed like a humble grocer to the dwarves at the outset of *The Hobbit*, and perhaps Frodo (Bilbo's heir) and Sam (the gardener) seemed of no more importance than shopkeepers to the evil Sauron. Still, it is not wise to underestimate the glory that can be earned by ordinary shopkeepers who were not bred for aristocratic combat. After all, Napoleon once remarked that England was a nation of shopkeepers, yet that nation played a crucial role in ending Napoleon's domination of Europe.

Frodo and his fellow hobbits receive great praise and glory at Aragorn's coronation at the end of *The Lord of the Rings*. But the praise is not the hoarse praise of warriors in the Homeric tradition. The glory is praise not of raw power but of the greatness achieved by the humble. Bilbo's achievement extends the classic taxonomy of heroism outlined in British historian Thomas Carlyle's (1795–1881) classic essay, "Hero-Worship."[17] Carlyle identifies many types of heroes, including the hero as divinity, prophet, poet, priest, artist, writer, and monarch. There should be an additional category: the hero as humble hobbit.[18]

The Making and Unmaking of Hobbits

While Tolkien in *The Hobbit* critiques the classical conception of glory, he also warns us about the danger of being too domestic. Without trials and adventure, he says, there would really be very little to talk about:

> Now it is a strange thing, but things that are good to have and days that are good to spend are soon told about, and not much to listen to; while things that are uncomfortable, palpitating, and even gruesome, may make a good tale, and take a deal of telling anyway.[19]

Good stories and conversations seem to be the key elements in Gandalf's mentoring of Bilbo. Bilbo needed to face adventure and danger lest he slip completely into the comfortable and unadventurous life of his neighbors.[20] Without a dangerous adventure, Gandalf would not have been able to say (with affection), "My dear Bilbo! . . . Something is the matter with you! You are not the hobbit that you were."[21] Indeed, Bilbo did win a kind of glory and was greatly honored in his old age by the elves at Rivendell.

But unlike the classic hero, Bilbo retains a love for the beauty of small domestic things amid all his high adventures and the praise he earns. Upon his return to the Shire, Bilbo might have lost some of his nice silver spoons, but he had learned from Beorn an important lesson about the limited value of glory and wealth. Beorn was not at all impressed by Thorin and Company's love for temporal wealth:

> They spoke most of gold and silver and jewels and the making of things by smith-craft, and Beorn did not appear to care for such things: there were no things of gold or silver in his hall, and few save the knives were made of metal at all.[22]

Tolkien may not have been consciously following Plato in subordinating glory to the good and the beautiful, but the ending of *The Hobbit* hints at a Platonic affirmation of worldly beauty as the key to what is truly important in life. Gandalf says:

> "You are a very fine person, Mr. Baggins, and I am very fond of you; but you are only quite a little fellow in a wide world after all."
>
> "Thank goodness!" said Bilbo laughing, and handed him the tobacco-jar.[23]

It is this love of tobacco, meals, gardens, and other simple goods that keeps the quest for excessive glory in check.

Socrates and his student Plato would have agreed. After all, in the *Symposium*, Plato's most famous dialogue about love and beauty, the conversation doesn't take place on the eve of battle (as it does in the Bhagavad Gita) or in a military camp (as it does in *The Iliad*). Rather, the setting is a party in which the participants try to outdo one another in wisdom and speech making. All participate in developing a philosophy of love, with the notable exception of an unruly warrior, Alcibiades. This famously handsome young man appears incapable of truly loving the beautiful; he is better at seduction, pleasure seeking, and the personal pursuit of glory—an ambition that eventually led him to betray Athens to its bitterest enemy, Sparta. Plato and Tolkien have pointed the way to a merrier world.[24]

NOTES

1. Plato, "The Apology," in *Dialogues of Plato*, trans. Benjamin Jowett (New York: Random House, 1937), 1:412–13.

2. Cicero, *De Officiis*, trans. George B. Gardiner (London: Methuen, 1899), 33.

3. Saint Augustine, *City of God*, trans. Henry Scowcroft Bettenson (Harmondsworth, UK: Penguin, 1972), 197.

4. A vivid portrait of ancient Greek glory may be found in book 15, lines 644–652; book 17, lines 412–419, 453–455, and 563–566; and book 19, lines 202–214. For a vivid overview of pagan glory, see William Durant, *The Story of Civilization: The Life of Greece* (Norwalk, CT: Eaton Press, 1992), 50.

5. Saint Augustine, *City of God*, 104.

6. J. R. R. Tolkien, *The Hobbit: or, There and Back Again* (New York: Del Rey/Ballantine Books, 2001), 285.

7. Cicero, *De Officiis*, 32.

8. J. R. R. Tolkien, *The Lord of the Rings: The Return of the King* (New York: Del Rey/ Ballantine Books, 2001), 175.

9. Aristotle (384–322 BCE), Plato's great pupil and the tutor of Alexander the Great, agreed. See his critique of honor as the chief good in Aristotle, *Nicomachean Ethics*, trans. Martin Ostwald (Englewood Cliffs, NJ: Prentice-Hall, 1969), 1095b22–29.

10. Tolkien, *The Hobbit*, 21–22.

11. Cicero, *De Officiis*, 30.

12. Tolkien, *The Hobbit*, 18.

13. Ibid., 15–16.

14. Ibid., 215–16.

15. Ibid., 293.

16. Ibid., 294.

17. Thomas Carlyle, *Past and Present* (New York: Charles Scribner's Sons, 1918), 40–46.

18. For an excellent analysis of hobbits as heroes, see Richard Purtill, *J. R. R. Tolkien: Myth, Morality, and Religion*, 2nd ed. (San Francisco: Ignatius Press, 2003), 59–77.

19. Tolkien, *The Hobbit*, 51. In one of his letters, Tolkien notes that one moral of *The Lord of the Rings* is that "without the high and noble the simple and vulgar is utterly mean; and without the simple and ordinary the noble and heroic is meaningless." Humphrey Carpenter, ed., *The Letters of J. R. R. Tolkien* (Boston: Houghton Mifflin, 1981), 160.

20. As Tolkien notes in a later story, Gandalf's plans to get rid of Smaug nearly failed because Bilbo had changed greatly in the years since Gandalf had last seen him. Bilbo "was getting rather greedy and fat, and his old desires had dwindled down to a sort of private dream." J. R. R. Tolkien, "The Quest of Erebor," in *Unfinished Tales of Númenor and Middle-Earth*, ed. Christopher Tolkien (Boston: Houghton Mifflin, 1980), 232.

21. Tolkien, *The Hobbit*, 302.

22. Ibid., 126.

23. Ibid., 305.

24. We wish to thank Eric Bronson and Gregory Bassham for their excellent insights on glory and hobbits; we are deeply grateful for their encouragement and contributions to our inquiry. We also wish to thank Elizabeth Clark for her brilliant assistance in researching and editing this chapter.

PRIDE AND HUMILITY IN *THE HOBBIT*

Laura Garcia

At the beginning of *The Hobbit*, Bilbo is remarkable for his very unremarkability. He is comfortably well-off and lives a respectably quiet and routine existence. No one would describe him as adventurous, we're told, in spite of rumored shenanigans among some relatives on his mother's side (the Took clan). He is in many respects a proper Englishman, possessing the virtues of hospitality, honor, and geniality.

Bilbo seems at first to be the very picture of humility as well, opening his larder to Gandalf and the thirteen strangers who come crowding into his home at Bag-End. He serves coffee, tea, wine, and ale along with seedcakes, mince pies, pork pies, salad, apple tarts, buttered scones, eggs, cold chicken, and pickles. But we also find that whenever Bilbo gets into serious trouble, it is because one of his good qualities has gotten a bit out of hand, threatening to turn a virtue into a vice.

His sense of honor, for example, makes him bristle when he overhears the dwarf Gloin complain that Bilbo "looks more like a grocer than a burglar." We're told that "he suddenly thought he would go without bed and breakfast to be thought fierce," which is no small spark of indignation in someone who hated to miss a meal as much as Bilbo did. "There is a lot more in [this hobbit] than you guess," Gandalf cautions the dwarves, "and a lot more than he has any idea of himself."[1]

Virtue in Middle-Earth

The importance of virtue, or moral character, runs like a thread through Tolkien's adventure story. The author clearly intends not just to entertain but to educate, and especially to support the claim at least as old as Socrates (ca. 470–399 BCE) that virtue leads to flourishing and vice to degradation. Moral theories can be distinguished by their answers to three fundamental questions: (1) Which kinds of moral judgments are the most basic? (2) Why should I be moral? (3) What makes an action right or wrong?

Regarding the first question, ancient Greek philosophers endorsed a moral theory, now called *virtue ethics*, that made judgments about virtuous character or virtuous actions fundamental. Other moral claims, about what is good (or valuable) and about moral laws and duties, were grounded in judgments about virtue. If Bilbo has a duty to try to protect his friends, for example, this is because loyalty is a virtue. Cheating at a riddle contest is bad because it's vicious to try to deceive someone.

Regarding the second question, Aristotle (384–322 BCE) claimed that a virtuous life, almost by definition, is one that enables a person to achieve his or her fullest potential. Moral virtues are character traits that lead to one's ultimate fulfillment as a rational, social animal, and all humans naturally seek happiness or fulfillment. In Aristotle's view, we ought to act morally because it is the only way to achieve self-fulfillment, and the desire for this kind of fulfillment is behind all of our other desires.

It is no accident that Tolkien's descriptions of Bilbo's contented home at Bag-End and of Elrond's gracious realm of Rivendell reflect the character of the people who live there. When our heroes descend into the valley toward the Last Homely House, we can almost hear the rushing water on the rocks below and smell the pine and oak trees. There is a warm glow from the fires below and the singing of elves among the trees. At last we meet Elrond, and we are not surprised to learn that "he was as noble and fair in face as an elf-lord, as strong as a warrior, as wise as a wizard, as venerable as a king of dwarves, and as kind as summer."[2]

Finally, regarding the third question, Aristotle's virtue theory held that actions deserve moral praise or blame solely because of the intentions and attitudes that motivate them. Judging others' acts to be morally right or wrong requires knowing what they were *trying* to do, even if they didn't succeed. Acting from virtuous motives is acting rightly, whereas acting from any vicious motive is morally wrong.

In our story, when the dwarves are released from the barrels they've been hidden in, they have a hard time forgiving Bilbo for coming up with such an uncomfortable escape plan. Their leader, Thorin, is especially annoyed: "Wet straw was in his draggled beard; he was so sore and stiff, so bruised and buffeted he could hardly stand or stumble through the shallow water to lie groaning on the shore." But Bilbo refuses to accept blame for this outcome, and rightly so, since he certainly hadn't meant to make the dwarves miserable. Hence his rather curt reply to Thorin: "Well, are you alive or are you dead?"[3]

It seems obvious that Tolkien, like Aristotle, operates from a virtue theory of morality. His highest praise is reserved for the virtuous, for characters of character, so to speak, and these folks make their decisions by considering what would be the loyal, courageous, or just thing to do. Our heroes in *The Hobbit*

often choose a path that even they believe is unlikely to produce a positive outcome—it's just the virtuous thing to do.

For example, when Bilbo escapes from the caves of the
goblins, he has no idea what has happened to Gandalf and
the dwarves, so even though he is reluctant to go back into the
dark mountain tunnels, we learn that "he had just made up his
mind that it was his duty, that he must turn back—and very
miserable he felt about it—when he heard voices."[4] Bilbo's
duty in this instance is easily defined in terms of the virtues:
the courageous and loyal thing to do is to come to the aid of
his friends.[5]

Something like Aristotle's virtue theory of morality ani-
mates much of Bilbo's story, and Tolkien even describes the
various creatures of Middle-earth by listing their moral qualities along with their physical characteristics. When we meet
the trolls, we find that "their language . . . was not drawing-
room fashion at all, at all," and they turn out to be sloppy,
argumentative, and not very bright. Goblins, on the other
hand, are fairly clever, but we find them disgusting from the
very start, since they whip and pinch the dwarves and plan
to eat the dwarves' ponies. Tolkien tells us that "goblins are
cruel, wicked, and bad-hearted" and so use their skills to make
weapons of mass destruction, forcing many of their captives
to work as slaves until they die for lack of air and water.[6] The
large, evil, and intelligent wolves, the wargs, are no better, and
in fact they operate in league with the goblins to plan an attack
on the few settlements of men still left in the shadow of the
Misty Mountains.[7]

Fortunately, there are more noble inhabitants of Middle-
earth, and our heroes are quite literally snatched from the fire
at one point by the Lord of the Eagles and his friends, even
though "eagles are not kindly birds. Some are cowardly and
cruel. But the ancient race of the northern mountains were the
greatest of all birds; they were proud and strong and noble-
hearted."[8] We have already met Elrond, almost the paradigm

of Aristotle's "great-souled man," and we instinctively trust Gandalf as well, although his character must be perceived more from his actions than from direct description.

Proud to Be a Hobbit

Moral virtues clearly play an important role in *The Hobbit*, and in general, humility is presented as a virtue and pride as a vice. But there are exceptions. The Lord of the Eagles is described as proud, and this is clearly meant as a compliment in the context (accompanied by adjectives like "strong" and "noble-hearted"). Near the end of the tale we meet Bard, a man of great skill and courage, who brings down Smaug the dragon with his last arrow, announcing for all to hear, "I am Bard, of the line of Girion; I am the slayer of the dragon!"[9] This is not exactly the picture of humility, even though Bard certainly deserves praise for his heroism.

Beyond these examples, however, pride is depicted as a vice and even as the fatal character flaw that leads to the ruin of the wicked: the giant spiders abandon their prey to pursue the invisible Bilbo because they are enraged by his taunts and name-calling, and Bilbo is able to discover Smaug's weak spot by appealing to his vanity and praising his vaunted invincibility.

Furthermore, when the heroes of the story come close to being captured or killed, it's often because they are in the grip of pride in one way or another. When Bilbo speaks to Smaug, he cannot resist the temptation to put in a parting shot about having stolen some of the dragon's treasure. "It was an unfortunate remark, for the dragon spouted terrific flames after him," and the incident gave rise to the proverb "never laugh at live dragons."[10]

Finally, Thorin's dwarvish pride is rekindled by his return to the mountain dwelling of his fathers, and it leads him into a needless dispute with the villagers of Lake-town and the Wood-elves over dividing the dragon's treasures. He begins to refer to himself as "Thorin son of Thrain, King under the Mountain," and a combination of pride and greed prevents him from recognizing the justice of others' claims. He even tells Bilbo, "You have mail [armor] upon you, which is made by my folk, and is too good for you."[11]

In fact, as Tolkien scholar John Rateliff notes, "Pride is the cardinal sin in Tolkien's ethos."[12] Morgoth's introduction of discord into the Music of the Ainur, the Noldorian elves' rebellion against the Valar, Galadriel's fall from grace and self-imposed exile to Middle-earth, the Númenoreans' attempt to conquer death by invading the Blessed Realm, Isildur's disastrous refusal to destroy the Ring after cutting it from Sauron's hand, Sauron's attempt to dominate the world and be worshiped as a God-king, Saruman's corruption and refusal of mercy, and Denethor's fall into madness and suicidal despair are all attributed by Tolkien to the sin of pride.[13]

Conversely, humility is consistently a central virtue in Tolkien's fantasy writings. For example, it is only through the remarkable humility of Frodo and Sam—their rare ability to resist the Ring's enticements to power and glory—that Sauron is defeated in *The Lord of the Rings*.

Tolkien was a devout Catholic, and his depictions of pride and humility are strongly influenced by classical Christian views of the moral virtues and vices. In classical Christian ethics, pride is regarded as one of the Seven Deadly Sins; in fact, it is considered the deadliest of the seven.

Tolkien's friend and Oxford colleague C. S. Lewis wrote that pride is "the great sin" because it separates one from both God and one's neighbors by creating a false view of one's merits before God and blotting out charity by leading one to look down on one's "inferiors." He added, "There is no fault which makes a man more unpopular, and no fault which we are more unconscious of in ourselves."[14]

John Hardon defines pride in the *Pocket Catholic Dictionary* as "an inordinate esteem of oneself" that may be manifested in various ways: "by glorying in achievements, as if they were not primarily the result of divine goodness and grace; by minimizing one's defects or claiming qualities that are not actually possessed; by holding oneself superior to others or disdaining them because they lack what the proud person has; by magnifying the defects of others or dwelling on them."[15]

As we have seen, however, Tolkien doesn't always speak of pride in negative terms. And Lewis pointed out that we often praise people for feeling justifiable "pride in" one's family, achievements, heritage, or school.[16] Is pride, then, sometimes a virtue and sometimes a vice? If so, it seems we are using the word in two different senses.[17] Aristotle's moral theory treated pride as a virtue, but St. Thomas Aquinas (1225–1274), a Catholic philosopher who adopted Aristotle's theory as largely correct, considered pride to be a vice.

One way to resolve this tension might be to say that pride is a secular virtue but a religious vice. But Aquinas rejected that option and even claimed that his treatment of pride is consistent with Aristotle's theory. To see whether he was right, we need to take a closer look at both thinkers' central discussions of pride.

Aristotle dealt with pride in book 4, chapter 3, of the *Nicomachean Ethics*, where he called it a virtue connected with "great and lofty matters" and especially with great honors or a reputation for (moral) greatness. Some translators call this virtue "pride," whereas others use the terms "high-mindedness" or "magnanimity." In a translation by W. D. Ross, Aristotle said, "Now the man is thought to be proud who thinks himself worthy of great things, being worthy of them; for he who does so beyond his deserts is a fool, but no virtuous man is foolish or silly."[18]

The virtuously proud man (and it was always a man, for Aristotle) is worthy of great things and so correctly believes himself to be worthy of them. The great things Aristotle had in mind here are not material things but honor, and honor itself is not a matter of fame or notoriety but a recognition of genuine value:

> If we consider him point by point we shall see the utter absurdity of a proud man who is not good. Nor, again, would he be worthy of honor if he were bad; for honor is the prize of virtue, and it is to the good that it is rendered. Pride, then, seems to be a sort of crown of the virtues; for it makes them greater, and it is not found without them. Therefore it is hard to be truly proud; for it is impossible without nobility and goodness of character.[19]

Aristotle commonly described moral virtue as a kind of mean between two extremes, where the moderate, or middle, way is the virtue and "too much" and "too little" are the opposed vices. In the case of pride, one vice involves thinking more highly of oneself than one actually deserves; Aristotle called this "vainglory" or "foolishness." The opposite vice is thinking of oneself less highly than one deserves, which in Ross's translation is called "undue humility."

Martin Ostwald's translation of the *Nicomachean Ethics* calls the relevant virtue "high-mindedness" rather than "pride," and the corresponding vices are "vanity" (thinking too highly of oneself) and "small-mindedness" (thinking too little of oneself). In a footnote, Ostwald defends his use of "high-mindedness" against another popular choice, "magnanimity," because the latter word has a rather narrow meaning in contemporary English. He notes that Aristotle's Greek term *megalopsychia* literally means "greatness of soul" and that Aristotle used it, as we have seen, to describe a kind of crown of perfect virtue.[20]

Aristotle contended that if one is, in fact, perfectly virtuous, it is proper to *believe* that one is deserving of great honor. Although it might seem that Aristotle was recommending something close to vanity for the truly noble, he would insist that "no honor can be worthy of perfect virtue," so it is impossible for a perfectly good person (if he exists) to overestimate the honor due to him.[21] With respect to the external goods of pleasure, wealth, and the like, Aristotle's great-souled man has a moderate attitude toward these things, being able to enjoy them but also able to do without them.

Humble Pie and Soul Food

What did Aquinas make of Aristotle's account? He had his work cut out for him, since in some translations Aristotle seemed to treat pride as a virtue and humility as a vice, whereas for Aquinas things were exactly the other way around. But Aquinas considered Aristotle's account to be largely correct, and he followed "the Philosopher," as he called him, in treating magnanimity or proper pride under the general category of temperance.

Temperance covers a variety of more specific virtues, and the Greeks considered it one of the four cardinal virtues, along with fortitude, justice, and prudence. The role of temperance is to regulate the natural appetites, so there are as many forms of temperance as there are natural appetites, including the desires for food and drink, sex, honor, and noble actions.

Like Aristotle, then, Aquinas described the virtuous attitude regarding noble actions as a proper or reasonable striving for great things, and he accepted greatness of soul as an appropriate description of this virtue. Aquinas explained that "the difficult good [one that is hard to achieve] has something attractive to the appetite, namely the aspect of good, and likewise something repulsive to the appetite, namely the difficulty of obtaining it."[22]

The difficult good in this case is virtue, or moral perfection, and Aquinas added that the two typical reactions we have to this good are two distinct virtues that we need in order to achieve the good. One spurs us on to keep striving for the good; this is Aristotle's virtue of greatness of soul, which could also be called a kind of proper pride in achieving this greatness. The other virtue prevents us from striving for a kind of excellence or perfection that is beyond our powers, and this is the virtue of humility.[23]

As we have seen, Aquinas's moral theory described two temptations that one might experience when faced with a difficult task: to give up without trying or to overestimate one's powers. Humility helps to prevent the latter mistake, and both ordinary life and Tolkien's stories are filled with proofs of its importance. But Aristotle placed even greater emphasis on the danger of underestimating one's power to achieve greatness of soul, and Tolkien clearly agrees with Aristotle on this point as well.

For example, although the dwarves were unimpressed with Bilbo at their first meeting, their opinion of him rises dramatically after their unfortunate encounter with the giant spiders. When Bilbo finally finds his friends after they were scattered in the pitch-black darkness of Mirkwood Forest, they are tied to a man (or to a dwarf) in great webbed bundles, hanging from the trees in the middle of the wicked spiders' den. Aided by his wits and the magic ring, Bilbo comes up with a plan to draw the spiders away and then circle back to free his friends.

The first part of the plan works a little too well, however: "As quick as lightning they came running and swinging towards the hobbit, flinging out their long threads in all directions, till the air seemed full of waving snares."[24] Soon the spiders have Bilbo completely surrounded, yet he plucks up his courage to taunt them with an insulting song:

> Here I am, naughty little fly;
> you are fat and lazy.
> You cannot trap me though you try;
> in your cobwebs crazy.[25]

Bilbo is able to cut through a weak part of the circle of webs with the help of his sword, Sting, but there is a fierce and lengthy battle before he and the dwarves are safe at last. The dwarves are deeply grateful, of course, and begin to look to Bilbo for leadership. "In fact they praised him so much that Bilbo began to feel there really was something of a bold adventurer about himself after all."[26] Tolkien seems to intend for us to agree with this sentiment and to be proud of Bilbo (in the good sense of "proud") for growing into the role that Gandalf expects of him.

Humble Heroes

With some of the minor characters in the story, we see similar examples of heroes in the making. When the dragon Smaug makes his fiery assault on the village, nearly everyone begins to flee from the flames, leaping into the water that surrounds the island town. Even the Master of the town abandons the fight to look for his gilded boat so he can escape to safety.

But one company of archers holds firm. "Their captain was Bard . . . a descendant in long line of Girion, Lord of Dale. . . . Now he shot with a great yew bow, till all his arrows but one were spent. The flames were near him. His companions were leaving him. He bent his bow for the last time."[27] Although his friends already "knew his worth and courage," it is in this final stand against the dragon that Bard truly comes into his own as having a rightful place among the great of soul. When the people learn that he has slain the dragon, they want to make him their king, and even though Bard has no desire to replace the Master of Lake-town, he does begin to develop a plan to lead a group of men northward and rebuild his ancestral town of Dale.

Among the dwarves, my two favorites are Fili and Kili, both because they are the youngest and because they are not as susceptible to the enchantment of the dragon's treasure. When Thorin refuses to share the treasure with the townsmen and the Wood-elves, "the others would not have dared to find fault with him; but indeed most of them seemed to share his mind—except perhaps old fat Bombur [my other favorite] and Fili and Kili."[28] When Thorin is fatally wounded in battle, we learn that "Fili and Kili had fallen defending him with shield and body, for he was their mother's elder brother."[29]

Nothing more is said of these two, but we are moved by their courage and loyalty and somehow unsurprised that they have grown into war heroes by now. Still, their death also brings to mind an earlier description of the bloody battle: "Already behind [Thorin] among the goblin dead lay many men and many dwarves, and many a fair elf that should have lived yet long ages merrily in the wood."[30]

Thorin himself, an older and more complex character, is tempted into an attitude of false pride, coming to believe that he and his companions are entitled to all of the dragon's treasure. He refuses to listen to the elves and the men who wish to claim their fair share of the spoils, and he even considers breaking his promise to give one-fourteenth of the treasure to Bilbo. Thorin is saved from this downward moral spiral by the onslaught of the goblin army, which unites dwarves, men, and elves in a desperate battle against their common enemies.

The elves and the men are the first to engage in the onslaught; they have some initial success in fending off the goblins, but late in the day a fresh wave of goblins attacks, joined by a host of wargs and "the bodyguard of Bolg, goblins of huge size with scimitars of steel."[31] With darkness approaching, Bard and his forces began to give ground, when "suddenly there was a great shout, and from the Gate came a trumpet call. They had forgotten Thorin! . . . In the gloom, the great dwarf gleamed like gold in a dying fire."[32]

Heedless of danger, "Thorin wielded his axe with mighty strokes, and nothing seemed to harm him. 'To me! To me! Elves and men! O my kinsfolk!' he cried, and his voice shook like a horn in the valley."[33] Thorin leads a strong rally against the goblins and wolves, but our heroes are saved in the end only by help from above in the form of the eagles. These are the same noble creatures who saved Gandalf and company from the fire set by the goblins in the forest. And it is another wise old bird, a thrush, who comes to Bard with the secret of the dragon's only vulnerability. Still, Tolkien's story makes us feel that it is worthwhile to stand for what is right and good even when that good is difficult to achieve, as Aquinas would have said—indeed, even when it threatens one's very life.

The central drama in the story, however, concerns Bilbo and his transformation from a homebody attached to routine and creature comforts to a hero who embarks on a quest (not alone, of course) to slay a wicked, man-eating dragon. At the beginning of the book, when Gandalf tells Bilbo, "I am looking for someone to share in an adventure that I am arranging, and it's very difficult to find anyone," Bilbo is quick to reply, "I should think so—in these parts! We are plain quiet folk and have no use for adventures. Nasty disturbing uncomfortable things!"[34]

But he permits himself to be swept into the adventure after all and returns to Bag-End a very different hobbit, having battled for his life and the lives of his friends against giant spiders, trolls, goblins, wargs, and the powerful dragon. Beyond these feats of courage and cleverness, he had braved the wrath of his companions the dwarves in an unsuccessful attempt to broker a peace between them and the men of Dain, a brave deed that won the praise of Gandalf: "Well done! Mr. Baggins! . . . There is always more about you than anyone expects."[35] "Anyone" here probably includes Bilbo himself!

Given Bilbo's reticence in the beginning, it may seem that he is guilty of vanity in attempting great deeds beyond his abilities. But Bilbo represents the vast majority of everyday folk who may not be looking for excitement but who often rise to deeds of heroism and selflessness in the face of danger or disaster. Perhaps we all have more about us than anyone expects. Bilbo is a reluctant hero at best, however, and when he returns home he hangs his sword above the mantel and contents himself thereafter with "writing poetry and visiting the elves."[36] Lest Bilbo come to think too highly of himself, Gandalf comes for a visit, as he did at the beginning of the story, and asks rather pointedly, "You don't really suppose, do you, that all your adventures and escapes were managed by mere luck, just for your sole benefit?"[37]

Attributing such remarkable success to luck or (worse) one's own greatness would manifest the kind of pride described above as "glorying in achievements, as if they were not primarily the result of goodness and grace." Assuming that things turned out so well because of one's own importance would be a more obvious sign of pride, the kind one might fall into without being fully aware of it. As it turns out, Gandalf needn't worry about Bilbo on either count. The story ends as it began, with a conversation between old friends. When Gandalf continues, "You are a very fine person, Mr. Baggins, and I am very fond of you; but you are only quite a little fellow in a wide world after all," Bilbo laughingly replies, "Thank goodness!" and passes the tobacco jar.[38]

NOTES

1. J. R. R. Tolkien, *The Hobbit: or, There and Back Again* (New York: Del Rey/Ballantine Books, 2001), 18, 19.

2. Ibid., 51.

3. Ibid., 193.

4. Ibid., 91.

5. The same virtue-centered approach is apparent in Bilbo's courageous decision to return to the dwarves and face the music after giving the Arkenstone to the Elvenking and the Lake-men in an attempt to broker peace: "I don't think I ought to leave my friends like this, after all we have gone through together. And I promised to wake up old Bombur at midnight, too!" Ibid., 273. The same approach to moral decision making is evident in Sam's decision to attempt to rescue Frodo from Minas Ithil rather than attempting the "greater good" of destroying the Ring in Mount Doom. J. R. R. Tolkien, *The Lord of the Rings: The Two Towers* (New York: Del Rey/Ballantine Books, 2001), 389–90.

6. Tolkien, *The Hobbit*, 62.

7. Ibid., 102. The wargs are actually demonic, not merely evil. Humphrey Carpenter, ed., *The Letters of J. R. R. Tolkien* (Boston: Houghton Mifflin, 1981), 381; and John D. Rateliff, *The History of* The Hobbit (Boston: Houghton Mifflin, 2007), 1:216–19.

8. Tolkien, *The Hobbit*, 104.

9. Ibid., 252.

10. Ibid., 227.

11. Ibid., 278. Thorin displayed a supercilious pride even before he set out on the Quest to recover the dragon's treasure. When Gandalf tried to convince him to take Bilbo along on the Quest, Thorin exhibited a "haughty disregard" of hobbits, dismissing them as "simpletons" and "food-growers." J. R. R. Tolkien, "The Quest of Erebor," in *Unfinished Tales of Númenor and Middle-Earth*, ed. Christopher Tolkien (Boston: Houghton Mifflin, 1980), 332–33.

12. Rateliff, *The History of* The Hobbit, 2:565.

13. J. R. R. Tolkien, *The Silmarillion*, ed. Christopher Tolkien (Boston: Houghton Mifflin, 1977), 16, 68–70, 278, 289; Tolkien, "The Quest of Erebor," 230, 274, 283, 390, 404; J. R. R. Tolkien, *The Return of the King* (New York: Del Rey/Ballantine Books, 2001), 283, 369; and Carpenter, *Letters*, 243.

14. C. S. Lewis, *Mere Christianity* (San Francisco: HarperSanFrancisco, 2001), 121–25.

15. John A. Hardon, *Pocket Catholic Dictionary* (New York: Image Books, 1985), 342.

16. Lewis, *Mere Christianity*, 127.

17. For a helpful discussion of the various senses of pride, see Richard Taylor, *Restoring Pride: The Lost Virtue of Our Age* (Amherst, NY: Prometheus Books, 1996), 30–39. Psychologists who study pride commonly distinguish between "authentic pride," which flows from real accomplishments, and "hubristic pride," which does not. Benedict Carey, "When All You Have Left Is Your Pride," *New York Times*, April 7, 2009.

18. Aristotle, *Nicomachean Ethics*, trans. W. D. Ross, Internet Classics Archive, http://classics.mit.edu/Aristotle/nicomachaen.4.iv.html.

19. Aristotle, *Nicomachean Ethics*, trans. Martin Ostwald (Englewood Cliffs, NJ: Prentice-Hall, 1969), IV.3, 1123b30–1124a4. All subsequent citations of the *Nicomachean Ethics* will be from this translation.

20. Ibid., 1124a.

21. Ibid., 1124a9.

22. Thomas Aquinas, *Summa Theologica*, trans. Fathers of the English Dominican Province (Notre Dame, IN: Ave Maria Press, 1948), II-II, Q. 161, a. 1, sed contra.

23. An obvious objection arises here, since there seems to be no mention of humility in Aristotle's theory. In fact, the correct estimation of one's own moral worth is what Aristotle called proper pride (or greatness of soul). The vices opposed to pride are small-mindedness, which underestimates one's value, and vanity, which overestimates it. But Aristotle left an opening here, devoting one sentence to the person who is not capable of moral greatness: "A man who deserves and thinks he deserves little is not high-minded, but is a man who knows his limitations." Aristotle, *Nicomachean Ethics*, IV.3, 1123b5). Ostwald notes that Aristotle here used the Greek term *sōphrōn*, defined in the glossary as "a person aware of his limitations in a positive as well as a negative sense: he knows what his abilities and nature do and do not permit him to do. He is a self-controlled man in the sense that he will never want to do what he knows he cannot or should not do." Ibid., 313–14. Although Aristotle did not use the term "humility" here, his description of this virtue seems to match Aquinas's account of humility as a virtue opposed to (improper) pride or vanity.

24. Tolkien, *The Hobbit*, 159.

25. Ibid., 160.
26. Ibid., 166.
27. Ibid., 250.
28. Ibid., 267.
29. Ibid., 292–93.
30. Ibid., 285.
31. Ibid., 284.
32. Ibid., 285.
33. Ibid.
34. Ibid., 4.
35. Ibid., 273–74.
36. Ibid., 304.
37. Ibid., 305.
38. Ibid.

"MY PRECIOUS"

Tolkien on the Perils of Possessiveness

Anna Minore and Gregory Bassham

The Hobbit combines several classic literary genres. It's a fairy tale about a magical world inhabited by imaginary beings such as elves, dwarves, trolls, and dragons. It's an adventure story that features dangers and hair-raising escapes as part of a perilous quest for guarded treasure. And it's a children's book that seeks to teach wholesome ethical values to young readers—"old-fashioned" values such as loyalty, honor, courage, mercy, generosity, and humility.

One of the clearest moral lessons in the book is the importance of keeping "precious" things like golden rings, fabulous jewels, and dragon's treasure in proper ethical perspective. Through his vivid portrayal of possessive characters, such as Gollum, Smaug, Thorin, and the Master of Lake-town, Tolkien cautions his young readers about the dangers of excessive materialism and greed.

The Social Costs of Greed

Greed, in the classic definition of Thomas Aquinas (1225–1274), is "an inordinate love of riches."[1] Because it involves desires that are inordinate or excessive, greed is, by definition, always a vice, or moral failing.

So what do the John Stossels, Ivan Boeskys, and Gordon Gekkos of the world mean when they bodaciously proclaim that "greed is good"?[2] They mean that self-interest and a desire for wealth often have good effects in free-market economies—that because of greed, start-ups get launched, well-paying jobs are created, goods get delivered to market efficiently, lifesaving medicines are developed, retirement accounts are funded, and philanthropists are able to give generously to worthy causes.[3]

All of this may be true and would probably be admitted by Aquinas. When he talked about greed (or "covetousness," in the standard translations), he was referring to a character trait that is, by definition, immoderate—that is, unbalanced and harmful. He was focused on the internal state of the covetous person's soul, not on the effects of greedy behavior on society. Nor did he deny that greed, like envy or pride, sometimes produces good consequences in the world.

According to Aquinas, greed is a vice, or character flaw, for two reasons: it violates our duty to love our neighbor, and it violates our obligation to love ourselves.[4] In other words, greed is an inordinate desire or disposition because it tends to have harmful effects on others and on ourselves.

Let's consider how greed can harm others. Philosophers have long recognized that an immoderate love of wealth is a primary cause of war, violence, crime, exploitation, corruption, and environmental damage. How many wars have been fought over booty or plunder? How many crimes have been motivated by a desire for ill-gotten gain? How many exploitative social systems have been built on a foundation of covetousness?

St. Thomas More (1478–1535) wrote in his classic *Utopia* that if money were abolished, "what a multitude of crimes [could be] pulled up by the roots! . . . Fraud, theft, robbery, quarrels, brawls, seditions, murders, treasons, poisonings, and a whole set of crimes . . . would at once die out. If money disappeared, so would fear, anxiety, worry, toil, and sleepless nights."[5]

And the problem, Plato (ca. 428–348 BCE) believed, is not confined to particular social or economic systems but is rooted in human nature itself. He observed in his own turbulent times that from an

> insatiable love of gold and silver, every man will stoop to any art or contrivance, seemly or unseemly, in the hope of becoming rich; and will make no objection to performing any action, holy, or unholy and utterly base, if only like a beast he have the power of eating and drinking all kinds of things and procuring for himself in every sort of way the gratification of his lust.[6]

So many social harms flow from humans' greedy impulses that utopian philosophers from Plato to St. Thomas More to Karl Marx (1818–1883) have proposed radical communal societies as the only possible cure. Other thinkers, such as the Greek Cynic philosopher Diogenes (ca. 412–323 BCE), the Chinese philosopher Lao-tzu (sixth century BCE), and the American naturalist Henry David Thoreau (1817–1862) have roundly condemned moneygrubbing and recommended instead a simple, self-reliant life in harmony with nature. Beorn himself would most likely agree with Thoreau's famous remark that "a man is rich in proportion to the number of things he can afford to let alone."[7] He would probably also like Lao-tzu's maxim that "he who is contented is rich."[8]

The idea that greed can lead to conflict and war is a central theme of *The Hobbit*. Thorin's consuming lust for the dragon's treasure and his pigheaded refusal to share any of it with other deserving parties nearly leads to a terrible three-way battle among the dwarves, the elves, and the Lake-men. The battle is avoided only because the three warring factions are attacked by the goblins, who are also partly motivated by desire for the treasure.[9] Only as he lies dying does Thorin come to his senses and recognize that "it would be a merrier world" if more of us valued simple pleasures over sparkly jewels.

Besides leading to war, crime, and violence, greed can impair human relationships in countless ways. As best-selling author Harold Kushner notes, greed can separate us from other people by creating a selfish and even obsessive focus on our own desires rather than the needs of others.[10] Great literary works like Jean-Baptiste Molière's *The Miser*, Honoré de Balzac's *Eugenie Grandet*, George Eliot's *Silas Marner*, and Charles Dickens's *A Christmas Carol* vividly portray how excessive money-mindedness separates and alienates us from others, including our loved ones. Recall, for example, how in Dickens's classic novel, Scrooge's miserliness leads to a cheerless solitary existence while he greedily exploits his poor underpaid clerk, Bob Cratchit.

In *The Hobbit*, Gollum provides an extreme example of the isolating effects of all-consuming possessiveness. Gollum lives alone and friendless on an island in the middle of a dark, cold subterranean lake. In *The Lord of the Rings*, we learn that Gollum acquired his magic ring by an act of murderous desire, that he used the ring to steal and commit other wicked deeds, and that he was eventually driven out of his community by his grandmother.[11]

By the time Bilbo encounters him, he has lived alone in the Misty Mountains for more than 450 years.[12] All that time, the lust for the ring slowly ate away at Gollum's mind and corrupted his will. Even Bilbo, despite Gollum's black-hearted treachery, couldn't help feeling a "pity mixed with horror" as he contemplated Gollum's sad, lonely, comfortless life.[13]

The tragic end of the Master of Lake-town—rather shocking for a children's book—offers another example of the isolating and alienating effects of greed. The Master, we're told, was what we today would call a booster: a forward-thinking, commercially minded politician who gave "his mind to trade and tolls, to cargoes and gold," rather than to "old songs."[14] When Lake-town is attacked by the dragon, the Master cowardly flees in his gilded boat and is nearly deposed by the angry Lake-people ("We've had enough of old men and the money-counters! . . . Down with Moneybags."[15])

Ultimately, the Master's avarice overcomes him and he comes to a bad end. "Bard had given him much gold for the help of the Lake-people, but being of the kind that easily catches such disease he fell under the dragon-sickness, and took most of the gold and fled with it, and died of starvation in the Waste, deserted by his companions."[16]

The Personal Costs of Greed

In Christian ethics, greed is considered one of the Seven Deadly Sins and, in fact, as the "root of all evil."[17] It's called the "root" of evil because, as Aquinas notes, having loads of money allows one to commit almost any sin.[18] Throughout the centuries, philosophers and religious thinkers have pointed to a multitude of ways in which an inordinate love of riches can skew one's personality and damage one's psyche.

Philosophers from the Buddha (560–480 BCE) to the ancient Greek Cynics to Thoreau have noted that greed creates a kind of psychic dependency, a bondage to the object of one's desires. In Thoreau's bucolic nineteenth-century United States, there was unquestionably "less noise and more green" than we find today. Yet even then it was becoming clear that the pursuit of the high-debt, high-consumption "good life" could become a rat race in which one loses both one's freedom and one's quality of life. Thoreau wrote the following:

> I have traveled a good deal in Concord; and everywhere, in shops and offices and fields, the inhabitants

have appeared to me to be doing penance in a thousand remarkable ways. . . . The mass of men lead lives of quiet desperation. . . . How many a poor immortal soul have I met well-nigh crushed and smothered under its load, creeping down the road of life, pushing before it a barn seventy-five feet by forty, its Augean stables never cleansed, and one hundred acres of land, tillage, mowing, pasture and wood lot! . . . Who made them serfs of the soil? . . . It is a fool's life, as they will find when they come to the end of it, if not before.[19]

In *The Hobbit* we see the burdening effects of possessiveness represented in both the ring and the dragon-sickness that afflicts Thorin and the Master. Gollum is a slave to the ring; it is his "precious," which he obsesses over day and night. (Only in *The Lord of the Rings*, of course, do we learn *how* enslaving the ring is.) The dragon-sickness—an overpowering lust for dragon-bewitched treasure—also causes a kind of obsessive craving that clouds its victims' thinking and ensnares their hearts. Only Bilbo is largely immune from the sickness. Although like most hobbits he is unusually "free from ambition or greed of wealth," even he at times feels the powerful enchantment.[20]

Philosophers have also pointed out how greed often *creates* more wants and needs than it satisfies. Cardinal John Henry Newman has observed, "A life of money-getting is a life of care"—that is, anxiety and concern.[21] Avaricious people are fretful people; they constantly compare themselves to others, envy those who have more, worry continually about losing what they have, and think day and night about how to get more.

Even worse, as contemporary philosopher Tom Morris notes, unlike most desires, greed tends to be insatiable: no matter how much covetous people have, they always want more. Morris points out that with money,

the concept of "enough" can't get a grip at all. What amount of money is enough? Everyone I know who has a little wants more. But it's even more interesting that everyone I know who has a lot wants even more. A reporter once asked John Rockefeller how much money it takes for a man to be happy. He replied, "A little bit more than he's got."[22]

Gollum offers a perfect illustration of how possessiveness leads to a fretful life. Gollum, we're told, "had brooded for ages on [the ring], and he was always afraid of its being stolen."[23] He "used to wear it at first, till it tired him; and then he kept it in a pouch next to his skin, till it galled him; and now usually he hid it in the rock on his island, and he was always going back to look at it."[24] His possessiveness, fueled by the corrupting influence of the ring, is understandable: He talks to the ring. It gives him food. It gives him power. It gives him unnaturally long life. It keeps him safe. It is his precious, and his entire life centers on it. Yet it's obvious that the ring doesn't make Gollum happy. Instead, it brings him misery, worry, and dependency.

Buddhism provides a non-Western lens through which to examine grasping characters like Gollum. A major difference between Christian and Buddhist thought is found in the concept of self. Unlike the common Western understanding of a physical body and a spiritual soul, Buddhism's view is that there is no self. For Buddhists, any concept of self and other is illusory and merely a manifestation of the mind. Yet far from leading to apathy or amorality, this understanding affirms that one's acts and attitudes are of paramount importance. The explanation of this paradox lies in the central Buddhist concept of *tanha*, or self-centered grasping and clinging. Buddhists believe that we are

possessive, greedy, hateful, angry, worried, and frightened because we think we have a self with needs, desires, and rights that must be honored and satisfied. Buddhists say we are deluded about this self. Our clinging to the idea is the cause of all of our problems and the reason we are reincarnated to lives of suffering over and over again. When we stop clinging to the notion of self, we can advance spiritually and eventually attain nirvana, an extinction of all craving that affords blissful release.[25]

According to Buddhism's Four Noble Truths, this self-centered craving is the major cause of human suffering and discontent. Hence, the right understanding of reality (*anatta*, or no-self) yields freedom and the cessation of afflictive, self-centered emotions. It results in both wisdom (*prajna*) and compassion (*karuna*) and thus seeks to reduce the suffering in the world. This is in contrast to greed, which—seeking to increase the power and possessions of a nonexistent self—is grounded in an illusion.

In Buddhism, therefore, the ultimate cause of hurtful actions is not voluntary wrongdoing but ignorance (*avidya*).[26] Only the ignorant would live in such a deluded manner and increase suffering. Thus, in Buddhism greed becomes a manifestation of ignorance and delusion. It is the result of being mired in *avidya*, which in turn involves being snared in *tanha*, based on the satisfaction of something that doesn't truly exist (the self). When right understanding replaces delusion, the manifestations of delusion (such as possessiveness and greed) can drop away. When right understanding is not reached, we are left with Gollum.

For Tolkien, then, greed is a major character flaw, not only because it fuels so much war, violence, and injustice but also because it offers a false promise of happiness. Greed is like a mirage in the desert, always receding into the distance just as we think we are approaching it. Although time and again we see the rich and famous living messed-up, out-of-control lives, we never learn the obvious lesson. Just ahead, just a little farther, the mirage always beckons.

Queer Lodgings

If greed and possessiveness aren't paths to enduring happiness and strong, peaceful communities, what are? In *The Hobbit*,

Tolkien depicts four happy, well-ordered communities: Bilbo's Shire, Elrond's Rivendell, the Wood-elves' forest realm, and Beorn's "queer lodgings" with his animal friends in the oak-wood. Elsewhere, one of us has examined the elves' secrets to happiness and well-ordered communities.[27] So here let's consider Beorn and Bilbo.

Beorn is a werebear, a skin-changer who, through his own magic, can change himself at will into the form of a gigantic bear. Together with his intelligent, talking animal friends, Beorn lives a life of natural rustic simplicity, raising bees for their honey, eating a vegetarian diet, quaffing home-brewed mead out of large wooden drinking bowls, and refusing to hunt or eat domestic or wild animals.

As Michael Brannigan points out in chapter 2, there are interesting parallels between Tolkien's depiction of Beorn and the ancient Chinese philosophy of Taoism. Taoist sages like Lao-tzu and Chuang-tzu (369–286 BCE) stressed the pursuit of happiness and inner peace through a life of simplicity, harmony with nature, tranquillity, nonstriving, and harmonizing of opposites (yin and yang).

Like Beorn, the early Taoist masters often led solitary lives as forest recluses, preferring a life of natural simplicity to the artificialities, stresses, and hypocrisies of civilization. Like Beorn, the Taoist sages sought to overcome dualities such as nature-human and human-animal. And like Beorn, they had little care for "gold and silver and jewels and the making of things by smith-craft."[28] For the voice of the Tao, they believed, was heard in soft summer breezes and the chatter of mountain brooks, not in the fiery roar of furnaces or in clanging hammers. In the words of Lao-tzu:

> There is no greater disaster than greed.
> He who is contented with contentment is always contented.[29]

In *The Hobbit*, we get only a glimpse at what life is like in the Shire; a much fuller picture is found in *The Lord of the Rings* and other works of Tolkien's. In those works we learn that the Shire-hobbits live simple, rustic lives in close-knit agrarian communities. They take great delight in simple pleasures such as eating and drinking, pipe smoking, gardening, attending parties, playing games, writing and receiving letters, composing family trees, and gathering at village pubs with friends and family.

Naturally cheerful, resilient, hospitable, and peaceable, the hobbits have no government to speak of and virtually no laws or crime. Most hobbits don't even lock their doors at night, and until the Battle of Bywater at the end of *The Return of the King*, no hobbit had ever killed another on purpose in the Shire.[30] Distrustful of technology and uncommonly free of possessiveness, the hobbits share a deep love for the Shire and are content with their simple lives and their largely unchanging communities. Basically, they live a lot like the Amish, except they have less religion and more beer.

One of the hobbits' most appealing features is their generosity. Hobbits love giving presents: in fact, they *give* presents on their birthdays rather than receive them.[31] Bilbo himself is a generous hobbit, and he grows increasingly so as *The Hobbit* unfolds. At the beginning of the tale we learn that Bilbo is a "very well-to-do hobbit" who lives alone in a large and very comfortable hobbit-hole, with multiple rooms: "bedrooms, bathrooms, cellars, pantries (lots of these), wardrobes (he had whole rooms devoted to clothes), kitchens, [and] dining-rooms."[32] Note the plural forms: pantries, kitchens. You get the idea—Bilbo was loaded.

All of this suggests that Bilbo was a bit of a hedonist who enjoyed his creature comforts and may have had—to a degree unusual in hobbits—a possessive streak. Certainly Bilbo is moved during the "unexpected party" by visions of "the jewels of the dwarves shining in dark caverns."[33] At one point he puts on his "business manner" and insists on hearing plain and clear about "risks, out-of-pocket expenses, time required and remuneration, and so forth."[34]

But during his adventure Bilbo grows in many ways, including in generosity. His act of surrendering the Arkenstone—a jewel worth "more than a river of gold"—is an act of stupendous generosity (not to mention courage).[35] Moreover, after the recovery of the treasure, he refuses to take his promised one-fourteenth share, being content with two small chests, one filled with gold and one with silver (plus a share of the buried trolls' gold that he and Gandalf retrieve on their return journey to the Shire).

In *The Lord of the Rings*, we learn that Bilbo gave away virtually all of the dragon-treasure and that his farewell 111th birthday party was an entertainment of extravagant generosity. Seventy-six years after he returned from his journey to the Lonely Mountain, Bilbo gave both Sting (his sword) and his priceless *mithril* coat to Frodo—kingly gifts indeed, for without them Frodo would never have survived the journey to Mordor.

From all this, Tolkien's central message is clear: Be generous. Take delight in food and cheer and song, not in hoarded gold. Count your riches in blessings, not in material possessions. Respect the wisdom of settled traditions and ways of life, and don't assume that all change is necessarily for the better. Focus on quality of life, not the number of toys you have. Simplify, simplify, simplify.

It is an old message, one expressed, as we've seen, by many philosophers and sages. Yet it is a message that has never been more timely.

NOTES

1. Thomas Aquinas, *Summa Theologica*, II-II, Q. 118, art. 4. Aquinas notes that in a broader sense, greed refers to an "immoderate love of possessing," whether of riches or other coveted things (II-II, Q. 118, art. 2). (Yes, that includes your collection of vintage Pabst beer cans.)

2. John Stossel, "Greed Is Good," *Townhall*, April 26, 2006, http://townhall.com/columnists/JohnStossel/2006/04/26/greed_is_good. Ivan Boesky, a disgraced Wall Street

financier, said in a 1985 commencement address, "Greed is all right, by the way. I think greed is healthy. You can be greedy and still feel good about yourself." Quoted in Bob Greene, "Boesky Learned Greed Wasn't Healthy after All," *Boca Raton News*, December 19, 1986, 3C. The punchier version of Boesky's remarks—"Greed is good"—was uttered by the Gordon Gekko character (Michael Douglas) in the 1987 film *Wall Street*.

3. This point is given classical expression in the metaphor of the "invisible hand" in Adam Smith, *The Wealth of Nations* (1776; repr., New York: Modern Library, 1937), 423. For a contemporary defense of free-market capitalism, see Deepak Lal, *Reviving the Invisible Hand: The Case for Classical Liberalism in the Twenty-First Century* (Princeton, NJ: Princeton University Press, 2006).

4. Aquinas, *Summa Theologica*, II-II, Q. 118, art. 1, ad. 2.

5. Sir Thomas More, *Utopia*, trans. and ed. Robert M. Adams (New York: W. W. Norton, 1975), 89–90.

6. Plato, *Laws*, trans. Benjamin Jowett, *The Dialogues of Plato* (New York: Random House, 1937), II: 581. Some would see resonances of this description in the conduct of Wall Street bankers and mortgage lenders, whose irresponsible greed, many believe, sparked the deep global recession that began in 2007.

7. Henry David Thoreau, *Walden* (1854; repr., Roslyn, NY: Walter J. Black, 1942), 106. Many of Thoreau's ideas are reflected in the contemporary voluntary simplicity movement, which touts the benefits of living a simple, low-consumption lifestyle, including less stress, more opportunities for leisure activities and personal growth, and less impact on the environment. For a classic introduction to the voluntary simplicity movement, see Duane Elgin, *Voluntary Simplicity: Toward a Way of Life That Is Outwardly Simple, Inwardly Rich*, rev. ed. (New York: Quill, 1993).

8. Lao-tzu, *Tao Te Ching*, trans. Lin Yutang, in Lin Yutang, ed., *The Wisdom of China and India* (New York: Modern Library, 1942), 602.

9. J. R. R. Tolkien, *The Hobbit: or, There and Back Again* (New York: Del Rey/Ballantine Books, 2001), 282.

10. Harold Kushner, *When All You've Wanted Isn't Enough: The Search for a Life That Matters* (New York: Summit Books, 1986), 52.

11. J. R. R. Tolkien, *The Lord of the Rings: The Fellowship of the Ring* (New York: Del Rey/Ballantine Books, 2001), 58.

12. J. R. R. Tolkien, *The Lord of the Rings: The Return of the King* (New York: Del Rey/Ballantine Books, 2001), 406.

13. Tolkien, *The Hobbit*, 87.

14. Ibid., 197.

15. Ibid., 253.

16. Ibid., 305.

17. 1 Timothy 6:10 ("the love of money is the root of all evil").

18. Aquinas, *Summa Theologica*, I-II, Q. 84, art. 1. Another reason is that greed, perhaps more than any other human passion, has the power to fix the mind and the heart on earthly rather than heavenly goods. For classic expressions of this theme, see Dante, *The Divine Comedy*, trans. John Ciardi (New York: W. W. Norton, 1977), 295–99 (Canto 19),

and Geoffrey Chaucer, "The Parson's Tale," in *Canterbury Tales* (Garden City, NY: International Collector's Library, 1934), 595–96.

19. Thoreau, *Walden*, 28, 29, 30, 32. As Aragorn remarks, "One who cannot cast away a treasure at need is in fetters." J. R. R. Tolkien, *The Lord of the Rings: The Two Towers* (New York: Del Rey/Ballantine Books, 2001), 185.

20. Humphrey Carpenter, ed., *The Letters of J. R. R. Tolkien* (Boston: Houghton Mifflin, 1981), 158; Tolkien, *The Hobbit*, 216, 237. In its extreme forms, avarice can literally be a kind of sickness—a true pathological condition. David Hume, "Of Avarice," in *Essays Moral, Political, Literary*, ed. Eugene F. Miller (Indianapolis, IN: Liberty Classics, 1987), 570–71.

21. John Henry Newman, "The Dangers of Riches," in *Parochial and Plain Sermons* (San Francisco: Ignatius Press, 1987), 448.

22. Tom Morris, *Philosophy for Dummies* (Foster City, CA: IDG Books, 1999), 308. See also Plutarch, "Of Avarice, or Covetousness," in *Moralia*, trans. Philemon Holland (London: Dent, 1911), 277; and Boethius, *The Consolation of Philosophy*, trans. V. E. Watts (Harmondsworth, UK: Penguin Books, 1969), 57.

23. Tolkien, *The Hobbit*, 82.

24. Ibid., 81.

25. Mike Wilson, "Schisms, Murder, and Hungry Ghosts in Shangri-la," *CrossCurrents*, Spring 1999, 26.

26. Socrates (ca. 470–399 BCE) also taught that virtue is knowledge and that no one does wrong willingly. See, for example, *Protagoras* 345d, *Meno* 78a, *Timaeus* 86d.

27. Gregory Bassham, "Tolkien's Six Keys to Happiness," in The Lord of the Rings *and Philosophy: One Ring to Rule Them All*, ed. Gregory Bassham and Eric Bronson (Chicago: Open Court, 2003), 49–60.

28. Tolkien, *The Hobbit*, 126.

29. Lao-tzu, "Tao Te Ching," in *A Sourcebook of Chinese Philosophy*, trans. and ed. Wing-Tsit Chan (Princeton, NJ: Princeton University Press, 1963), 162. Such Taoist parallels shouldn't be pressed too far, of course. There are certainly features of Beorn, such as his fierceness and appalling temper, that reflect his roots in Norse mythology as a werebear berserker (literally, "bear-shirt"), rather than a placid Taoist sage. For more on Beorn's Norse origins, see John Rateliff, *A History of* The Hobbit (Boston: Houghton Mifflin, 2007), 1:256–60.

30. Tolkien, *The Fellowship of the Ring*, 111; Tolkien, *The Return of the King*, 310.

31. Tolkien, *The Fellowship of the Ring*, 28.

32. Tolkien, *The Hobbit*, 1.

33. Ibid., 16.

34. Ibid., 22.

35. Ibid., 268.

TOLKIEN'S JUST WAR

David Kyle Johnson

> War must be, while we defend our lives against a
> destroyer who would devour all; but I do not love
> the bright sword for its sharpness, nor the arrow
> for its swiftness, nor the warrior for his glory. I love
> only that which they defend: the city of the Men of
> Númenor.
>
> —Faramir, in *The Two Towers*[1]

Tolkien's works of fantasy are filled with scenes of battle and
war.[2] Whether it's the titanic battles of *The Silmarillion* that literally reshaped Middle-earth, the Quest of Erebor and the Battle
of Five Armies in *The Hobbit* that ultimately saved Rivendell
and the Shire, or the three great battles of *The Lord of the
Rings*, Tolkien frequently writes about war, often in stirring and
heroic terms.

You might imagine that Tolkien held romantic notions of war, but that isn't so. As a British officer in World War I, he became intimately acquainted with the horrors and the waste of war. Tolkien himself fought in the Battle of the Somme (1916), in which more than a million people were killed or wounded, including an Austrian corporal named Adolf Hitler, who was wounded by a British shell three weeks before Tolkien was put out of action by trench fever.

As Tolkien scholars Janet Brennan Croft and John Garth have demonstrated, there are many resonances of Tolkien's war experiences in his works of fantasy. For example, the Dead Marshes, with its lifeless war-torn bodies looking up from pools of water, reflected Tolkien's experience of seeing thousands dead at the western front.[3] No one who reads Tolkien's heartrending tale of the Nirnaeth Arnoediad (the Battle of Unnumbered Tears) can imagine that he glorified or romanticized war.[4]

But all the same, Tolkien did think that war is sometimes morally justified. The Rohirrim's defense of Helm's Deep, the Ents' destruction of Isengard, Gandalf's rallying of the forces of Gondor to defend their city, and Aragorn's mustering of the Dead to come to the aid of Minas Tirith are all presented as noble and heroic actions. As Sam says in the film version of *The Two Towers*, "there's some good in this world, Mr. Frodo, and it's worth fighting for." Tolkien surely would have agreed.

But not all examples of warfare in Tolkien's writings are so noble or morally clear-cut. The Battle of Five Armies, the climactic battle of *The Hobbit*, started over treasure, after all. The situation, you'll recall, is this: Smaug is dead, Lake-town has been destroyed, and Thorin and his companions are besieged with the dragon's treasure in the Lonely Mountain. Thorin thinks the treasure should all be theirs because it was wrongly taken from their ancestors, but Bard and his fellow Lake-towners believe that they are owed a portion of the treasure.

Bard isn't alone. Backing him up is the Elvenking (Thranduil, Legolas's father) and an army of Wood-elves. The elves originally set out for the Lonely Mountain because they think the treasure might be unguarded and prime for the taking. But after seeing the plight of the Lake-men, the elves decide to help them out—even fighting on their behalf to help them recover a fair share of the gold. Thorin calls for reinforcements, and the dwarves of the Iron Hills show up to defend the dwarves' claims on the treasure. Thorin refuses to compromise, and the armies prepare to duke it out.

As the three armies are about to go to war, Gandalf appears and warns them that a giant army of goblins, wargs, wolves, and vampire bats is about to attack. The goblins are angry about the death of the Great Goblin but are mostly interested in the treasure and conquering the North. The armies of men, dwarves, and elves decide that Gandalf is right, so they put their differences aside and join forces. And when things start looking bad, the army of Great Eagles swoops in to save the day, with the shape-shifter Beorn in tow. Once the battle is won, everyone makes nice and splits up the treasure. There is nothing like a common enemy to solve a dispute.

Was this battle justified? Let's look at what philosophers have had to say about the morality of war to see if this war was really worth its weight in gold.

War! Huh! What Is It Good For?

Pacifists argue that war is not acceptable in any circumstances. Human life is intrinsically valuable, and in war human lives are deliberately taken, so they conclude that war can never be justified. Pacifists often point to the number of innocents killed in war—accidentally and otherwise—to bolster their position. They also point out that combatants in war are often innocent. After all, combatants are usually forced to fight by their governments and would rather be home with their families.

Finally, pacifists argue that violence can never actually solve anything—war always does more harm than good, and even though war may seem to solve problems, it always just creates bigger ones.[5]

But those who object to the pacifists have quite a few possible replies. Human life is valuable, they say, but doesn't that mean that one is justified in defending it? If you can stop the killing of thousands of innocents in Rohan simply by killing Saruman, shouldn't you? If you don't, aren't you devaluing human life? Innocents may be killed in war, but isn't having a few innocents killed better than letting thousands of innocents, or an entire group of people, be killed?

And it's unclear that violence *never* solves anything, the nonpacifists argue. Millions of people died in Europe during World War II, but if the Allies had not fought and won, Hitler might have conquered most of the world and exterminated the Jews. Wasn't defeating fascism and stopping the Holocaust worth it? And although many enemy combatants are innocent in the sense that they were forced to fight by their governments, they *are* trying to kill someone else. Doesn't one have a right to self-defense? If a peaceful country is invaded, doesn't it have a right to defend itself? And wouldn't it be okay for other nations to help it by forcing out the invaders?

Considerations like these led classical philosophers and early Christian thinkers to develop the just-war theory, which sets forth the conditions under which war can be morally justified. There are two aspects of just-war theory.[6] First, *jus ad bellum* (the right to go to war) dictates the conditions under which fighting a war is justified. Second, *jus in bello* (right conduct within war) dictates the methods by which a war may justly be fought.

St. Augustine (354–430) tried to reconcile war with the pacifist teachings of Jesus. His arguments were later developed by Thomas Aquinas (1225–1274) and again by more recent philosophers and theologians. Although there are different versions of just-war theory, the various renditions have many common elements.

The *jus ad bellum* criteria focus on the purpose of a war and are as follows. For a war to be just, it must be started by a *legitimate authority*; if you are not the leader of a population, you cannot rightfully call that population to war. The war must be for a *just cause*; personal jealousy or pride (such as Thorin's rejection of Bard's reasonable proposals) or lust for power (like Sauron's megalomania) are not just causes for war. However, defense against an unwarranted invasion or power grabbing (like Faramir's many skirmishes across the domain of Gondor) is justified.

The purpose of the war must be *proportional*. That is, the anticipated benefits of waging the war must outweigh the harm you are going to have to inflict. In fact, you have to be *reasonably sure you can win the war* before you wage it; if you know you'll lose, surrender would accomplish the same thing but with less loss of life. War also has to be the *last resort*; if economic sanctions can achieve the same results, you should use those instead.

We see Tolkien playing around with the concept of economic sanctions to prevent war in the buildup to the Battle of Five Armies. Dain has just arrived from the Blue Mountains with a large army of dwarves. Dain's envoy is met by Bard. Tolkien writes the following:

> Bard, of course, refused to allow the dwarves to go straight on to the Mountain. He was determined to wait until the gold and silver had been brought out in exchange for the Arkenstone; for he did not believe that this would be done, if once the fortress was manned with so large and warlike a company.[7]

As we see, Bard toys with the idea of sanctions against Thorin, hoping that the lure of the Arkenstone will prove too powerful. Once Dain is able to reinforce Thorin, sanctions won't work and Bard will have to resort to force.

Once a war has begun, just-war theory specifies rules for determining how it may be justly conducted. The *jus in bello* criteria focus on specific military actions in the war and are as follows. Individual military actions must be *rightly directed* toward a *legitimate military objective* and must be *proportional*; in this case, proportionality refers to a specific military action; the benefit derived from it must outweigh the harm it will do, and it should do the minimum amount of harm necessary to accomplish that goal.

Again, *legitimate authority* is required; a military action cannot justifiably be done without appropriate approval. In addition, the action must be *necessary* and *sufficient* for the military objective; the military objective must be achievable by, and only by, the use of force. Finally, the military action must show *discrimination*; no matter what the goal is, noncombatants may never be the intentional target of a military action.

These standards are only guidelines, however. What counts as a just cause, for example? The standards don't tell us. There are obvious examples of what counts, like national defense against an all-destroying invader. But what about taking back one's ancestral homeland from a long-established occupying power? What about a preemptive war against a grave but uncertain foreign threat? What about stopping the spread of intolerant ideologies that deny basic human rights?

Moreover, these just-war standards are not all-or-nothing. If a nation's leader declares war on an invading force knowing that his army can repel the invasion but will probably fight recklessly, his declaration could still be moral—his war is simply not as just as it could be. In addition, if a soldier learns that another branch of the military is using more force than necessary to accomplish its goals, that soldier is not obligated to declare the war unjust, throw down his weapons, and walk home.

A war can still be a just war, and a soldier be justified in fighting in it, even if it doesn't meet all the standards. As Tolkien himself notes, even if in desperation Aragorn and the forces of the West "had bred or hired orcs and had cruelly ravaged the lands of other Men as allies of Sauron, or merely to prevent them from aiding him, their Cause would have remained indefeasibly right."[8]

The Battle of Five Armies

With these traditional just-war principles in mind, let's now ask whether the Battle of Five Armies was justified. The question of the battle's justification can be divided into two parts. First, let's ask whether the men, dwarves, or elves would have been justified in fighting over the treasure.

Each army was led by a legitimate authority—the dwarves by Thorin and Dain, the men by Bard, and the elves by Thranduil—so that criterion is met. But was it a last resort? Were the means proportional? And was there a chance of success? In the case of the men, the answer seems to be yes. They bargained in good faith with Thorin at length before finally resorting to force—even using the Arkenstone as a bargaining chip to prevent the fighting.

As Thranduil notes, the combined forces of the elves and the men had an excellent chance of winning the war, and given that the Lake-men needed their portion of the treasure to rebuild their town, the war's harm would have been justified by the good of reconstruction (although, I grant, such things are hard to determine). Moreover, as Bard notes, part of the treasure was stolen by the dragon from his ancestor, Girion of Dale; it was the dwarves who provoked the dragon's attack on Lake-town; the Lake-men helped the dwarves when they were in need; and it was Bard, not the dwarves, who slew the dragon and thus delivered the treasure.

The elves are a slightly different case. Initially, they are not unlike the goblins: showing up to take some treasure because they think it is unguarded. But after they arrive and see the plight of the men, they change their tune and offer to help them. Thranduil, who is king of a "good and kindly people," even seems to explicitly acknowledge that war should be fought only as a last resort and only if it is winnable.[9] When Bard suggests attacking the dwarves as they approach the Mountain, the Elven-king says the following:

> Long will I tarry, ere I begin this war for gold. The dwarves cannot pass us, unless we will, or do anything that we cannot mark. Let us hope still for something that will bring reconciliation. Our advantage in numbers will be enough, if in the end it must come to unhappy blows.[10]

The dwarves, in contrast, seem to be far less justified. Their fighting certainly wasn't a last resort—they simply could have given up the one-twelfth portion of the treasure that Bard requested. In fact, the main causes of their fighting seem to have been greed and pride, and those certainly are not just causes. Moreover, it was the dwarves who began the actual hostilities. As Gandalf says, Thorin was "not making a very splendid figure as King under the Mountain."[11]

Next we need to ask whether the five-way battle that actually happened was justified. The goblins are clearly in the wrong. None of their motivations (revenge for the just killing of the Great Goblin, greed, lust for dominion) are just causes.

The men, the elves, and the dwarves, however, are obviously fighting a war of self-defense (and defense of others) against a host of murderous invaders—a perfectly just cause. The other conditions seem to be met as well. The uneasy coalition knows that there is no bargaining with enraged goblins and that they would all be killed unless they fight back, so the fighting seems to be a last resort and proportional. And given that they have three armies, the chance of success is reasonable. So their fighting seems justified. And since the Eagles and Beorn are helping their just cause, they seem to be justified in their fighting as well.

All in all, just-war theory confirms what most of us—and most of Tolkien's young readers—would think about the rights and wrongs of the Battle of Five Armies. The dwarves were acting wrongly in not sharing the treasure, and the goblins were acting unjustly in trying to take the treasure that was not theirs. The elves, the dwarves, and the men were fighting a just battle against the goblins and the wolves. But there is one more thing to consider: Did Tolkien himself really believe that wars could be just?

Was Tolkien Really a Just-War Theorist?

Doubts about whether Tolkien endorsed (or fully endorsed) traditional just-war principles stem from two sources in Tolkien's writings: passages that appear to support pacifism and passages that exalt mercy over justice or cast doubt on the right of mortal creatures to decide who deserves to live or die. Let's look at examples of such passages.

Two major figures in *The Lord of the Rings*—Tom Bombadil and Frodo Baggins—appear to adopt views that are at least substantially pacifist. Bombadil, the powerful and mysterious nature spirit featured in *The Fellowship of the Ring*, refuses to take or use the Ring and has, Tolkien says, "renounced control" and adopted "a natural pacifist view, which always arises in the mind when there is a war."[12] Tolkien clearly portrays Bombadil as an ancient, holy, and immensely powerful being.[13] Should we say, then, that Tolkien endorses Bombadil's pacifism as his own?

The answer is no, because Tolkien makes clear that Bombadil is a special case. Bombadil renounces all interest in questions "of the rights and wrongs of power and control" in order to devote himself fully to the contemplation and enjoyment of nature for its own sake. He is thus like a monk who takes a special vow to abandon earthly pleasures and concerns in order to focus on higher things.

"The view of Rivendell," Tolkien says, "is that [Bombadil's renunciation] is an excellent thing to have represented, but that there are in fact things with which it cannot cope; and upon which its existence depends. Ultimately only the victory of the West will allow Bombadil to continue, or even to survive."[14] Thus Tolkien does not endorse Bombadil's pacifist view as a generally applicable principle.

A second example of apparent pacifism in *The Lord of the Rings* is Frodo's refusal to use weapons or to condone unnecessary violence or retribution in kicking "Sharkey" (Saruman) and his men out of the Shire at the conclusion of *The Return of the King*.[15] Does Frodo—Tolkien's heroic and almost Christlike suffering servant—speak here for Tolkien himself?

He does not. Tolkien makes this clear in a letter:

> Frodo's attitude to weapons was personal. He was not in modern terms a "pacifist." Of course, he was mainly horrified at the prospect of civil war among Hobbits; but he had (I suppose) also reached the conclusion that physical fighting is actually less ultimately effective than most (good) men think it is![16]

So Tolkien sees Frodo, like Bombadil, as a special case, not as a model for all to follow.

Tolkien was a Christian, and the traditional Christian virtues of pity, mercy, and compassion loom large in both *The Hobbit* and *The Lord of the Rings*.

Consider Tolkien's take on Gollum. Early in *The Fellowship of the Ring*, when Frodo laments that Bilbo didn't stab Gollum when he had the chance, Gandalf retorts as follows:

> Pity? It was Pity that stayed his hand. Pity, and Mercy: not to strike without need. . . . Many that live deserve death. And some that die deserve life. Can you give it to them? Then do not be too eager to deal out death in judgment. For even the very wise cannot see all ends.[17]

Although such remarks are more about killing on an individual level and could be applied more directly to issues like capital punishment, it could very well be a pacifist creed. Even if the invader deserves death for invading, are we qualified to "play God," to deal out death and judgment? Besides, even the wise cannot know whether fighting, even in self-defense, will bring about a greater good. Shouldn't one therefore play it safe and not fight?

Tolkien pretty clearly did not accept a complete pacifist reading of Gandalf's remark, as a close look at the original passage in *The Hobbit* makes clear. As Gollum blocks his exit, Bilbo thinks to himself that he

> must get away, out of this horrible darkness, while he had any strength left. He must fight. He must stab the foul thing, put its eyes out, kill it. It meant to kill him. No . . . Gollum had not actually threatened to kill him, or tried to yet.[18]

Since it would not be an act of self-defense, killing Gollum would not have been justified. But the passage also suggests that if Gollum *had* threatened to kill Bilbo, or tried, Bilbo would have been justified in killing him if this was necessary to save his own life. So it seems that Tolkien does think that killing can be justified.

Other passages in Tolkien's works provide even stronger evidence that he believed some wars were just. In *The Silmarillion*, not only the good elves but even the demigods themselves (the Valar) join in battle to defeat the original Dark Lord, Morgoth. In *The Lord of the Rings*, patently good characters such as Gandalf, Aragorn, Legolas, and Sam all take up arms to defend the West from Sauron and his all-destroying armies. Each of these heroes would no doubt agree with Faramir's view, expressed in the quote at the beginning of this chapter, that "war must be, while we defend our lives against a destroyer who would devour all."

But the clearest evidence of Tolkien's views on the morality of war is found in his letters. Writing in April 1944 to his son

Christopher, who was then training as a bomber pilot in South Africa, Tolkien comments as follows:

> The utter stupid waste of war, not only material but moral and spiritual, is so staggering to those who have to endure it. And always was (despite the poets) and always will be (despite the propagandists)—*not of course that it has not [been] and will be necessary to face it in an evil world.* But so short is human memory and so evanescent are its generations that in only about 30 years there will be few or no people with that dire experience which alone goes really to the heart. The burnt hand teaches most about fire.[19]

Here Tolkien makes clear that war—however tragic, wasteful, and foolishly glorified—is an unavoidable evil in an evil world. In another letter to Christopher, he notes that in real life there are many orclike characters, vicious and cruel, and in war they are usually found on both sides (not just Sauron's). He then says:

> In real (exterior) life men are on both sides: which means a motley alliance of orcs, beasts, demons, plain naturally honest men, and angels. But it does make some difference who are your captains and whether they are orc-like per se! And what it is all about (or thought to be). It is even in this world possible to be (more or less) in the wrong or in the right.[20]

Here he seems to notice that how a war is fought has something to do with whether it is justified and that it seems to be possible to be "in the right" during war. Elsewhere Tolkien says something similar:

> There are clear cases: e.g. acts of sheer cruel aggression, in which *right* is from the beginning wholly on one side. . . . That being so, the *right* will remain an inalienable

possession of the right side and justify its cause throughout. . . . The aggressors are themselves primarily to
blame for the evil deeds that proceed from their original
violation of justice. . . . They at any rate have no right
to demand that their victims when assaulted should not
demand an eye for an eye and a tooth for a tooth.[21]

It is clear, then, that Tolkien did believe that war, however
tragic and destructive, could sometimes be morally justified.

But perhaps Tolkien did not agree with all the traditional
criteria of just-war theory. For example, just-war theory says
that wars may be fought only if there are "serious prospects of
success."[22] Did Tolkien agree? It would seem not. The Battle
of Helm's Deep was supposedly unwinnable, as was the
Battle of the Morannon at the gates of Mordor. Since Tolkien
clearly considered these battles justified, it would seem the
odds of success were irrelevant to him. (After all, Gandalf himself admits there was ever only a "fool's hope" for Frodo's success.[23]) Thus, it seems that Tolkien disagreed with that aspect
of just-war theory.

But not so fast! The just-war theory suggests surrender in
an unwinnable war, mainly because it gets the same result with
less loss of life. But when one is fighting Uruk-hai or orcs, one
knows surrender will just make things worse. In addition, some
just-war theorists suggest that fighting a hopeless battle can
be justified, if it's in defense of key values.[24]

Since the Battle of the Morannon was fought to distract
Sauron while Frodo and Sam chucked the One Ring into the
fires of Mount Doom, that seems to be in defense of a key
value: the freedom of the Free Peoples of Middle-earth. And
maybe the biggest clue that Tolkien actually agreed with this
principle is found in his depiction of Denethor as he sends
Faramir to defend the river at Osgiliath, knowing the cause to
be hopeless. Denethor is clearly portrayed as being mad. Even
Gandalf tells Faramir not to rashly throw his life away.[25]

But the truth is, Tolkien just doesn't tell us enough to know for sure whether he agreed with every aspect of just-war theory or not. Still, there is no doubt that Tolkien believed strongly that "there's some good in this world . . . and it's worth fighting for."[26]

NOTES

1. J. R. R. Tolkien, *The Lord of the Rings: The Two Towers* (New York: Del Rey/Ballantine Books, 2001), 314.

2. For a comprehensive treatment of the theme, see Janet Brennan Croft, *War and the Works of J. R. R. Tolkien* (Westport, CT: Praeger, 2004).

3. For additional examples, see John Garth, *Tolkien and the Great War: The Threshold of Middle-Earth* (Boston: Houghton Mifflin, 2003), 311–12.

4. J. R. R. Tolkien, *The Silmarillion*, ed. Christopher Tolkien (Boston: Houghton Mifflin, 1977), 192–95.

5. For a useful overview of pacifist arguments and viewpoints, see Jan Narveson, "At Arms' Length: Violence and War," in *Matters of Life and Death: New Introductory Essays in Moral Philosophy*, ed. Tom Regan, 2nd ed. (New York: McGraw-Hill, 1986), 137–42.

6. For a helpful overview, see Brian Orend, "War," *Stanford Encyclopedia of Philosophy*, Stanford University, http://www.Plato.stanford.edu/entries/war. Because of limitations of space, there are complexities to the traditional just war theory that can't be delved into here.

7. J. R. R. *The Hobbit: or, There and Back Again* (New York: Del Rey/Ballantine Books, 2001), 279.

8. Humphrey Carpenter, ed., *The Letters of J. R. R. Tolkien* (Boston: Houghton Mifflin, 1981), 244.

9. Tolkien, *The Hobbit*, 255.

10. Ibid., 280.

11. Ibid., 277.

12. Carpenter, *Letters*, 179.

13. There is considerable debate among Tolkien scholars about who, or what, Bombadil is. For one plausible answer, see Gene Hargrove, "Who Is Tom Bombadil?" University of North Texas College of Arts and Sciences, http://www.cas.unt.edu/~hargrove/bombadil .html. Hargrove, a philosopher and Tolkien expert at the University of North Texas, argues that Bombadil is Aulë, the archangelic demigod who created the dwarves.

14. Carpenter, *Letters*, 179.

15. J. R. R. Tolkien, *The Lord of the Rings: The Return of the King* (New York: Del Rey/ Ballantine Books, 2001), 310, 314.

16. Carpenter, *Letters*, 255.

17. J. R. R. Tolkien, *The Lord of the Rings: The Fellowship of the Ring* (New York: Del Rey/Ballantine Books, 2001), 65.

18. Tolkien, *The Hobbit*, 86–87.

19. Carpenter, *Letters*, 75–76 (emphasis added).

20. Ibid., 82.

21. Ibid., 242–43.

22. *Catechism of the Catholic Church* (Mahwah, NJ: Paulist Press, 1994), 555.

23. Tolkien, *The Return of the King*, 83.

24. National Conference of Catholic Bishops, *The Challenge of Peace: God's Promise and Our Response* (Washington D.C.: U.S. Conference of Catholic Bishops, 1984), 42–43.

25. Tolkien, *The Return of the King*, 85.

26. A huge special thanks goes to my good friend Caleb Holt, whose godlike knowledge of Tolkien and literary prowess greatly contributed to this chapter.

"PRETTY FAIR NONSENSE"

Art and Beauty in *The Hobbit*

Philip Tallon

What can *The Hobbit* show us about the philosophy of art? Or perhaps we might ask, what could *one* hobbit tell us about this subject? If, for instance, Bilbo had to give a lecture on art at the museum at Michel Delving, what would he say? This chapter will attempt to answer this question by looking at some key themes in Tolkien's thought and seeing how these themes are present in *The Hobbit*.

Once you start looking, it's easy to see that aesthetics (the area of philosophy concerned with art and beauty) is fundamental to understanding the world of *The Hobbit* and the views of its creator. Whether it's the magical map Gandalf gives Thorin, Gollum's clever riddles in the dark, the ring of power Bilbo finds, the artistic way Gandalf weaves his story for Beorn, or the peerless beauty of the Arkenstone of Thrain, the arts are continually a key feature in the story.

Works of art are to *The Hobbit* what surveillance gadgets and secret documents are to spy movies: integral elements that drive the plot. The story of *The Hobbit* is a journey through a world of craftsmanship, artifacts, and artistry. From his insular and routinized world within the protected Shire, Bilbo journeys out and experiences a wider and weirder world than he could have ever imagined.

Of course, hobbits themselves are not a terribly artistic race. Although their pipe smoking is described by them as an art, and all hobbits, Tolkien says, learn the art of cooking, it seems that most hobbit craftsmanship is dedicated to practicality and comfort. If Bilbo had never journeyed forth from the Shire, it seems doubtful that he would have had much to say about artistry or beauty, except perhaps to note the best way to pack a pipe or to suggest what kind of beer goes best with roast mutton.

Tolkien and the Art for Art's Sake Movement

Tolkien, who lived from 1892 to 1973, was born at the end of a century that saw a huge change in the conception of art and beauty. In the Middle Ages, art served as the handmaiden of the church, illustrating (both figuratively and literally) the text of the Christian worldview. By the nineteenth century, the idea that art ought to conform itself to the message of the church, or serve primarily to confirm moral and spiritual values, had long been eroded.

Through changes in aesthetics set in motion a century before by Immanuel Kant (1724–1804), it was no longer widely assumed that art could or should serve as a vehicle for instruction or moral improvement. Around the time Tolkien was born, it was widely assumed that art existed in a realm that was indifferent or perhaps even hostile to truth and morality. Oscar Wilde (1854–1900) expressed this prevalent mood well when he remarked that "art is out of the reach of morals, for her eyes are fixed upon things beautiful and immortal and ever-changing. To morals belong the lower and less intellectual spheres."[1]

This development, which Wilde participated in and gave voice to, is often known as the "art for art's sake" movement. It left morality and teaching behind in the way that schoolchildren leave their books in the classroom when going out for recess. Art was relieved from having to *do* anything. James Whistler (1834–1903), the famous painter of mothers, wrote, "Art should be independent of all claptrap—should stand alone . . . and appeal to the artistic sense of eye or ear, without confounding this with emotions entirely foreign to it, as devotion, pity, love, patriotism and the like."[2]

Today the idea that art exists in a separate sphere from other realms of human importance is widely assumed in Western culture. The phrase "art for art's sake," or its Latin equivalent, *ars gratia artis*, is commonly quoted as a standard view of creativity. It is even the motto of the Hollywood studio MGM, which, appropriately, coproduced *The Hobbit* movies.

Tolkien agreed with the art for art's sake movement, but only up to a point. Like Whistler and Wilde, Tolkien believed that art should not be seen as mainly practical or utilitarian. For instance, Tolkien expresses a cordial dislike of forms of literature, such as allegory, that explicitly seek to teach a message.[3] Although Tolkien was a Christian, he didn't believe that art should simply be the handmaiden of the church; he saw artistic creation as a worthy end in itself and not merely a means to a greater purpose.

With words that sound somewhat like Whistler, Tolkien writes, "Art and the creative (or, as I should say, sub-creative) desire seems to have no biological function, and to be apart from the satisfactions of plain ordinary biological life."[4] In other words, Tolkien saw no direct practical need for creativity; unless one sells a lot of art, it doesn't put bread on the table or a roof over one's head.

Furthermore, Tolkien seemed to *favor* the impracticality of art as a real benefit, noting, for example, that the elves "are primarily artists," whose magic is "Art and not Power, sub-creation not domination and tyrannous re-forming of Creation."[5] Writing about the dangers of technology, Tolkien laments that humans are not more elvish in this regard:

> There is the tragedy and despair of all machinery laid bare. Unlike art, which is content to create a new secondary world in the mind, it attempts to actualize desire, and so to create power in this World; and that cannot really be done with any real satisfaction. Labour-saving machinery only creates endless and worse labour.[6]

All of this is to say, that for Tolkien, creativity wasn't first and foremost about *doing* anything practical. In this way he echoes themes from the art for art's sake movement.

"Just for the Fun of It"

At the height of their power and creativity, the dwarves also saw art as intrinsically valuable, making objects simply for enjoyment. At the beginning of *The Hobbit*, they drop in on Bilbo, bringing him into the adventure. Describing what they have lost in their long exile from the Lonely Mountain, Thorin tells of better times:

> Altogether those were good days for us, and the poorest of us had money to spend and to lend, and leisure to make beautiful things just for the fun of it, not to speak of the most marvelous and magical toys, the like of which is not to be found in the world now-a-days.[7]

Creation "just for the fun of it" seems to be an activity also shared by other races in *The Hobbit*. We see Gandalf blowing smoke rings, and we hear elves singing. The wizard isn't above a bit of playing around (remember also his famous fireworks), and neither are the elves. When Thorin and Company approach Elrond's house, they hear singing from the trees: "So they laughed and sang in the trees; and pretty fair nonsense I daresay you think it. Not that they would care; they would only laugh all the more if you told them so."[8]

Tolkien was similarly unconcerned with whether modernist critics would judge his fantasy writings to be nonsense. Tolkien invented and endlessly elaborated his world of Middle-earth with no sense that it could ever be anything more than a private amusement. "I am a very serious person and cannot distinguish between private amusement and duty," Tolkien writes, adding, "I work only for private amusement, since I find my duties privately amusing."[9]

Writing much later, Tolkien confesses that it was only his friend and fellow scribbler C. S. Lewis who convinced him to publish much of his writing, including *The Lord of the Rings*. "Only from [Lewis] did I ever get the idea that my 'stuff' could be anything more than a private hobby."[10] Most of Tolkien's colleagues at Oxford would have thought his artistic creation "pretty fair nonsense," but Tolkien himself, like the elves and the dwarves, had a healthy appreciation of creativity "just for the fun of it."

"They Too May Perceive the Beauty of Eä"

Unlike many of the doctrinaire art for art's sake writers, however, Tolkien does make room for a moral dimension in artistic creation, especially pointing out how creativity and the appreciation of beauty are signs of moral and spiritual health.[11] In many places in *The Hobbit*, Tolkien uses sensitivity to beauty as a kind of moral thermometer to test when a person (or a race of people) has a healthy level of virtue or moral excellence.

Good creatures in Tolkien's Middle-earth tend to be creative and responsive to beauty, and bad creatures do not. After their narrow escape from the trolls, Thorin and his companions find some elvish blades among the trolls' belongings. Gandalf realizes immediately that the blades, with their "beautiful scabbards and jeweled hilts," could not have been made by trolls.[12]

Tolkien also notes that the goblins' songs are more like croaking than singing, and as a further sign that goblins "are cruel, wicked, and bad hearted," Tolkien states that they "make no beautiful things, but they make many clever ones." Indeed, Tolkien notes that goblins most likely invented some of the machines used today to kill many people at once.[13] This contrasts with the way Tolkien praises elves as "primarily artists" who seek "Art and not Power." Clearly, Tolkien is suggesting that good creativity is aimed at bringing about beauty and enjoyment, not death and destruction.

Artistic creation is a sign that we can love something other than ourselves. The dwarves' very existence sprang from this good desire to create out of love. In *The Silmarillion*, Tolkien tells how Aulë the Smith (one of the Valar, the almost godlike angelic beings of Middle-earth) wanted something else to love and so created a race of tough little people who, like Aulë, are smiths. When Aulë gets in trouble with Ilúvatar, the God figure of Middle-earth, for creating living creatures without permission, Aulë explains why he created the dwarves behind Ilúvatar's back:

> I desired things other than I am, to love and to teach them, so that they too may perceive the beauty of Eä [the physical universe], which thou hast caused to be. For it seemed to me that there is great room in Arda [Earth and its solar system] for many things that might rejoice in it, yet it is for the most part empty still. . . . Yet the making of things is in my heart from my own making by thee.[14]

Here Aulë indicates why he wanted to make the dwarves in the first place: because he thought the world could use some other creatures to enjoy its beauty. Because of this entirely good intention on Aulë's part, Ilúvatar does not destroy the dwarves but lets them become a race of Middle-earth.

Contrast Aulë's motivation with that of Saruman when the latter creates an improved breed of sun-resistant super-orcs (Uruk-hai), and you can clearly see the difference between moral creativity and the immoral desire for domination and corruption. Aulë just wants to create out of creative benevolence and enjoyment; Saruman, with his "mind of metal and wheels," wants domination, no matter how ugly his creations are.[15]

It's easy to see, then, that aesthetic appreciation and craftsmanship are positive moral indicators in the world of *The Hobbit*. This connects with St. Augustine's view of virtue as an *ordo amoris*, or "right ordering of the loves."[16] Tolkien, well schooled in the tradition to which Augustine contributed, seems to agree that good people (and good hobbits, good dwarves, and good Valar), appreciate good art, whereas evil beings lack a proper taste for beauty. Perhaps the best example of this from *The Hobbit* is what Thorin says about dragons in his first meeting with Bilbo:

> Dragons steal gold and jewels, you know, from men and elves and dwarves, wherever they can find them; and they guard their plunder as long as they live (which is practically forever, unless they are killed), and never enjoy a brass ring of it. Indeed they hardly know a good bit of work from a bad, though they usually have a good notion of the current market value; and they can't make a thing for themselves, *not even mend a little loose scale of their armour*.[17]

Dragons cannot appreciate the beauty of anything, nor can they make anything or even mend a scale in their armor. This is especially significant for Bilbo, since he is the one who spots the hole in Smaug's armor and reports it to the thrush, who then reports it to Bard, who kills the dragon by aiming an arrow at the hole, which the dragon, because of his incapacity for artistry, neglected to fix. The whole book hinges on the simple fact that dragons are not artistic and do not truly care about beauty, only the possession of material wealth.

Several characters in *The Hobbit* are afflicted with dragon-sickness, a mad, magically induced lust for dragon-hoard treasure, including the Master of Lake-town, who was given a good measure of the gold from the mountain to rebuild the town, but he fled with it and "died of starvation in the Waste."[18] Similarly, Thorin becomes obsessed with the beauty of the Arkenstone after the dwarves regain possession of the mountain. "It was like a globe with a thousand facets; it shone like silver in the firelight, like water in the sun, like snow under the stars, like rain upon the Moon!"[19]

Thorin's obsession with the Arkenstone is different from the dragon's or the Master's greed, because he is driven primarily by the beauty of the object he seeks, but it still affects Thorin in a similar way. Thorin is temporarily driven mad by his desire to recover the Arkenstone (which Bilbo secretly possesses). This shows that even beautiful things can cause us to stray from our moral compass, just as the desire for another good, such as justice or truth, can cause us to act immorally.

But it must still be noted that Thorin is corrupted in a way that a dragon, or a merely greedy person, could never be. His desire for the Arkenstone goes beyond its value. As Thorin says, "The Arkenstone of my father . . . is worth more than a river of gold in itself, and to me it is beyond price."[20]

"The Love of Beautiful Things"

At the beginning of *The Hobbit*, Bilbo is rudely interrupted from his peaceful Baggins existence. Gandalf, who does the disrupting, expresses his disappointment that as a Took (an adventurous folk), Bilbo is so wary of adventures making him late for dinner. But when Thorin takes out his beautiful golden harp and begins to play a song about the Lonely Mountain, the rest of the dwarves join in. The song moves Bilbo:

> As they sang the hobbit felt the love of beautiful things made by hands and by cunning and by magic moving through him, a fierce and a jealous love, the desire of the hearts of dwarves. Then something Tookish woke up inside him, and he wished to go and see the great mountains, and hear the pine-trees and the waterfalls, and explore the caves, and wear a sword instead of a walking-stick.[21]

Listening to the beautiful song, Bilbo is awakened to the wider world and deeper values. Tolkien's view of beauty in *The Hobbit* is similar to that of Elaine Scarry, a contemporary philosopher of art. In her book *On Beauty and Being Just*, Scarry argues against the art for art's sake idea that beauty exists in a separate realm from morality. For Scarry, "beauty prepares us for justice," because when we see something beautiful, this "is bound up with an urge to protect it, or act on its behalf."[22] Through the song, Bilbo gets a little bit of the "desire of the hearts of dwarves" and shares their burning desire to recover the treasure stolen by the dragon.

Iris Murdoch (1919–1999), a moral philosopher and fellow Oxfordian of Tolkien's, also connected the appreciation of beauty to ethical imperatives of concern for others:

> In intellectual disciplines and in enjoyment of art and nature we discover value in our ability to forget self, to be realistic, to perceive justly. We use our imagination not to escape the world but to join it, and this exhilarates us because of our ordinary dulled consciousness and an apprehension of the real.[23]

This sort of awakening is exactly what we see in Bilbo as he first encounters the beauty of the dwarves' song. Before this, Bilbo could think only of comfort and a pleasing routine. Adventures were merely "nasty disturbing uncomfortable things" that "make you late for dinner."[24] After hearing the song, however, Bilbo can sense that there might be more important things in life. Something wakes up inside him, and he wants to experience something more than his comfortable, easygoing life.

So Bilbo, standing in front of the *mithril* coat loaned to the museum there at Michel Delving, would no doubt say that beauty and art are not just good to create in themselves (although they are that), nor are they merely signs of moral health (although they are that, too); rather, they fire the imagination and kindle in the heart a desire for higher, nobler, and more difficult things. In conclusion, Bilbo would no doubt graciously acknowledge that this is only a little window on the big field of the arts, because he is just a little hobbit in a wide world, after all.

NOTES

1. Oscar Wilde, "The Critic as Artist," in *Intentions* (London: Methuen, 1913), 190–92.

2. James McNeill Whistler, *The Gentle Art of Making Enemies* (New York: Courier Dover, 1967), 127.

3. J. R. R. Tolkien, *The Lord of the Rings: The Fellowship of the Ring* (New York: Del Rey/Ballantine Books, 2001), x.

4. Humphrey Carpenter, ed., *The Letters of J. R. R. Tolkien* (Boston: Houghton Mifflin, 1981), 145.

5. Ibid., 146, 192.

6. Ibid., 88.

7. J. R. R. Tolkien, *The Hobbit: or, There and Back Again* (New York: Del Rey/Ballantine Books, 2001), 23.

8. Ibid., 49.

9. Carpenter, *Letters*, 218.

10. Ibid., 33.

11. Tolkien remarks that one of his goals in writing his tales of Middle-earth was "the encouragement of good morals." Ibid., 194.

12. Tolkien, *The Hobbit*, 42.

13. Ibid., 62.

14. J. R. R. Tolkien, *The Silmarillion*, ed. Christopher Tolkien (Boston: Houghton Mifflin, 1977), 41.

15. J. R. R. Tolkien, *The Lord of the Rings: The Two Towers* (New York: Del Rey/Ballantine Books, 2001), 76.

16. Augustine, *The City of God*, trans. Philip Devine (Cambridge, MA: Harvard University Press, 1966), 4:536.

17. Tolkien, *The Hobbit*, 23 (emphasis added).

18. Ibid., 305.

19. Ibid., 231.

20. Ibid., 268.

21. Ibid., 15–16.

22. Elaine Scarry, *On Beauty and Being Just* (Princeton, NJ: Princeton University Press, 2001), 88.

23. Iris Murdoch, *The Sovereignty of the Good* (London: Routledge & Kegan Paul, 1970), 93.

24. Tolkien, *The Hobbit*, 4.

HOBBITUS LUDENS

Why Hobbits Like to Play and Why We Should, Too

David L. O'Hara

Every two years, athletes gather from all over the world so that they can play together in the Olympic Games. When you add up the training, the travel, and the facilities, the Olympics cost billions of dollars. Add to that the amount we spend on professional sports around the world, and you might start to wonder: Aren't there more important ways for us to use that money? You know, ending world hunger, curing cancer, endowing chairs for philosophy professors—that sort of thing?

But the verdict of history seems to be that every culture considers playing to be an important part of a well-lived life. So here's a question: How seriously should we take playing?

Football, Golf, and Other Games
Hobbits Play

If *The Hobbit* is any indicator, J. R. R. Tolkien seems to think we should take it very seriously. After all, this is a book about a hobbit. If you're a hobbit, a good part of your life is devoted to recreation of various kinds: games, parties, fireworks, gossiping, visiting friends and neighbors, throwing stones and darts, wrestling, singing, mushroom raiding, beer drinking, and blowing smoke rings.[1]

It's true that hobbits are "skilful with tools" and doubtless worked hard to maintain their "well-ordered and well-farmed countryside."[2] (Somebody has to grow and prepare all the food hobbits need for their six meals a day!) But it's evident that Tolkien's hobbits spend far more time at recreation and leisure activities than most people do today.

Still, it's not just the hobbits who play. Elves sing and party in the woods at night. The people of Lake-town are fond of festivity (although one or two are grim fellows). Even characters you wouldn't think of as playing well with other children like to play: Gollum suggests that Bilbo play a riddle game with him, and Gandalf wins Beorn's hospitality through playful acting and storytelling. By night, Beorn plays even harder with the local bears. Smaug can't resist playing Bilbo's dangerous game of wits. And nearly everyone in *The Hobbit*—even the goblins—makes songs and music.

Tolkien even writes about sports.[3] He tells us that hobbits invented golf when Bullroarer Took whacked the head off the goblin king Golfimbul and the head rolled into a rabbit hole. After Thorin and Company leave Rivendell on their journey to the Lonely Mountain, they find themselves in the mountains, in a storm, surrounded by giants who are "hurling rocks at one another for a game, and catching them, and tossing them down into the darkness where they smashed among the trees far below, or splintered into little bits with a bang."

Thorin complains, "This won't do at all! If we don't get blown off, or drowned, or struck by lightning, we shall be picked up by some giant and kicked sky-high for a football."[4] That's not just a throwaway line; it tells us something important about Middle-earth—namely, that dwarves know about football (aka soccer).

I'm only half kidding. It actually tells us something else: even giants play games. Maybe this is why Gandalf believes that he'll be able to find a "more or less decent giant" to plug up the goblins' "front porch."[5] Play may seem unimportant in the grand scheme of things, but it may also be what connects us most to one another.

Think of Gollum when he meets Bilbo. The presence of a hobbit reminds Gollum of the most pleasant part of his former life, when he would play at riddles with his friends: "Asking them and sometimes guessing them had been the only game he had ever played with the other funny creatures sitting in their holes in the long, long ago, before he lost all his friends and was driven away, alone, and crept down, down, into the dark under the mountains."[6]

Moments like these make Gollum less of a monster and more of a person. We feel closest to animals when they are at play; if they play, they're like us. In fact, if someone didn't play at all, we would doubt that he or she was fully human. Along these lines, the German philosopher Friedrich Schiller (1759–1805) asked, "But why call it a *mere* game, when we consider that in every condition of humanity it is precisely play, and play alone, that makes man complete?"[7]

Okay, you may say, big deal: hobbits golf and dwarves play soccer. That doesn't exactly make *The Hobbit* the Middle-earth version of *Sports Illustrated*. True enough—but there's a lot more playing in the story than we hear about. When the Company is in Rivendell, Tolkien tells us the following information:

> It is a strange thing, but things that are good to have and
> days that are good to spend are soon told about, and not

much to listen to; while things that are uncomfortable, palpitating, and even gruesome, may make a good tale, and take a deal of telling anyway. They stayed long in that good house.... Yet there is little to tell about their stay.... I wish I had time to tell you even a few of the tales or one or two of the songs that they heard in that house.[8]

They spent at least two weeks in Rivendell, but there's not much to report, because it was mostly spent in rest and recreation.

Besides, playing means more than sports. Think about all the ways we use the word "play" in English. Dramatic performances are called plays, and actors used to be called players. When people make music, we say that they are playing their instruments. We play with Play-Doh (no surprise there), with sand on the beach, and with things on our desks. We are at play when we fish or hunt, and we call the animals we pursue "game." Crosswords, telling jokes, singing, dancing, making art—all of these things are kinds of play.

What Play Is Not

So what do all of these activities have in common? What is play? Let's start with ruling out some things that play is not.

Play Is Not a Lack of Seriousness

We might be tempted to think of play as a lack of seriousness, but in fact, the more intensely we play, the more serious we become about it. Just think about how a child plays at make-believe games. If you play guitar in a garage band or play pickup basketball with friends, you expect the people you play with to take playing seriously.

Schiller thought of play as superlative seriousness, saying, "Man is only serious with the agreeable, the good, the perfect; but with Beauty he—*plays*." Schiller takes beauty to be something higher than the merely "agreeable, good, and perfect," and so play, which is focused on beauty, is something higher than being serious.[9]

Play is, in a sense, too serious to be called merely "serious," so we call it "play."

Play Is Not Laziness

Play is also not merely relaxation or laziness. Thomas Aquinas (ca. 1225–1274) wrote in his *Summa Theologica* that while *acedia*, or "slothfulness," was definitely a sin, rest and recreation were so important that he thought people would continue to engage in them in heaven.[10]

On a more mundane level, athletes who take their games seriously train hard for them. Hobbits are another example of this: when they play, they play hard. Imagine the planning involved in Bilbo's birthday party in *The Fellowship of the Ring*, or the hard work that must have gone into making Bag-End the festive place it was: "It was a hobbit-hole, and that means comfort," we are told.[11]

Serious comfort comes only through hard work and careful planning. Charles S. Peirce (1839–1914) said that play is practically the opposite of laziness: "Play, as we all know, is a lively exercise of one's powers."[12] When we play, we bring all our resources to bear on what we're doing.

Play Is Not Childishness

Play is also not folly or childishness, even if it seems so at first glance. Tolkien illustrates this through the most playful of people in *The Hobbit*: the elves of Rivendell. When Bilbo and Company arrive at Rivendell, they are met by elves laughing and singing in the trees.

"And pretty fair nonsense I daresay you would think it," says Tolkien. "Not that they would care; they would only laugh

all the more if you told them so. They were elves, of course. . . .
Even decent enough dwarves like Thorin and his friends think
them foolish (which is a very foolish thing to think), or get
annoyed with them."[13]

Of course, these "foolish" elves "know a lot and are wondrous folk for news," and by the time the dwarves left Elrond's
house, "their plans were improved with the best advice."[14]
Without Elrond's knowledge of runes, the dwarves would still
be on Smaug's doorstep wondering how to get in. Or they
would be dragon-barbecue.

The Goodness of Play

Philosophers often find it useful to trace the history of an idea
in order to better understand it. Since the ancient Greeks gave
us both philosophy and the Olympics, let's look at what they
thought about play. In ancient Greek, there's a close connection
between the words for "play" (*paidia*) and "education" (*paideia*).
The Greeks considered education to be something that comes
out of leisure, because leisure is time spent seeking things that
are beautiful and enjoyable, not just working to get things
that are necessary.

It always surprises my students to learn that our word
"school" comes from the Greek word *scholé*, which means "leisure." School may not feel like leisure, but if we had no time free
from subsistence farming and fighting off cave bears, we would
not have time to study things for their own sake. The Athenian
statesman Pericles (ca. 495–429 BCE) defended the Athenian love
of play and of *scholé* in his famous funeral oration, saying that
the Athenians "loved beauty frugally, and loved wisdom without
growing soft."[15] In this one sentence Pericles summed up for us
two important observations: play has to do with learning, and
play is concerned with beauty.

With that in mind, it might be helpful to think about play in
terms of ethics. One of the things philosophers do is distinguish

among different kinds of good things. Some good things, like money, are desirable because they help us get other things. Other good things, like love, are desirable simply for their own sake and not as a means to an end. In between these two is a third kind of good, which is desirable both for its own sake and because it gets us other good things.[16] So which kind of good is play?

A number of people have argued that play is the first kind of good, because when we play we can learn useful things in an enjoyable way. Xenophon (ca. 431–355 BCE) wrote that anyone who wanted an education should learn to hunt.[17] Then, he said, if you have any money left over, you should study the other subjects. Xenophon believed that in the playful pursuit of wild game, young men would learn all the lessons they needed to succeed in life and in war.

Similarly, King Edward III of England (1312–1377) outlawed the playing of ball games; he wanted to make Englishmen better archers by forcing them to play with bows rather than balls. Edward then used the English longbow to defeat the Scots and to mow down the flower of the French nobility at Crécy.

More peacefully, the famous educator Maria Montessori (1870–1952) claimed that play is the work children do. It's often the case that if we're having a good time, we're learning. That's one of the ideas behind this book, after all: that you'll have fun learning philosophy through it.

Others, like Socrates (ca. 470–399 BCE), have argued that at least a certain kind of play is closer to the second kind of good: something that is good purely for its own sake. Plato (ca. 428–348 BCE) told us that Socrates believed that the most valuable kind of play was philosophy. Devoting yourself to playing with the loftiest ideas is like sowing beautiful gardens in thought.[18] Playful, philosophical thinking becomes its own reward.

Aristotle (384–322 BCE) disagreed with Socrates on this point. In his famous *Nicomachean Ethics*, Aristotle argued that play isn't the highest thing but that it is an example of the third type of good: because play has a kind of beauty to it, it's desirable for its own sake, but it is also essential for preparing us for other things that are worthwhile. In his words, "we play in order that we might be serious."[19]

Adventurous Play: Bilbo's Education

Play obviously trains us. As the poet Alexander Pope (1688–1744) said, "'Tis education forms the common mind / As the twig is bent so the tree's inclined."[20] And play is part of education. This helps us to understand a bit more why Bilbo was the right man—er, hobbit—to play the burglar.

Although the dwarves doubted that Bilbo would be any good as a burglar, Gandalf knew something they did not about hobbits: they "can move very quietly, and hide easily . . . and they have a fund of wisdom and wise sayings that men have mostly never heard or have forgotten long ago."[21] Clearly, much of this comes from playing games like hide-and-seek, listening to stories, and singing songs. Part of the fun of *The Hobbit* is watching how, with each subsequent adventure, Bilbo himself discovers how well his life in the Shire has prepared him for his adventures. When the dwarves are captured by spiders in Mirkwood, we learn that:

> Bilbo was a pretty fair shot with a stone. . . . As a boy he used to practise throwing stones at things . . . and even grown up he had still spent a good deal of his time at quoits, dart-throwing, shooting at the wand, bowls, ninepins and other quiet games of the aiming and throwing sort—indeed he could do lots of things, besides blowing smoke-rings, asking riddles, and cooking, that I haven't had time to tell you about.[22]

Bilbo's boyhood pastimes, as was often the case in days "when there was less noise and more green,"[23] were an education for adventure. This comes as no surprise to philosophers, actually. Joseph Esposito describes play as openness to possibility. Part of why we engage in sports is precisely that we do not know the outcome. A game is not a game if the outcome is wholly determined before play begins. We play not just for exercise or to win, but to experience the very encounter with possibility that playing presents. He writes,

> Rock-climbing is sport and not simply healthy exercise because it contains a moment of possibility—the foothold or grasp on the rock which might give way without notice. In sport-fishing it is the strike of the fish at the lure or the bait. . . . When nature has occasion to play with us, as also in sailing, surfing, hunting, gliding, etc., then these activities go beyond mere leisure activity and become occasions of sportive play.[24]

Similarly, Drew Hyland says that play involves a "stance of responsive openness" to new experiences.[25] Maybe this explains Bilbo's Tookish side. When Tooks long for adventure, they are not acting in an unhobbitlike way. On the contrary, they are taking the hobbits' love of play to its natural end: if you love play, it is because you love possibility; and the greatest possibilities we call "adventures."

To paraphrase Schiller, the life of a hobbit is good and comfortable, but it needs some adventure to make it complete. Bilbo isn't motivated by wealth, fear, patriotism, or anything else external to the adventure; he goes on the adventure for its own sake.[26]

Playing with Fire: Gandalf and the Goblins

But not all playing is equal, in part because it is not all equally oriented toward the beautiful. I said before that nearly everyone in Middle-earth plays. It's probably irreverent to say this, but Gandalf and the goblins have a couple of things in common. First, they both like songs. Second, they both play with fire. In both cases, of course, Gandalf's play is better than the goblins' play.

Let's start with the fire. Gandalf has a gift for fireworks, and this makes him the life of the Shire's best parties. The fireworks are also sometimes useful for things like distracting goblins and igniting wargs. Like Bilbo's childhood games, Gandalf's play has focused on beauty, and it has turned out to be useful as well.

The goblins like explosions too. We read:

> Goblins are cruel, wicked, and bad-hearted. They make no beautiful things, but they make many clever ones. . . . It is not unlikely that they invented some of the machines that have since troubled the world, especially the ingenious devices for killing large numbers of people at once, for wheels and engines and explosions always delighted them, and also not working with their own hands more than they could help.[27]

Gandalf plays with fireworks because they are beautiful; goblins tinker with explosions only *because they are useful*. The difference between these two approaches has to do, once again, with possibility. Goblins don't want possibilities or adventures; they want to do things with less work.

The goblins' attitude toward play is even clearer in their singing. Their songs have no wonder, beauty, or mystery in them. They sing to make one another work: "Hammer and tongs! Knocker and gongs! . . . Work, work! Nor dare to shirk!"[28] Contrast this song with Rivendell's festive songs; the song of the barrel-boatmen, who marvel at nature; or the hopeful, prophetic songs of Lake-town. Whether with tongs or in songs, goblins love cleverness, not beauty.

Playing by the Rules: Riddles and Ethics

Cleverness is overrated, or at least it is not as important as play and beauty. The title of this chapter comes from *Homo Ludens*, a book about philosophy and play by the Dutch historian

Johan Huizinga (1872–1945). Huizinga's title plays on *Homo sapiens*, the name we gave our species to emphasize our cleverness at knowing how to do things. Huizinga thought that the people who came up with that name were like wargs barking up the wrong tree. It's not cleverness that makes us what we are, but play.

Huizinga claimed that philosophy itself was born in wordplay—specifically, in riddles.[29] In ancient Athens men who called themselves Sophists taught others how to speak cleverly so they could win elections and court cases. Sophists would challenge one another with riddles to establish their rank as thinkers. Into this environment came Socrates, the first great Western philosopher, who detected something important behind the apparent silliness of riddles.

In riddles, we play with the multiple meanings of words and playfully explore the connections among things that may not seem to be connected. In a way, this is the beginning of metaphysics (the study of what is ultimately real) and epistemology (the branch of philosophy that studies knowledge and belief). It also provides insight into ethics, or how we ought to live with others.

Thorin's frequently quoted deathbed speech suggests that he too has learned that a playful life may in fact put us most deeply in touch with ethics and the best kind of life.[30] Maybe this is why Schiller claimed, "Man plays only when he is in the full sense of the word a man, and he is only wholly Man when he is playing."[31]

For Schiller and Aristotle, play was a kind of intermediate good. It is desirable in itself, but it also unites all our other thinking. When we play, our encounter with the beauty of possibility allows us to join our sense impressions with more general ideas, rules, and definitions. To put it more simply: it is play that allows us to know what is ethical. If we are *Homo sapiens* (knowing humans), it is only because we are first *Homo ludens* (playing humans).

Recreation and Subcreation

This view of play is close to Tolkien's view, apparently. In several of his books, Tolkien offers pictures of what it means to be an artist. Art, he suggests, is a kind of play in which we imitate the highest ethic, the divine. Tolkien called this process "subcreation."

An example of this is found in *The Silmarillion*, when Aulë explains to Ilúvatar (God) why he made the dwarves without the latter's knowledge. Aulë describes his creation as play: "The making of things is in my heart from my own making by thee; and the child of little understanding that makes a play of the deeds of his father may do so without thought of mockery, but because he is the son of his father."[32] Tolkien didn't write his stories of Middle-earth for profit as much as for recreation, or, as he would have said, subcreation: the creative, playful work of an artist imitating the divine.

The Limits of Play

Still, Tolkien reminds us that play has its limits. For instance, the quote above from *The Silmarillion* suggests that not all play is equal. Aulë recognizes that were he to mock Ilúvatar in his play, Aulë himself would be degraded by it and would deserve reproach. Remember what Aristotle said: play is important, but it aims at preparing us to be serious.

Immanuel Kant (1724–1804) agreed with this.[33] Play, he said, exercises our skills, but without work and discipline we will never gain skills or cultivate our minds. Kant warned that play holds dangers as well, especially in the way we treat other people when we play. When we play, we mustn't treat other people as playthings. In fact, Kant said that giving children the things they want does not spoil them; the main way to spoil a child is for the parent to treat the child like a toy to be played with. This,

Kant suggested, is a failure to respect the person that the child is becoming.

The danger in play, then, is the failure to take others as seriously as they deserve to be taken. Tolkien gives us lots of examples of this. As Bilbo said, "Never laugh at live dragons!"[34] Or recall Gandalf before Orthanc in *The Two Towers* when he said, "Those of you who wish may come with me [to speak to Saruman], but beware! And do not jest! This is not the time for it." When Pippin asked what the danger was, Gandalf replied that the greatest danger was for those who "ride to [Saruman's] door with a light heart" and so fail to take a wizard's power of speech as seriously as they ought to do.[35] Tolkien knew that words may be fun to play with, but they can also be powerful and dangerous.

The Professor at Play

Tolkien's friend C. S. Lewis (1898–1963) knew the power of well-crafted words as well as anyone, and he read *The Hobbit* and loved it. In his 1937 review of *The Hobbit*, Lewis confirmed the playfulness of Tolkien's work. Lewis wrote, "*The Hobbit*, though very unlike *Alice* [*in Wonderland*], resembles it in being the work of a professor at play."[36] As Lewis predicted in his review, the professor's play gave us an enduring classic. What greater testimony to the importance of play do we need?

NOTES

1. As Pippin says good-naturedly to young Bergil (who threatens to stand him on his head or lay him on his back), "We know some wrestling tricks in my little country." J. R. R. Tolkien, *The Lord of the Rings: The Return of the King* (New York: Del Rey/Ballantine Books, 2001), 29.

2. J. R. R. Tolkien, *The Lord of the Rings: The Fellowship of the Ring* (New York: Del Rey/Ballantine Books, 2001), 1. Indeed, prior to his journey to the Lonely Mountain,

Thorin disdained hobbits as a race of "food-growers." J. R. R. Tolkien, "The Quest of Erebor," in *Unfinished Tales of Númenor and Middle-Earth*, ed. Christopher Tolkien (Boston: Houghton Mifflin, 1980), 332.

3. Tolkien himself was a scrappy (if undersized) athlete in his youth. When Tolkien attended a class reunion at King Edward's School, he found he was remembered more for his prowess in rugby than as a scholar. Humphrey Carpenter, ed., *The Letters of J. R. R. Tolkien* (Boston: Houghton Mifflin, 1981), 70.

4. J. R. R. Tolkien, *The Hobbit: or, There and Back Again* (New York: Del Rey/Ballantine Books, 2001), 57.

5. Ibid., 95.

6. Ibid., 73.

7. Friedrich Schiller, *On the Aesthetic Education of Man*, trans. Reginald Snell (Mineola, NY: Dover, 2004), 79.

8. Tolkien, *The Hobbit*, 51.

9. Schiller, *On the Aesthetic Education of Man*, 79.

10. Thomas Aquinas, *Summa Theologica*, Part I, Q. 73, art. 2; Part II-II, Q. 35; and Part III, Q. 84.

11. Tolkien, *The Hobbit*, 1.

12. Charles S. Peirce, "A Neglected Argument for the Reality of God," in *The Essential Peirce* (Bloomington: Indiana University Press, 1998), 2:436.

13. Tolkien, *The Hobbit*, 49.

14. Ibid., 52.

15. Quoted in Thucydides, *The Peloponnesian War*, 2.40.

16. This distinction of the three types of good is found in Plato, *The Republic*, 2.357b–d.

17. Xenophon, "Cynegetica," in *Xenophon in Seven Volumes*, trans. E. C. Marchant (Cambridge, MA: Harvard University Press, 1971), 7:373.

18. Plato, *Phaedrus*, 276d. See also Arthur A. Krentz, "Play and Education in Plato's *Republic*," Boston University, http://www.bu.edu/wcp/Papers/Educ/EducKren.htm; and Drew Hyland, *The Question of Play* (Lanham, MD: University Press of America, 1984), 139–63.

19. Aristotle, *Nicomachean Ethics*, 1176b33. This is a loose translation; the exact translation is "to play in order that one might be serious."

20. Alexander Pope, *Epistles to Several Persons*, 1.102.

21. Tolkien, *The Hobbit*, 70. Gandalf also points out that Smaug has never *smelled* hobbits—a big advantage, given the dragon's keen nose. Tolkien, "The Quest of Erebor," 333.

22. Tolkien, *The Hobbit*, 158.

23. Ibid., 3.

24. Joseph L. Esposito, "Play and Possibility," *Philosophy Today*, Summer 1974.

25. Hyland, *The Question of Play*, 139.

26. I am indebted to Tolkien scholar Matthew T. Dickerson for this insight.

27. Tolkien, *The Hobbit*, 62.

28. Ibid., 60–61.

29. Johan Huizinga, *Homo Ludens* (Boston: Beacon Press, 1950), 146–57.

30. Tolkien, *The Hobbit*, 290.

31. Schiller, *On the Aesthetic Education of Man*, 80.

32. J. R. R. Tolkien, *The Silmarillion*, ed. Christopher Tolkien (Boston: Houghton Mifflin, 1977), 43.

33. Immanuel Kant, *On Education*, 2.55, 4.65–69.

34. Tolkien, *The Hobbit*, 227.

35. J. R. R. Tolkien, *The Lord of the Rings: The Two Towers* (New York: Del Rey/Ballantine Books, 2001), 260.

36. C. S. Lewis, "The Hobbit," in *On Stories* (San Diego: Harcourt, 1982), 81.

PART THREE

RIDDLES AND RINGS

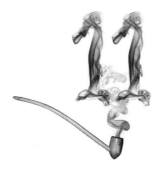

"THE LORD OF MAGIC AND MACHINES"

Tolkien on Magic and Technology

W. Christopher Stewart

The Hobbit features a lot of magic, some whimsical and some practical. When Bilbo first encounters Gandalf, it's clear that he already knows him by reputation as the "wandering wizard" responsible for the splendid fireworks displays he remembers from the Old Took's Midsummer's Eve celebrations, as well as the tales of "dragons and goblins and giants and the rescue of princesses and the unexpected luck of widows' sons." It was Gandalf too, recalls Bilbo, who "gave old Took a pair of magic diamond studs that fastened themselves and never came undone until ordered."[1]

Lots of other objects sprinkled throughout *The Hobbit* have magical properties, are made "by magic," or are manipulated by means of magic.[2] During the "unexpected party" at Bag-End at the beginning of the story, Thorin and Gandalf engage in a smoke-ring competition. As Thorin's huge smoke rings floated off "wherever he told one to go," Gandalf sent a smaller smoke ring right through each of them, after which they would "go green and come back to hover over the wizard's head."[3] Later, in the midst of his negotiations with Bilbo back in Bag-End, Thorin makes reference to "the most marvelous and magical toys" fashioned in the workshops under the mountain by his ancestors, "the like of which is not to be found in the world now-a-days."[4]

Examples of less whimsical and more practical applications of magic include Gandalf's lighting the end of his magic staff to provide illumination in dark places. In Bilbo's encounter with the trolls, his first serious attempt to demonstrate his prowess as a burglar is foiled when a troll's magical purse blurts out, "'Ere, 'oo are you?" as Bilbo draws it from his pocket. After their eventual escape from the trolls, aided both by the timely return of Gandalf and the arrival of dawn (which, by the magical laws of Middle-earth, causes the trolls to turn to stone), the dwarves buried the pots of gold they found in the trolls' cave, "putting a great many spells over them" to protect them until their hoped-for return. In Mirkwood, the party is relieved to discover that whether "because of some magic" or by other means, the nasty cobwebs that fill the woods do not stretch across the path they're traveling on.[5]

Other examples of magic include the fires of the wood-elves in Mirkwood, which would alight and then just as suddenly go out "by magic" whenever intruders stepped into the clearings, and the moon-letters on Thror's map, which Elrond explains "can only be seen when the moon shines behind them, and what is more, with the more cunning sort it must be a moon of the same shape and season as the day when they were written."[6] In the battle with the goblins in the Misty Mountains, we encounter ancient elf-made blades such as Gandalf's Glamdring the Foe-hammer and Bilbo's Sting, which gleam "with rage" whenever goblins are around. And amid the treasure recovered from Smaug by the dwarves are magical harps that have remained in tune despite their very great age.[7]

Like human attempts to manipulate nature through science, Middle-earth magic works according to very definite rules. More than once we're told of spells that fail to work, such as Gandalf's repeated attempts to use incantations to open the stone door blocking the entrance to the trolls' cave or the "fragments of broken spells of opening" with which the dwarves unsuccessfully tried to open the secret door into the Lonely Mountain.[8]

In Middle-earth, magic is not a means by which you can *violate* the principles that govern how the world works. It's not a power that lets you do anything you can imagine. We're told early in the story that even Gandalf can't do everything, though he could, of course, "do a great deal for friends in a tight corner." Gandalf's great magical skills are largely the fruit of years of patient study and practice, and his special talents with bewitchments involving fire and lights (such as the impressive fireworks that open the film version of *The Fellowship of the Ring*) are the result of a special study of the subject over many years. Gandalf does the best he can with these skills whenever he finds himself in a tight corner, such as his escape from the goblins "in a terrible flash like lightning in the cave," his rescue of the entire party shortly thereafter as he extinguished the goblins' great fire "into a tower of blue glowing smoke . . . that scattered piercing white sparks all among the goblins," and the flaming pinecones he hurled down from a tree when he and his companions were trapped by wolves.[9]

Even magical events in the "secondary world" of Middle-earth must fit with the laws of that world, which makes Tolkien's magic very different from what most people think of as "miracles."[10] The Scottish philosopher David Hume (1711–1776) famously defined a miracle as "a violation of the laws of nature." Since experience is our only guide in "matters of fact," and "uniform experience" lies behind our faith in the laws of nature, Hume said, it's never reasonable to believe any human testimony that a miracle has occurred.[11]

Although genuine miracles do occur in Middle-earth—such as Gandalf's return to life in *The Two Towers*—they are apparently quite rare. When the residents of Middle-earth fear magical powers, it is not because they believe that those who wield them are capable of violating the laws of nature but rather because they suspect (often correctly) that others' knowledge of those laws is vastly superior to their own, enabling their adversaries to produce effects that are more sophisticated and potentially more dangerous than they are capable of producing themselves.

Moreover, magic can be strong or weak, just like other natural forces such as electricity, gravity, and magnetism. Think, for example, of the scene in Mirkwood Forest when Bilbo hopefully suggests that the magic of the enchanted stream is probably not strong enough to harm one if one only touches a bit of wet rope.[12] Magic has its limits, such as when we're told that "even magic rings are not much help against wolves," who "smell keener than goblins, and do not need to see you to catch you."[13]

In the course of *The Hobbit*, we also learn that although Bilbo's magic ring makes you completely invisible, it doesn't conceal your shadow in daylight (it only makes it "shaky and faint"), as Bilbo discovers in his escape from the goblins' cave. Nor does the magic ring conceal his wet footprints, the trail of drippings from his wet clothes, or the sound of his muffled sneezes in his escape from the Wood-elves.[14]

So although a magic ring may not provide "complete protection in a goblin charge, nor . . . stop flying arrows and wild spears," it does help a great deal "in getting out of the way" and preventing your head from being "specially chosen for a sweeping stroke by a goblin swordsman."[15] Even the dwarves appreciate that "some wits, as well as luck and a magic ring . . . are very useful possessions."[16]

One of the first and most interesting things we learn about hobbits is that "there is little or no magic about them," apart from the "everyday sort which helps them to disappear quietly and quickly when large stupid folk like you and me come blundering along," which is more a matter of stealth than actual magic. In addition to their ability to move quietly and hide easily, we're told that they "do not easily lose their sense of direction underground," owing to their being "more used to tunneling than we are."[17]

In the prologue to *The Lord of the Rings*, we learn that hobbits have "a close friendship with the earth," and have never, in fact, studied magic of any sort. And although hobbits are skillful with tools and adept at many crafts, they "do not and did not understand machines more complicated than a forge-bellows, a water-mill, or a hand loom," nor do they "hurry unnecessarily."[18]

In their attitude toward machines and metalwork, hobbits contrast sharply with goblins, who "make no beautiful things, but . . . many clever ones." Goblins are particularly good at making tools for tunneling (an art at which they are surpassed only by the dwarves), as well as weapons and instruments of torture. Moreover, goblins are blamed for having "invented some of the machines that have since troubled the world, especially the ingenious devices for killing large numbers of people at once, for wheels and engines and explosions always delighted them, and also not working with their hands more than they could help." At the time of *The Hobbit*, however, "they had not advanced (as it is called) so far" as present-day humans in inventing weapons of mass destruction.[19]

The Will to Magic

The cynicism in Tolkien's remark about the advances of the goblins in the creation of terrible weapons provides a clue to at least one important message underlying Tolkien's treatment of magic in *The Hobbit* and developed more fully in *The Lord of the Rings*: that just because we *can* do something "magical" by scientific means doesn't mean that we *should* do it.

Goblins were created by Morgoth, the original Dark Lord of Middle-earth, in mockery of elves. We don't learn much about the history of the elves in *The Hobbit*, but what we do learn is very instructive. We're told, for instance, that even though the Wood-elves of Mirkwood are cousins of the High Elves of the West, the Wood-elves are "more dangerous and less wise" than the High Elves, who journeyed to Faerie in the West where they "lived for ages, and grew fairer and wiser and more learned, and invented their magic and their cunning craft in the making of beautiful and marvelous things, before some came back into the Wide World."[20]

Tolkien insists that "magic" is not quite the right word for the special craft of the elves. "Enchantment" is a better word, because what the elves practice is more akin to art than it is to "Wizardry of Magic, properly so called."[21] The aim of elfish "magic" is not so much to produce a change in the physical world as to create a secondary world in our minds to delight, inspire, or instruct.

Magic, by contrast, seeks to actualize our desire for things that do not present themselves to us naturally in the course of our experience or that cannot be obtained by means of our "inherent inner powers or talents" and are thus achievable only by artificial means (and even then without "any real satisfaction"). In this way magic, unlike the enchantments of the elves, seeks "to create power" by producing real effects in the physical world.[22]

The magic of the elves, however, is art "delivered from many of its human limitations: more effortless, more quick, more complete." As art, its object is subcreation rather than the "domination and tyrannous re-forming of Creation."[23] Herein lies the contrast between the "magic" of Faërie (like Galadriel's mirror) and "the vulgar devices of the laborious, scientific magician," as well as the link between the latter sort of magic and modern technology, much of which serves the same purpose in our world as Saruman's genetically engineered superorcs (the Uruk-hai) or Sauron's magical battering ram, Grond.[24]

In one of his letters, Tolkien distinguishes *magia* (or magic proper) from *goeteia* (a Greek word meaning "charm" or "jugglery"), which seeks not to produce real effects in the physical world but instead to create illusions. (As such, *goeteia* is closer to what we typically mean by the sort of stuff on sale in magic shops or performed by professional stage magicians.)

Neither is inherently good or bad, but it becomes so as the result of a magician's (or scientist's) "motives or purpose or use." The supremely bad motive is "domination of other 'free' wills." Both the forces of good and the forces of evil use *magia* and *goeteia*, but the evil ones use *magia* "to bulldoze both people and things" and *goeteia* "to terrify and subjugate." The goetic effects of the elves are not intended to deceive, although they may deceive others accidentally. The elves themselves are never deceived by *goeteia*. Gandalf and the elves, in fact, are rather sparing in their use of *magia*, which they tend to employ only for "specific beneficent purposes," such as escaping from danger (good examples are Gandalf's frequent use of fire and lights and the fires of the Wood-elves in *The Hobbit*).[25]

The forces of evil in Middle-earth are attracted to machinery for many of the same reasons that they are drawn to magic. Indeed, given that the "mark of a mere Magician" in contrast to an enchanter is the "greed for self-centered power," this is precisely what we should expect.[26] *Magia's* "basic motive" is "immediacy: speed, reduction of labour, and reduction also to a minimum (or vanishing point) of the gap between the idea or desire and the result or effect."[27]

The "tragedy and despair of all machinery laid bare" is that like magic, it springs from impatience and "the desire for Power, for making the will more quickly effective."[28] Thus, because "the Enemy" in Middle-earth (Sauron) is "always 'naturally' concerned with sheer Domination" and impatient for quick results, he is also "the Lord of magic and machines."[29]

All of these distinctions are only hinted at in *The Hobbit*, although the story clearly presupposes a distinction between "good" and "bad" magic. The spiders of Mirkwood, for example, do not like the "good magic" that seems to linger in the places where the fires of the Wood-elves accompanied their revelries. At the end of *The Hobbit*, Gandalf finally explains the "pressing business away south" that prevented him from accompanying the party into Mirkwood. He left them for a time to attend a council of the "white wizards"—"masters of lore and good magic"—and to drive the "black sorcerer" known only as "the Necromancer" in *The Hobbit* from his "dark hold in the south of Mirkwood."[30]

The ring that Bilbo discovers quite accidentally (or so it seems) in Gollum's cave is the supreme technological artifact of Middle-earth. Although in *The Hobbit* we are told only that it is a "ring of power," it subsequently becomes the link between *The Hobbit* and *The Lord of the Rings*, acquiring capital letters in the process. Its "primary symbolism" is "the will to mere power, seeking to make itself objective by physical force and mechanism, and so also inevitably by lies."[31] (Note the word "inevitably.")

Part of its allure for mortals is its utility in the ill-conceived quest to achieve immortality by device or magic (not unlike the philosopher's stone of Renaissance alchemists), which Tolkien identifies as one aspect of the "supreme folly and wickedness" of mortals that leads "the small to a Gollum, and the great to a Ringwraith."[32] (Elsewhere, Tolkien says that "death and the desire for deathlessness" is what his tales of Middle-earth are all about.[33])

The "frightful evil" that arises from the rush to deploy "magic and machines" to achieve one's aims arises "from an apparently good root"—namely, "the desire to benefit the world and others." What eventually perverts this aim, however, is that the intended benefit is pursued "speedily and according to the benefactor's own plans" rather than in harmony with the cosmic purpose and design of "the One," Ilúvatar the creator.[34]

Part of the deceptiveness of the Ring in Middle-earth, and the lure of technology in ours, is not delusion but rather a limited or partial view of the world. Applied science is always undertaken with a view to solving a particular problem, and we often become blind to everything else in our pursuit of a solution, heedless of consequences we do not intend. (Think for a moment about lifesaving medical technologies or cell phones.)

Tolkien is sympathetic to the impulse of pure science—the pursuit of knowledge for its own sake without any thought of *doing* something with the knowledge acquired. In *The Lord of the Rings*, Tom Bombadil is an embodiment of this disinterested pursuit of knowledge; he is driven solely by a sense of wonder, which in part explains his attitude of indifference toward the Ring, the sole purpose of which is to control and manipulate, as well as its failure to have any discernible effect on him.[35]

In contrast, Sauron, somewhat repentant after the overthrow of Morgoth, lingered in Middle-earth with a view to rehabilitating what he perceived to be a ruin "neglected by the gods," but he eventually became "a thing lusting for Complete Power," caring only for such instruments of magic or technology that could help him achieve his evil ends.[36]

Tolkien considers the machine to be the most obvious modern form of "the desire to make the will more quickly effective," and "more closely related to Magic than is usually recognized."[37] Reflecting on the century and a half since the beginning of the Industrial Revolution in England, he observed that "labour-saving machinery only creates endless and worse labour." Furthermore, the fact of human depravity ensures that "our devices not only fail of their desire (to improve our lives) but turn to new and horrible evil." In Tolkien's view, the inevitable transition "from Daedalus and Icarus to the Giant

Bomber" is decidedly "not an advance in wisdom," and he considers it symptomatic of "a worldwide mental disease that only a tiny minority perceive it."[38]

In 1945, Tolkien wrote to his son Christopher, "Well, the first War of the Machines seems to be drawing to its final inconclusive chapter—leaving, alas, everyone the poorer, many bereaved or maimed and millions dead, and only one thing triumphant: the Machines." In words that will resonate with fans of *The Matrix* films, he added, "As the servants of the Machines are becoming a privileged class, the Machines are going to be enormously powerful. What's their next move?"[39]

The problem is that all too often we develop and deploy technologies more rapidly than we develop the conceptual resources to reflect on their implications. (Think, for instance, of the rapid developments taking place at the moment in genetic engineering or on the Internet, or of atomic energy in the first half of the twentieth century.) Like magic, technology both accelerates and amplifies the effect of our actions on the world, including those actions that stem from erroneous or malicious intentions. Too often, as Tolkien notes, our desire for speed, power, and control outstrips our ability to think responsibly about long-term consequences and deeper values:

> If there is any contemporary reference in [my tales of Middle-earth] at all it is to what seems to me the most widespread assumption of our time: that if a thing can be done, it must be done. This seems to me wholly false. The greatest examples of the action of the spirit and of reason are in *abnegation*.[40]

Only very recently, in the blink of an eye, have humans acquired the power to dramatically alter earth's climate, to clone ourselves, to greatly extend old age through medical interventions, to propagandize millions through mass media, and to exterminate whole populations with weapons of mass destruction. Has our wisdom kept pace with our technology?

Tolkien's Vision of Nature and the Modern World

Tolkien connects the triumph of machines, made possible by the rise of modern science, with the suppression of the human spirit. In the history of the actual world, magic developed for thousands of years alongside and in close relationship with what we now think of as science. Integral to both magic and science is a philosophy of nature—that is, an understanding of what we mean by "nature," distinct from the practical applications of our understanding of nature. Tolkien insists that the materialism underlying modern science, despite its obvious and impressive achievements, has also had an increasingly obvious and disastrous effect on the satisfaction of "certain primordial human desires" he believes to be deeply rooted in the human spirit, most particularly the desire to experience a sense of connection to the natural world and a "communion with other living things."[41]

In this regard, Beorn—a powerful and unpredictable shape-shifter, of whom even Gandalf is wary—provides another sharp contrast to the goblins' fascination with machines. After their escape from the goblins in the mountains, Thorin and his companions arrive at the house of Beorn, a being who is "under no enchantment but his own" and who shows little interest in the dwarves' talk of "gold and silver and jewels and the making of things by smith-craft," since there are few such items anywhere in his hall. Beorn "loves his animals as his children," and even appears to be a vegetarian.[42] His harmony with nature is so close that he is capable of changing his form from man to bear, and he communes closely with other animals, some of whom also appear to possess magical powers.

The antithesis of Beorn, in Tolkien's tales of Middle-earth, is Saruman, a corrupt wizard who uses magic and technology to pursue his dreams of power and domination. Saruman transforms Isengard into a moonscape, invents high explosives, and uses genetic engineering to breed an elite Delta force of superorcs—all to pursue his warped vision of "Knowledge, Rule, Order." In contrast to the makers of three elfish Rings of Power, "who did not desire strength or domination or hoarded wealth, but understanding, making, and healing, to preserve all things unstained," Saruman possessed "a mind of metal and wheels" that seeks only the swiftest and most efficient means to dominate other wills.[43]

As Lynn Thorndike documents in his definitive *History of Magic and Experimental Science* (1958), magic was, from its origins in antiquity, not simply an operative art or technique but a way of looking at the world and understanding our relationship to nature. The idea that the natural world (including the human body) is nothing more than a complex machine represents a momentous development in the history of our grappling with the natural world and in the history of our culture as a whole. Some regard it as a leading cause of the sense of alienation and estrangement from nature into which we've fallen in the past few centuries, despite (and in some cases because of) advances in our technical mastery of nature.

In this climate of uncertainty and alienation, *The Hobbit* invites us to consider whether it might after all be "possible for a rational man, after reflection, . . . to arrive at the condemnation, implicit at least in the mere silence of 'escapist' literature, of progressive things like factories, or the machine-guns and bombs that appear to be their most natural and inevitable, dare we say 'inexorable,' products."[44]

The American philosopher and naturalist Henry David Thoreau (1817–1862) urged us to price a material possession or technological advancement not in dollars and cents but in terms of the amount of "life required to be exchanged for it."[45] Similarly, Tolkien invites us to recall a time when there was "less noise and more green," when there were some, at least, who, like the hobbits, understood that there is more to life than increasing its speed.[46]

NOTES

1. J. R. R. Tolkien, *The Hobbit: or, There and Back Again* (New York: Del Rey/Ballantine Books, 2001), 5.

2. Ibid., 15.

3. Ibid., 13.

4. Ibid., 23.

5. Ibid., 36, 43, 140.

6. Ibid., 53.

7. Ibid., 239.

8. Ibid., 206.

9. Ibid., 65, 60, 64, 102.

10. J. R. R. Tolkien, "On Fairy-Stories," in *The Tolkien Reader* (New York: Ballantine Books, 1966), 37.

11. David Hume, *Enquiry Concerning Human Understanding* in *The Empiricists* (New York: Anchor Press, 1974), 390, 390, 391.

12. Tolkien, *The Hobbit*, 143.

13. Ibid., 99.

14. Ibid., 187.

15. Ibid., 283.

16. Ibid., 166.

17. Ibid., 2, 70.

18. J. R. R. Tolkien, *The Lord of the Rings: The Fellowship of the Ring* (New York: Del Rey/Ballantine Books, 2001), 1–2.

19. Tolkien, *The Hobbit*, 62.

20. Ibid., 166.

21. Tolkien, "On Fairy-Stories," 52.

22. Humphrey Carpenter, ed., *The Letters of J. R. R. Tolkien* (Boston: Houghton Mifflin, 1981), 87–88.

23. Ibid., 146.

24. Tolkien, "On Fairy-Stories," 10.

25. Carpenter, *Letters*, 199–200. As one of the elves of Lothlórien says to Frodo, "we put the thought of all that we love into all that we make." Tolkien, *The Fellowship of the Ring*, 416.

26. Tolkien, "On Fairy-Stories," 53.

27. Carpenter, *Letters*, 200.

28. Ibid., 87, 145.

29. Ibid., 146.

30. Tolkien, *The Hobbit*, 299. Later, Tolkien came to identify the Necromancer with Sauron, the Dark Lord of *The Lord of the Rings*.

31. Carpenter, *Letters*, 160.

32. Ibid., 286.

33. Ibid., 262.

34. Ibid., 146.

35. Ibid., 192.

36. Ibid., 151.

37. Ibid., 146.

38. Ibid., 88. In Greek mythology, Daedalus made wings of feathers and wax, which Icarus used to escape from the Labyrinth, only to perish when he flew too near the sun and it melted his wings.

39. Ibid., 111.

40. Ibid., 246.

41. Tolkien, "On Fairy-Stories," 13, 15.

42. Tolkien, *The Hobbit*, 136.

43. Tolkien, *The Fellowship of the Ring*, 301; J. R. R. Tolkien, *The Lord of the Rings: The Two Towers* (New York: Del Rey/Ballantine Books, 2001), 76.

44. Tolkien, "On Fairy-Stories," 63.

45. Henry David Thoreau, *Walden* (Roslyn, NY: Walter J. Black, 1942), 55.

46. Tolkien, *The Hobbit*, 3.

INSIDE *THE HOBBIT*

Bilbo Baggins and the Paradox of Fiction

Amy Kind

As the doorbell to his hobbit-hole rings time and time again on that fine April morning, Bilbo becomes increasingly flustered. What's a hobbit to do when thirteen dwarves turn up unexpectedly, all of them convinced that he's an accomplished burglar who's meant to help them reclaim their stolen treasure from a fearsome dragon? Prodded by Gandalf and his own long-suppressed Tookishness, Bilbo reluctantly agrees to join the dwarves' quest. Things aren't too bad, initially (despite his being without a pocket handkerchief), but after several weeks on the road, both the terrain and the weather take a turn for the worse. Wet, hungry, and homesick, Bilbo feels sorry for himself—and we, the readers, feel sorry for him, too.

This isn't the only time we pity Bilbo as we read *The Hobbit*. One can't help but feel sorry for him when he's stuck uncomfortably in a tree, the wild wolves howling below, or when he wakes up alone and apparently abandoned in the total darkness of the goblins' cave, or when he's sitting glumly on the doorstep of the Lonely Mountain, pining for home.

And our feelings of pity give way to all sorts of other emotional reactions as Bilbo's adventure continues. We're fearful when he's captured by the hungry trolls, we're anxious as he trades riddles with Gollum, we're joyful when the eagles rescue him and his companions from the treetops, we're indignant when Thorin denounces him for giving away the Arkenstone, and we're proud when he musters the courage to travel down the tunnel alone to face the terrible Smaug.

But all of this raises an intriguing philosophical puzzle: How can we have these emotions about Bilbo—and why should we care what happens to him at all—when we know that Bilbo is a fictional creature and never existed at all? Our emotional reactions to fictional characters and events are, as Gollum might say, very "tricksy," indeed.

Paradoxes in the Dark

Philosophers refer to this puzzle as the *paradox of fiction*: How can we be rational in having emotional responses to fiction? Although there were hints of this puzzle in Aristotle's (384–322 BCE) discussion of the cathartic effects of tragic drama, Samuel Johnson's (1709–1784) preface to William Shakespeare's plays, and Samuel Taylor Coleridge's (1772–1834) works, it didn't attract significant philosophical attention until the mid-1970s, when it was brought to prominence through the works of philosophers Colin Radford and Kendall Walton.[1] The paradox can be laid out clearly in terms of three mutually inconsistent claims.[2]

First, it seems virtually undeniable that we have emotional responses to fiction. When we read *The Hobbit* or see it on-screen, we are moved by the characters and events depicted. This gives us what we'll call the *emotion condition*: we have genuine and rational emotional responses to characters like Bilbo.

Second, in order for us to have genuine and rational emotional responses to someone or to some situation, those responses must be properly coordinated with our beliefs; that is, we must believe that the person really exists or that the situation has really occurred. (Something that exists or occurs only fictionally does not *really* exist or occur.) Another way of saying this is that emotions require *existence beliefs*. Radford argues "that I can only be moved by someone's plight if I believe that something terrible has happened to him. If I do not believe that he has not and is not suffering or whatever, I cannot grieve or be moved to tears."[3] That gives us the *coordination condition*: in order for us to have genuine emotional responses toward someone, we must believe that he or she really exists.

Third, the emotional responses we have when we knowingly engage with a piece of fiction aren't properly coordinated with what we believe. We don't have the relevant existence beliefs. We might on occasion mistake fiction for fact, but without such confusion, we don't take the fictional characters of our imagination to be real. This gives us the *belief condition*: we do not believe that Bilbo really exists.

Each of these three claims seems true when considered on its own, but when they're considered together, we're faced with an inconsistency. Even for those of us fond of riddles, the paradox of fiction is not easy at all.

Confusticate and Bebother!

Sometimes we can resolve a paradox by showing that despite the initial appearance, the claims making up the paradox aren't really inconsistent after all. With the paradox of fiction, this strategy seems like a nonstarter; it's hard to see any way that all three claims could jointly be true. So a solution to the paradox requires us to reject at least one of the three claims. But just as most of the many paths and passes through the Misty Mountains were "cheats and deceptions and led nowhere or to bad ends," none of our three options for solving the paradox of fiction makes for an easy philosophical journey.[4]

On first reflection, denying the emotion condition looks like an especially rocky road. How on (Middle-)earth could we deny that we have genuine or rational emotional responses when engaging with works of fiction? It's therefore surprising, perhaps, that both Radford and Walton themselves make exactly this argument, though in different ways. Radford accepts that we experience genuine emotions in response to fiction, but he denies that they are rational. Walton, however, denies that our engagement with fiction involves genuine emotions at all.

Let's look at Radford's response first. Independent of whether he's given us an adequate solution to the paradox of fiction, his claim that emotions can be unreasonable might seem odd in its own right, for there's a natural inclination to think that emotions are outside the sphere of rationality altogether. Scottish philosopher David Hume (1711–1776) famously suggested, "'Tis not contrary to reason to prefer the destruction of the whole world to the scratching of my finger."[5] Hume was making a point about desires, or what he called the *passions*, but we might think that a similar point applies to emotion.

Suppose we adopt the *pure feeling view* of emotions usually attributed to William James (1842–1910), a view that identified emotions with bodily sensations. When we perceive that we are in danger, our bodies undergo all sorts of physical changes: our pulses race, our faces become flushed, and we start to sweat. For James, the emotional state of fear is just the bodily sensation that accompanies all of these physiological responses.[6] Since it seems doubtful that bodily sensations can be judged to be rational or irrational, the pure feeling view seems to suggest that emotions too cannot be judged to be rational or irrational.

Yet it's clear that we do routinely characterize emotions as being either rational or irrational. Consider Shakespeare's Iago, a man who accuses his wife, Emilia, of having an affair, despite having no real evidence whatsoever of any unfaithfulness on her part. This jealousy is very naturally characterized as unreasonable or irrational. Or consider someone who experiences great joy over something completely trivial: like the discovery that he's really got twelve pocket handkerchiefs left in his drawer, not just eleven. This exuberance too seems most naturally characterized as unreasonable or irrational.

Consider one more case. One day the local paper reports that a mountain lion has been spotted in a nearby residential area, preying on small pets that have been left outside overnight. Lots of emotions would likely be aroused by reading the story: fear of the dangerous animal on the loose, pity for the families who lost their Chihuahuas or kittens, and anxiety about our own dear Fluffy outside in the yard. But now suppose that the next day the paper reports that all the mountain lion sightings have proved false and that all of the apparent pet abductions were found to have been perpetrated by high school pranksters; all the missing pets have now been returned to their owners completely unharmed. Any fear that we continue to feel about the mountain lion would at this point be unwarranted and irrational. It doesn't make any sense to fear the mountain lion prowling around town now that we know there isn't one.[7]

In his effort to solve the paradox of fiction by denying the emotion condition, Radford would claim that our fear of Smaug is like the irrational fear of the mountain lion. Given that we know that Smaug doesn't exist, our fear of him is irrational. For Radford, all the emotions that we experience when reading *The Hobbit*—and, in fact, all the emotions we experience when reading any works of fiction—are irrational in this way: "Our being moved in certain ways by works of art, though very 'natural' to us and in that way only too intelligible, involves us in inconsistency and so incoherence."[8]

A strong reason to doubt Radford's rejection of the emotion condition stems from the distinctions we draw among the emotional reactions we have to fiction; surely they cannot *all* be dismissed as unreasonable. Although it wouldn't be appropriate to fear the kindly elf Elrond, our fearful reaction to Smaug is quite a different matter. After all, as Thorin tells us, Smaug is a "most specially greedy, strong and wicked worm."[9]

Contemporary philosopher Martha Nussbaum gives us a fruitful way to defend the rationality of our responses to fiction by arguing that such responses enable us to cultivate moral character. By engaging with fiction, we're provided with insights into the experiences of others that we do not usually otherwise have access to, and we are thereby better able to develop our moral sensibilities. It seems implausible to dismiss our emotional reactions to fiction as irrational given the important role they play in our moral education.[10]

Quasi-Bewutherment

The second strategy for denying the emotion condition comes from adopting a view we might call *emotional irrealism*.[11] In this view, even though it may seem undeniable that we experience a cascade of emotions—fear, anxiety, pity, and joy—when reading about Bilbo, we're mistaken. All we're really experiencing are *quasi-emotions*.

The primary proponent of emotional irrealism is Kendall Walton, a philosopher who's had a profound influence in aesthetics—the philosophy of art—over the last forty years or so. According to Walton, to accept the emotion condition "is to tolerate mystery and court confusion."[12] Although we naturally report being terrified by the on-screen depiction of the advance of Saruman's Uruk-hai forces during the Battle of Helm's Deep, this report should not be taken literally. Our hearts may be relentlessly pounding, we might be sweating and gasping for breath, and our knuckles may be white as we clutch the armrests of the theater seats we're sitting in, but it's nonetheless a mistake to describe these involuntary responses as indicative of genuine terror. Since we lack a belief that the Uruk-hai are really advancing toward us, we cannot be terrified of them. Rather, our reactions to the film are best described as analogous to the reactions we have when we are playing ordinary games of pretend.

In support of this point, Walton asks us to consider a young boy playing a game of monsters with his father:

> The father, pretending to be a ferocious monster, cunningly stalks the child and, at a crucial moment, lunges viciously at him. The child flees, screaming, to the next room. The scream is more or less involuntary, and so is the flight. But the child . . . is perfectly aware that this father is only "playing," that the whole thing is "just a game," and that only make-believedly is there a vicious monster after him. He is not really afraid.[13]

Just as movies and novels encourage us to imagine certain characters and to make believe that the depicted events are real, they also encourage us to make believe that we have the relevant emotions.

In addition to providing a solution to the paradox of fiction, emotional irrealism nicely solves a related puzzle about our emotional responses to fiction. Emotions usually motivate us to action. For instance, when we fear something, we tend to do something to try to avoid it or to prevent it from happening. But our apparent fear of Saruman's advancing army doesn't motivate us to take any actions at all. Rather, we just sit passively in our seats. If this apparent fear is just make-believe, however, then we have a nice explanation for our passivity; there's no reason for us to take action if we're not feeling genuine fear.

Still, despite the fact that emotional irrealism can provide solutions to these philosophical problems, it is highly questionable. When you're watching the Peter Jackson film *The Fellowship of the Ring* and feeling anguish about Gandalf's fall from the Bridge of Khazad-dûm, it doesn't make you feel any less sad to be reminded that he's only a fictional character—nor does the reminder make the sadness feel any different or any less real. The fear and anxiety that we feel when we read *The Hobbit* certainly *feel* exactly like genuine fear and anxiety to us, so much so that we mistake the former for the latter.

In response, emotional irrealists like Walton dismiss the surface similarity of our subjective impressions, arguing that we shouldn't be misled by our inability to distinguish pretend fear from real fear. From a distance, we might be unable to distinguish Kili from Fili, but we shouldn't draw any conclusions about their identities from the fact that we can't tell them apart. Quasi-fear might feel just like real fear to us, but that in itself is not enough to make it a genuine emotion.

It's hard to be fully satisfied by that response. When Bilbo nears home on his return journey, he reaches a place "where the shapes of the land and of the trees were as well-known to him as his hands and toes."[14] We seem to know our own emotions just as well, so it's hard to accept a theory that suggests we are systematically mistaken about the kinds of experiences we're having when we engage with fiction.

Moreover, additional problems can be raised for the emotional irrealist by a closer scrutiny of Walton's analogy to games of make-believe. When we engage with fiction, we are remarkably unable to control our emotional responses. How can we fail to be moved by Bilbo's adventure? We don't really have any choice but to be disgusted by Gollum, to fear the wild wargs, and to delight in Bilbo's safe return home.

Likewise, try as we might, we cannot bring ourselves to fear the hobbits of the Shire. In playing games of make-believe, we have much freer rein over our emotional responses. As Noël Carroll has argued, if our emotional responses to fiction were merely the result of make-believe, then they should be able to "be engaged at will"—we should be able to turn them both on and off as we choose.[15]

Thus, it seems we should prefer a solution to the paradox of fiction that allows us to recognize our emotional responses to fiction as genuine. It's just too implausible to dismiss them as the products of make-believe. We need to consider our other alternatives for solving the paradox of fiction.

Out of the Frying Pan and into the Fire?

Unfortunately, denying the belief condition—that we don't believe Bilbo exists—doesn't seem to work, either. It's hard to swallow the idea that we ever believe that the events depicted by *The Hobbit* are real, that we somehow mistake it as a factual travelogue. Even when we're completely captivated by Tolkien's magical prose, we don't believe that Bilbo really exists. What some philosophers suggest, however, is that we "half believe" that he really exists. After all, we do talk of being *absorbed by* fiction, of getting *lost in* what we read.[16] Such talk might even be especially appropriate about works of fantasy, through which we *escape* to the fictional world created.

Tolkien himself suggests something like this in his essay "On Fairy-Stories." Arguing that escapism is one of the main functions of fantasy, Tolkien suggests that the successful fantasy writer "makes a Secondary World which your mind can enter. Inside it, what he relates is 'true': it accords with the laws of that world. You therefore believe it, while you are, as it were, inside."[17] On this way of looking at things, we can distinguish our beliefs inside the story from our normal beliefs. Although we don't normally believe that Bilbo exists, we can believe it inside the story.

The success of this response to the paradox comes down to whether we can make sufficient sense of the notion of inside-the-story belief, or half belief, and even if we can, whether it can do the philosophical work we need it to do. If we really have beliefs—even weak or half beliefs—about the fictional works we engage with, then it seems these beliefs would be manifested in our behavior.

While watching the early scenes of *The Fellowship of the Ring*, for example, would we really sit passively in our seats if we had the belief—even the half belief—that Black Riders were coming to get us? Walton has convincingly argued that even just a hesitant belief or a mere suspicion that Black Riders were on their way "would induce any normal person seriously to consider calling the police [or the 'Shirriffs'] and warning his family."[18] Even the least Tookish of us would surely do *something*, if only to run and take cover.

Given the difficulty of rejecting either the belief condition or the emotion condition, other philosophers have tried instead to reject the coordination condition, that we must believe something really exists to have a genuine emotional response toward it. We might note, however, that the case for the coordination condition is usually made by considerations of emotions like pity and fear. When we consider other emotions, the case is considerably less compelling. Berys Gaut invites us to reflect on our feelings of disgust:

> It is odd to say that one has to know whether something really occurred if one is to be disgusted at the thought of it. If I describe in vivid and detailed fashion the jam-and-live-mouse sandwich that I breakfasted on the other day, you might well feel disgusted, without supposing that I am telling the truth.[19]

It's quite natural here to want to say that it's the very thought of the sandwich that disgusts us, and this gives rise to a view often referred to as the *thought theory*. Roughly speaking, the thought theorist claims that mere thoughts, rather than existence beliefs, are enough to ground emotional responses. Just as the thought of the sandwich is enough to give rise to a feeling of disgust even though we don't believe that it actually exists, the thought of Bilbo can give rise to a feeling of pity for him even though we don't believe that he actually exists.

Peter Lamarque advocates a version of the thought theory in terms of *mental representations*: "Mental representations or thought-contents can be the cause of emotions such as fear and pity quite independently of beliefs we might hold about being in personal danger or about the existence of real suffering or pain."[20] Lamarque thus suggests that we amend the coordination condition. In order for us to have genuine and emotional responses toward someone, we needn't believe that he or she really exists; rather, all we need to do is to form mental representations of his or her situation.

Unlike the original coordination condition, this amended condition allows us to make sense of our engagement with fiction. When we read *The Hobbit*, we imagine the adventure that's described and the characters who participate in it, and we use our imaginations to form mental representations (mental images) of the characters depicted. Moreover, for Lamarque, these mental representations are the source of our emotions; when we pity and fear fictional characters, it's the mental representations to which we direct our emotions. Thus, the thought theory provides a solution to the paradox of fiction.

But should we accept the thought theory? On the one hand, there does seem to be something right about it. We engage with works of fiction through the imagination, and it seems plausible that our imaginings would come into play to explain away the paradox. On the other hand, when we think more closely about exactly what the thought theory commits us to, it becomes harder to endorse. Lamarque's solution to the paradox of fiction depends on the bold assertion that "the fear and pity we feel for fictions are in fact directed at thoughts in our minds."[21]

When we read *The Hobbit*, our emotional responses are responses not to the character Bilbo himself—after all, he's a fictional character who we know doesn't exist—but rather to the mental images of him that we've formed when reading about his exploits. Likewise, my fear of Smaug is really a fear of my mental image of Smaug.

But whereas dragons (were they to exist) would be genuinely terrifying, mental images of dragons aren't (or needn't be). After all, it's not the mental image of a dragon that's fire-breathing, it's the dragon itself that's fire-breathing. So I'm not worried that my mental image of Smaug is going to kill my mental image of Bilbo with a fiery roar. Rather, I'm worried that Smaug himself is going to kill Bilbo himself with a fiery roar.

The basic paradox of fiction arises because we can't answer questions like these: *What* do we fear? *Whom* do we pity? Emotions, unlike moods, are always directed at something in particular; they always have objects. As Gaut explains, "A mood, such as happiness or sadness, need not have an intentional object: someone can simply be happy or sad without being happy or sad about *anything*. An emotion in contrast has an intentional object: I am afraid of something, I pity something."[22]

But what's the *something* in the case of fiction? There's no existing object to serve this function. Thought theorists provide such an object: thoughts (or, more specifically, mental representations or images). Unlike Bilbo himself, my thought of Bilbo is a really existing thing. But unfortunately for the thought theorist, it doesn't seem like the right kind of existing thing to make sense of our emotional reactions to fiction.

Living with Bewutherment

Confronted with one of Gollum's riddles, Bilbo "had a feeling that the answer was quite different and that he ought to know it, but he could not think of it."[23] We might feel something similar about the paradox of fiction. On the one hand, given how natural and commonplace our emotional reactions to fiction are, it seems that it should be an easy matter to explain them. On the other hand, try as we might, a satisfactory solution to the puzzle continues to elude us.

At this point, I think our best option is to take a second look at the coordination condition. We saw earlier that the thought theorist's attempt to amend this condition runs into trouble. But perhaps it was a mistake to try to hold on to the condition at all, even in an amended form. Maybe we'd do better to reject it entirely. Although it may be true that emotions are often grounded in existence beliefs, that doesn't mean they must *always* be grounded this way.

In an influential article, Richard Moran has suggested that it's not just in the case of fiction that we have emotional reactions without the relevant existence beliefs. Rather, once we reflect on the vast array of our ordinary emotional repertoire, "it begins to look like comparatively little of one's emotional attention concerns objects in the actual here and now."[24] I admire Tolkien, even though I know full well that he's no longer alive. I might also feel sorrow that many of Tolkien's closest friends died in World War I, and I might regret that he didn't publish more works in his lifetime.

As Moran points out, emotions like regret and remorse are essentially backward looking and thus are often directed at things that do not presently exist. Yet we don't consider these emotions to be at all puzzling. We might also direct our emotions at future objects or events that don't presently exist; for example, I might fear the floods that will come from the melting of the polar ice caps. I can even have emotions about things that can't possibly exist, like a trip back in time to sit in on a meeting of Tolkien's famous Oxford discussion group, the Inklings.

Furthermore, just as the mere thought of something disgusting can generate disgust, there seems to be a whole class of emotions that aren't tied to existence beliefs. Moran provides us with several examples:

> Whatever air of paradox there might be in the idea of pity or fear directed at what are mere characters, there is none at all in the idea of, say, mirth and merriment directed at events one knows to be staged, or at tales concerning salesmen and chickens who never really lived.[25]

He later adds pleasure, boredom, anxiety, and suspense to the list. All of these reactions seem entirely independent from the relevant existence beliefs.

To solve the paradox of fiction, we'd certainly need some additional explanation for why the coordination condition seems to us so plausible, and it would also be nice if we had an alternative explanation of the relationship between our emotions and our beliefs. But reflection on considerations like those offered by Moran provides us with at least some resolution to the paradox we find ourselves in. We might still be somewhat bewildered and bewuthered, but at least we can have some confidence that the bewilderment and bewutherment that we're feeling are genuine after all.

NOTES

1. Colin Radford, "How Can We Be Moved by the Fate of Anna Karenina?" *Proceedings of the Aristotelian Society* 49 (1) (1975): 67–80; and Kendall Walton, "Fearing Fictions," *Journal of Philosophy* 75 (1) (1978): 5–27. Other influential discussions of the puzzle appear in Gregory Currie, *The Nature of Fiction* (Cambridge, UK: Cambridge University Press, 1990); and Nöel Carroll, *The Philosophy of Horror, or, Paradoxes of the Heart* (London: Routledge, 1990). For a very clear overview of the paradox and various proposals for dealing with it, see Steven Schneider, "The Paradox of Fiction," *Internet Encyclopedia of Philosophy*, http://www.iep.utm.edu/f/fict-par.htm).

2. My formulation of the argument is indebted to Tamar Szabó Gendler and Karson Kovakovich, "Genuine Rational Fictional Emotions," in *Aesthetics and the Philosophy of Art*, ed. Matthew Kieran (Oxford, UK: Blackwell, 2006), 241–53.

3. Radford, "How Can We Be Moved by the Fate of Anna Karenina?", 68.

4. J. R. R. Tolkien, *The Hobbit: or, There and Back Again* (New York: Del Rey/Ballantine Books, 2001), 55.

5. David Hume, *A Treatise of Human Nature* (Oxford, UK: Clarendon Press, 1985), 416.

6. William James, "What Is an Emotion?" *Mind* 9 (1884): 188–205.

7. Perhaps in some situations your residual fear is not irrational. For example, you might never have realized before that mountain lions came down from the hills into populated areas, or you might have forgotten this fact; now, having been alerted to or reminded of that possibility, you fear that one of the mountain lions living in the hills will make its way down into town. This fear might not be irrational, but notice that it's not the fear of a nonexistent mountain lion roaming about town; rather, it's the fear of an actual mountain lion not yet roaming about town.

8. Radford, "How Can We Be Moved by the Fate of Anna Karenina?", 78.

9. Tolkien, *The Hobbit*, 23.

10. Martha Nussbaum, *The Fragility of Goodness* (Cambridge, UK: Cambridge University Press, 1986); see also Gendler and Kovakovich, "Genuine Rational Fictional Emotions," 252.

11. The term *emotional irrealism* comes from Berys Gaut, "Reasons, Emotions, and Fiction," in *Imagination, Philosophy, and the Arts*, ed. Matthew Kieran and Dominic McIver Lopes (London: Routledge, 2003), 15.

12. Walton, "Fearing Fictions," 6.

13. Ibid., 13.

14. Tolkien, *The Hobbit*, 302.

15. Carroll, *The Philosophy of Horror*, 74. Carroll makes his argument about works of horror, but they seem to apply equally well to works of fantasy.

16. Schneider, "The Paradox of Fiction."

17. J. R. R. Tolkien, "On Fairy-Stories," in *Poems and Stories* (New York: Houghton Mifflin, 1994), 167.

18. Walton, "Fearing Fictions," 7.

19. Gaut, "Reasons, Emotions, and Fiction," 17.

20. Peter Lamarque, "How Can We Fear and Pity Fictions?" *British Journal of Aesthetics* 21 (4) (1981): 296.

21. Ibid., 293.

22. Gaut, "Reasons, Emotions, and Fiction," 16.

23. Tolkien, *The Hobbit*, 78.

24. Richard Moran, "The Expression of Feeling in Imagination," *Philosophical Review* 103 (1) (January 1994): 78; see also Gendler and Kovakovich, "Genuine Rational Fictional Emotions," 249.

25. Moran, "The Expression of Feeling in Imagination," 81. Tolkien tells us that "it is a strange thing, but things that are good to have and days that are good to spend are soon told about, and not much to listen to; while things that are uncomfortable, palpitating, and even gruesome, may make a good tale, and take a deal of telling anyway." Tolkien, *The Hobbit*, 51. Perhaps this explains why philosophers worrying about the paradox of fiction have focused so much on fear and pity rather than mirth and merriment.

PHILOSOPHY IN THE DARK

The Hobbit and Hermeneutics

Tom Grimwood

Imagine that one day you wake up and find a note, written by an exiled dwarf king, apparently asking you to meet him at a nearby pub in ten minutes. It's not a particularly lucid note. In fact, it leaves several key points somewhat ambiguous. You may well wonder what it all might mean. You might, like Bilbo, throw caution to the wind and follow the instructions regardless. But you might also stop and ask yourself the following: How do I know what this note means? What determines the note's meaning? And how do I know that I've found the right meaning?

If you were to ask these questions, you'd be thinking about the theory of interpretation, what philosophers call *hermeneutics*. Usually associated with the interpretation of texts, hermeneutics asks fundamental questions about how we interpret meaning through any object or medium (writing, speaking, signing, painting, acting, and so on).

In *The Hobbit*, these types of questions are explored by Bilbo and Gollum in the chapter titled "Riddles in the Dark." In the course of the chapter, each character attempts to outwit the other in a game of riddles. During the course of the game, Bilbo and Gollum are challenged on several levels of understanding. They must understand where they are and who the other is and, most important, solve each other's riddles. Each riddle offers a variety of possible interpretations, but according to the rules of the game, there is only one correct answer. As impromptu philosophers of interpretation, Bilbo and Gollum grapple with the classic problem of how to assign fixed meaning to vague or ambiguous language.

The Rules of Riddles

Thorin's note may well be easy enough to understand without the interventions of philosophy. But if you were confronted with a different message, which seemed to deliberately play on the slipperiness of language, it might be worth stopping to think about how you would answer. Consider this question that Gollum poses to Bilbo:

> What has roots as nobody sees,
> Is taller than trees,
> Up, up it goes,
> And yet never grows?[1]

The riddle is a question, but unlike most questions, it does not supply us with an obvious frame of reference that would allow an immediate answer. We can see that this question is asking what has aspects of a tree but is not a tree. How we interpret such a question, and how we know when we have arrived at the correct answer, will involve constructing a frame of reference for ourselves.

To make this less of a (Misty) mountainous task, there are fortunately certain rules at work in Bilbo and Gollum's game of riddles that may help us here. The game is, after all, "sacred and of immense antiquity."[2] There are two participants (the game would have little meaning played on one's own). One gives the other a riddle. The riddle has an answer, known by the riddler.

Of course, at the beginning of the game, at least, neither Bilbo nor Gollum simply asks the other to guess what he is thinking without any clues (later in the discussion, when Bilbo asks Gollum to guess what's in his pockets, these rules are bent, if not broken, but we'll deal with that problem later). The key to the success of the riddle is to tell the audience what this answer is while hoping that the audience will not guess what it is. Think about Bilbo's first effort:

> Thirty white horses on a red hill,
> First they champ,
> Then they stamp,
> Then they stand still.[3]

Because it is a riddle, we know that Bilbo isn't actually talking about thirty horses—otherwise, the answer would simply be "horses," which would hardly make a game of it—but something similar to thirty horses. In other words, the goal of the message seems to be both to *communicate* an answer—in this case, "teeth"—and to *not* communicate an answer. Only when the riddle fails to be understood has it succeeded as a communication. In short: there is a meaning, but the meaning is in disguise (or "in the dark"). In this way, the riddle plays a particular type of ironic mischief in the task of understanding.

Bilbo's End: Intentionalism

There are two interlinking issues at stake in the game of riddles. First, we need to know the answer to the riddle. This is determined quite straightforwardly by the riddler; technically, whatever answer is given should be judged either wrong or right by the poser of the riddle. Second is the slightly more complicated interpretative aspect. Before we can answer the riddle, we need to understand the meaning of the words and how they work in the riddle. This move presupposes that we have some idea of what "meaning" actually is.

The most commonsense answer would perhaps be "a message means what its author intended it to mean." The goal of interpretation is thus to discover what this original intention was. The view that the meaning of a message is identical to its author's intention is called *intentionalism*. One of the best-known defenders of intentionalism is educator and former University of Virginia English professor E. D. Hirsch Jr.

Bilbo is, as we know, all about common sense, and his focus on the intentions of his fellow riddler is for good reason. He suspects that Gollum wants to eat him. Indeed, he seemingly agrees to play the game of riddles only to buy time while trying to figure out what Gollum is and how dangerous he might be. Accordingly, the questions he asks about Gollum's riddles are often not so much "What do these words mean?" but rather "What does this creature *intend* them to mean?" In these cases, the act of understanding the text of the riddle is the same as understanding the intended reference of the words. This is made all the easier for two reasons: (1) the answers to Gollum's first few riddles are fairly reflective of his immediate surroundings— "mountain," "dark," "fish"—and (2) Bilbo has heard many of the riddles before, presumably in a less hostile environment where he was able to confirm the riddler's intention.

There is, however, an obvious problem with treating the author's intention as the determiner of meaning, as Bilbo discovers. If the only way of ascertaining the meaning of a riddle is through the author's intention, how do we know for certain what the author's intention is? There are a few possible answers to this question.

We could, perhaps, simply ask the author what he meant. This is not an option for Bilbo, unfortunately, and it would rather destroy the whole point of the game. In fact, it might not be an entirely reliable option for anybody, since in order to understand the author's message, we are asking the author to give us yet another message. This is fine if we've simply misheard or require clarification from the author. But if the second message is as unclear as the first, then one may find oneself in something of a vicious cycle.

Alternatively, if the author is absent or unwilling to reveal his intention, we could try to determine the intention for ourselves from the clues left in both the message and the author's behavior or history. This seems to be the strategy that Bilbo has opted for when he asks Gollum, "Well, what is it? . . . The answer's not a kettle boiling over, as you seem to think from the noise you are making."[4]

For Hirsch, language is always an instrument of the user, and it cannot create or determine meaning on its own. After all, if language were self-determining, we would not have so many disagreements over interpretation. He says, "A word sequence means nothing in particular until somebody either means something by it or understands something from it."[5]

Riddle Me This, Professor Hirsch

In many ways, Hirsch's theory is intended to provide some certainty in the interpretation of texts. But it is "tricksy" to talk of definite knowledge in this context, even if intentionalism is by far the most commonsense way of thinking about meaning. Bilbo himself seems to discover more by chance and common knowledge than by guessing Gollum's hidden intentions. Gollum's fifth riddle is tough for Bilbo, and merely thinking about Gollum's motive—that he wants to eat the hobbit—doesn't seem to help:

> This thing all things devours:
> Birds, beasts, trees, flowers;
> Gnaws iron, bites steel;

Grinds hard stones to meal;
Slays king, ruins town,
And beats high mountain down.[6]

In this case, Gollum's rather choice wording of the riddle seems to heighten Bilbo's fear. When one encounters words that refer to devouring all things, from birds to mountains, uttered by one's possible future devourer, the words' implications may go well beyond the limits of the game. It is only a lucky sequence of events that enables Bilbo to guess the correct answer: "time."

Indeed, Hirsch admits that words sometimes have a kind of meaning separate from the author's intention: certain words will evoke various reactions from different readers or listeners. As we know from Gimli and Legolas's very different reactions to the Glittering Caves of Aglarond, "caves" will mean one thing to a dwarf and quite another to an elf.[7] According to Hirsch, there is a difference between "meaning," which is determined purely by the author (in this case, the answer to the riddle, as determined by Gollum) and "significance," which is a message's "meaning to" a particular reader or listener (its import or subjective connotations). In this view, a text's meaning remains fixed and unchanging, but its significance varies from person to person.

Philosopher Monroe Beardsley (1915–1985) argued, however, that the issue is not whether the meaning of the message and the intention of the author coincide or whether the meaning of the message is sufficient evidence of the author's intention, for all theories of interpretation admit that these are often the case. Rather, the question is whether a message's meaning and the author's intention are *one and the same thing*.[8] From one perspective, it would seem that far more of Bilbo's understanding may be based on the significance of Gollum's riddles than on their intended meaning.

Furthermore, Hirsch admits that language, while not the source of "meaning," is nevertheless the source of "intelligibility." An author cannot simply claim that the words she uses mean whatever she wants them to mean. I cannot make "Baltimore Ravens fan" mean "brainless pinhead," regardless of my grid-iron loyalties. Moreover, texts that have many authors, such as committee reports, constitutional provisions, and, indeed, many riddles and jokes, may be perfectly intelligible yet not have any shared "original intent."[9] But if language is shared in this way, does this not affect the idea that the author is the *sole* determiner of a text's meaning?

Gollum and Gadamer

These criticisms of intentionalism do not deny that riddles have an author, an intention, or an answer. Rather, the criticisms suggest that one's interpretation of a riddle's meaning cannot be reduced to the mere recovery of the riddler's intention. While the riddler may determine the answer to the riddle, our way of interpreting the communication so that we can reach that answer involves a wider appreciation of how meaning is created and communicated.

With this in mind, we can see in Gollum's responses to Bilbo's second and third riddles the reflection of a slightly different approach to interpretation.

> An eye in a blue face
> Saw an eye in a green face.
> "That eye is like to this eye"
> Said the first eye,
> "But in low place,
> Not in high place."[10]

This riddle is more complex than the earlier examples. "Eyes" and "faces" are immediately problematic terms. First, our tendency to read human characteristics into the world in literature, myth, and so on, means that these two images have a potentially wider application to any number of things in the world than the more defined image of a horse or a tree.

Second, as it turns out, the riddle is actually referring to two different types of things (the sun and a daisy) with the same descriptive image. Rather than trying to understand Bilbo's motive for such words, which could lead to innumerable scenarios involving the author's experience of eyes and faces, Gollum relates the text of the riddle to his own experience of the world:

> He had been underground a long long time, and was forgetting this sort of thing. . . . Gollum brought up memories of ages and ages and ages before, when he lived with his grandmother in a hole in a bank by a river. "Sss, sss, my preciouss," he said. "Sun on the daisies it means, it does."[11]

In this way, Gollum follows a model of interpretation proposed by perhaps the most influential philosopher of hermeneutics in the twentieth century, Hans-Georg Gadamer (1900–2002). For Gadamer, our interpretations are always situated in a particular historical context. We think in terms of our experiences and our acquired knowledge. This provides us with a horizon for understanding. Such a horizon provides us with a set of prejudices that enable us to understand the object of interpretation.

This notion of prejudice is not meant in the negative sense of an irrational bias against someone or something. Rather, "prejudice" means the set of predispositions by which we recognize something as meaningful. Our education, for example, teaches us to read in a certain language, thus prejudicing us to see certain shapes and signs as letters and words. If we were not educated in that language, we would not be able to understand it.

For Gadamer, it is our prejudices that make understanding possible. We are always within the act of interpreting the world and are thus able to adapt and develop our prejudices and widen our horizons of understanding. Thus, understanding is not simply a process of reconstructing the original thought

behind the message, which is located within its own historical context or horizon. Rather, "understanding" is a dialogue
between the interpreter and the object of interpretation and
the fusion of the two horizons. In other words, to "understand"
is to understand oneself in the subject matter.[12]

Now, properly speaking, Gollum is not a historically situated being; he is a fictional character. Nevertheless, his understanding of Bilbo's riddles is based on the (fictional) history
of his own existence and the horizon this gives him. Whereas
Bilbo begins the game by locating the meaning of the riddle
in terms of Gollum's intention—the meaning is determined by
the answer, which has been decided by Gollum beforehand—
Gollum himself attempts to understand each riddle by reflecting on his own experience.

For Hirsch's intentionalism, both author and reader are
taken as relatively stable entities, but Gadamer's hermeneutic
theory recognizes that we are in part formed by our engagement and fusion with other horizons of understanding. We do
not simply submit to an idea but instead understand that idea
within our own realm of experience. Thus, Gollum is able to
guess the answer to Bilbo's riddle:

> A box without hinges, key, or lid. Yet golden treasure
> inside is hid.[13]

He does so by reflecting on his experience of

> thieving from nests long ago, and sitting under the river
> bank teaching his grandmother, teaching his grand-
> mother to suck—"Eggses!" he hissed. "Eggses it is!"[14]

When faced with a communication that invokes a horizon
we are not familiar with—for example, a philosophy book
written in the 1600s or the language of the elves from the
days "when all the world was wonderful"—we obviously do
not abandon our individual positions, situated as we are in our
own horizons in the here and now.[15] But it would be a mistake,

according to Gadamer, to attempt to appropriate the message completely into our individual horizons, because then we would merely be seeing everything as we want to see it.

This could certainly be pleasant for a while. But we must remember that our individual horizons, made up of all of our experiences, are essentially changing and fluctuating frames of reference. If you've ever had a conversation with somebody who only sees things his or her way, you'll know how important it is to see our horizons of understanding as something we negotiate rather than appropriate.

In contrast, attempting to reconstruct the original horizon in its entirety is also futile, for this would empty the message of any significance for us. This, according to Gadamer, was Hirsch's fundamental mistake: by situating meaning in the intention of the author alone, we do not account for the changing significance of meaning from person to person. But we don't simply arrive at a message in a vacuum. Consequently, the role of personal engagement with a message is essential, as we see in Gollum:

> These ordinary aboveground everyday sort of riddles were tiring for him. Also they reminded him of days when he had been less lonely and sneaky and nasty, and that put him out of temper.[16]

It is no small irony that Gollum, who is portrayed throughout Tolkien's sagas as a lone, loathsome individual, should seek understanding through dialogue with another. Gollum, however, continually talks in dialogue—not to another person, but to either his own alter ego, Sméagol, or to his beloved "precious," the ring.

Indeed, Gadamer's model of dialogue is not limited to an actual conversation between two people. Rather, the model of dialogue is just that: a model to explain how understanding occurs. As a model, it describes the structure in which any encounter with an object of understanding is formed, whether this is a work of art, a book, another person, or a riddling halfling.

What's in Bilbo's Pocketses?

This model of dialogue involves certain commitments, however, just as the riddle game involves certain rules, which we outlined earlier. Dialogue, according to Gadamer, is meaningful because of the goodwill of the participants: the shared understanding that one person has something to say and another wants to understand it. But we have already seen how this creates problems for the intentionalist theory of meaning.

From the point that Bilbo asks Gollum to guess "What's in my pocket?", communication between the two seems to break down. The goodwill of the dialogue is notably absent as both parties descend to shouting repeated questions at each other. This ending to the game raises two questions: (1) Is Bilbo's final riddle entirely fair? (2) How does Gollum's interpretative method help or hinder him in determining the answer?

On the one hand, from the intentionalist standpoint, there is an intention within the question and an answer to the riddle, so the question does at least have meaning. There *is* something in Bilbo's pocket, and that something is of huge significance to the story, not just of Bilbo and Gollum but of Middle-earth itself. Furthermore, it is not something that Gollum is unaware of—it is his own ring, which he will shortly discover is missing. Hence, Bilbo declares that he has won the contest fairly (although he admits that the ancient laws may not consider his last puzzler a genuine riddle).

On the other hand, from the perspective of Gadamer's dialogical theory of interpretation, Bilbo's final riddle clearly disrupts the sense of dialogue that gives any interpretation meaning. In other words, it is not the fact that there is an answer that seems to upset the game but rather that Bilbo has disrupted the tentative spirit of goodwill at work in the game itself. His question is simply an inquiry, not a statement that provides clues or communicates a message without asserting it too obviously. This has implications for the underlying point of the game.

It leaves Gollum with no horizon to fuse. It is not surprising, then, that Gollum appropriates this question and interprets the message purely in terms of his own experience.

As a result, when Gollum finally arrives at the truth as we know it—that Bilbo has "stolen" his "precious" from him—it is "true," in a sense, only to the extent that Gollum has created that truth from his inner dialogue. He cannot objectively prove that Bilbo has the ring, but this doesn't matter, given his interpretive approach. As we've seen, Gollum is not tied to seeing the meaning of Bilbo's riddle as identical with his intention, so he is justified in arriving at the conclusion on his own.

Out of the Frying Pan

Philosophers could go at it hammer and tongs over whether Bilbo really wins the game of riddles or not. But the purpose of this chapter has simply been to show how the game of riddles throws out a range of problems for interpretation, even within its relatively established rules. The problems of interpretation don't stop once the formal riddles end. Indeed, from *The Hobbit*'s opening chapter, when Bilbo is confronted with the arrival of a troupe of uninvited yet expectant dwarves, Bilbo is challenged throughout the book with different scenarios that he must interpret and understand in order to survive.

Whether riddling or not, words are often slippery customers that can mean one thing to one person and something quite different to another. Even a simple statement such as "Good morning!" can give a wizard as wise as Gandalf problems in understanding: "Do you wish me a good morning, or mean that it is a good morning whether I want it or not; or that you feel good this morning; or that it is a morning to be good on?"[17]

As with many branches of philosophy, our everyday approach to the philosophy of interpretation is often assumed rather than questioned (indeed, Bilbo is less than impressed with Gandalf's wordplay). But while it might seem pretentious to talk of interpreting a children's book such as *The Hobbit*, it's important to see that interpretation in the hermeneutic sense is something that goes on all the time, and the way in which we interpret meaning is closely bound up with particular philosophical traditions and presuppositions.

We can never achieve a position where we see the world "as it is" outside our own interpretation. (Even if we could, communicating this to anybody else would place us back where we started, since he or she would in turn have to interpret what we were saying.) In reading this chapter, you will have probably already made several fundamental hermeneutic assumptions about what the meaning of the text is and how it might be verified. (Is the meaning of the text what I, the possibly "tricksy" author, intend it to mean? Or is it what you, the reader, take it to mean? Or is it something else?)

In turn, because I am writing this in order that you understand what I'm trying to say, I am also making certain presuppositions about the nature of communication. For example, I write in English, so that like Röac the raven, speaking in the common speech to the dwarves on the Lonely Mountain, I am more likely to be understood by an audience that speaks that language.

This being the case, it is also true that certain situations will bring our assumed notions of meaning and understanding to our attention more acutely than others. When we are faced with an unclear or ambiguous message, as we are in a game of riddles, our interpretive approach is often brought into sharp relief.

NOTES

1. J. R. R. Tolkien, *The Hobbit: or, There and Back Again* (New York: Del Rey/Ballantine Books, 2001), 73.

2. Ibid., 80.

3. Ibid., 74.

4. Ibid., 76.

5. E. D. Hirsch Jr., *Validity in Interpretation* (London: Yale University Press, 1967), 4.

6. Tolkien, *The Hobbit*, 77.

7. J. R. R. Tolkien, *The Lord of the Rings: The Two Towers* (New York: Del Rey/Ballantine Books, 2001), 165–67.

8. Monroe Beardsley, *Aesthetics* (New York: Harcourt, Brace, 1958), 25.

9. Tolkien claimed that all but two of the riddles—"Thirty White Horses" and "No-Legs"—were his own creation. John D. Rateliff, *The History of* The Hobbit (Boston: Houghton Mifflin, 2007), 1:169.

10. Tolkien, *The Hobbit*, 74–75.

11. Ibid., 75.

12. Hans-Georg Gadamer, *Truth and Method* (London: Continuum, 2004), 294.

13. Tolkien, *The Hobbit*, 75.

14. Ibid., 76.

15. Ibid., 215.

16. Ibid., 75.

17. Ibid., 4.

PART FOUR

BEING THERE AND
BACK AGAIN

SOME HOBBITS HAVE ALL THE LUCK

Randall M. Jensen

The Roman philosopher Seneca (ca. 4 BCE–65 CE) famously remarked that "luck is when knowledge meets preparation." That may be true for Stoics, but apparently not for hobbits.

Bilbo has no prior knowledge of any of the places he is about to visit, and he never took the time to learn about the wider world until well into his adventure. As for preparation, Bilbo embarks on his dangerous adventure without his hat, walking stick, and pocket handkerchief. And though he goes in search of treasure, his own money is carelessly forgotten, left at home.

Still, Bilbo is chosen as the lucky fourteenth member of the dwarves' company, and, as Thorin remarks, he does prove to be "possessed of good luck far exceeding the usual allowance."[1] Bilbo and his companions narrowly escape becoming troll-jelly when Gandalf returns from the wilds "in the nick of time."[2] They barely avoid being crushed by falling boulders in the high passes of the Misty Mountains.[3]

Bilbo is "saved by pure luck" when he inadvertently hits on the correct answer ("Time!") to one of Gollum's riddles when he was only intending to ask for more time to respond.[4] He luckily pulls his hands out of his pockets just before Gollum guesses "Handses!" as the answer to Bilbo's unintended riddle, "What do I have in my pockets?"[5]

By "sheer luck," Dori stumbles upon Bilbo, sleeping like a log, in the pitch-black night of Mirkwood Forest.[6] Later that evening, Bilbo wakes up just as a giant spider is about to wrap him up for dinner.[7] In the Elvenking's cellars, Bilbo experiences "luck of an unusual kind" when the guards unwittingly drink an exceptionally "heady vintage" and fall sound asleep, allowing Bilbo to steal their keys.[8]

Most important, in a moment that appears pregnant with luck, Bilbo finds a small ring in the dark in the seemingly endless maze of goblin caves. What are the odds of such a thing? Only with this magic ring is he able to save himself from Gollum and the goblins, rescue his companions from hungry spiders and unfriendly elves, sneak up on Smaug, and survive the Battle of Five Armies.

Luck indeed looms large in Tolkien's beloved classic. In this chapter we fellow conspirators will embark on an adventure of our own to see what philosophical treasure can be found by reflecting on the nature and moral importance of luck. We will have no need for the talents of a burglar, and several expert philosophers await us at the Green Dragon Inn.

Aristotle and the Riddle of Luck

The great Greek philosopher Aristotle (384–322 BCE) often approached a philosophical topic by posing a series of questions or puzzles about it. As he famously put it, philosophy begins in wonder—or, perhaps, in *riddles*. In his treatment of luck (*tuche*, in Greek), Aristotle observed that while we talk a lot about luck in our ordinary explanations of what's happening in the world around us, some philosophers deny the reality of luck.[9] In fact, the more we think about luck, the more we may suspect that we don't quite know what we're talking about. What is luck, anyway?

Aristotle offered three key insights that will help us solve some of the puzzles we'll encounter. First, something that happens most or all of the time isn't a matter of luck; lucky events are unusual and hence generally unexpected. Second, luck isn't an independent, stand-alone cause but is found instead in a "coincidence" of causes. Third, something can be lucky (or unlucky) for an agent only if it is outside of the person's control. Each of these points can be illustrated by looking at lucky episodes in Bilbo's journey.

Recall Bilbo's passage under the Misty Mountains and through the maze of goblin caves, especially his dramatic exit through the well-guarded back door. When Bilbo relates this escape to his companions, they naturally want to know how he did it. His opening answer, "Oh, just crept along, you know—very carefully and quietly," doesn't satisfy them, and rightly so.[10] No doubt some of them not only regarded Bilbo with newfound respect, as Tolkien tells us, but also thought of him as one very lucky hobbit. And if the events had really happened as Bilbo says they did, he would have been extraordinarily lucky indeed!

If someone of Bilbo's stature were to scurry around a cave teeming with enemies, dodging them and jumping over them, he would nearly always be caught. For someone to avoid capture in such circumstances would be very unusual, and thus it would be entirely appropriate to see it as a matter of luck: good luck for the escapee and bad luck for the captors. However, we wouldn't see a captive of such a chase as a victim of bad *luck*, even though it would be awfully dreadful for him, because his capture was to be expected. As Aristotle's first insight stated, luck isn't found in what happens all or most of the time. When a regular, predictable event befalls someone, whether it's a benefit or a harm or neither, it's just not a matter of luck. We invoke luck in our explanations when something surprising happens.

Of course, as we know, Bilbo's story is a lie because of its crucial omission. Imagine that he had been more forthcoming and told his audience of the magic ring he'd found. If he then went on to explain how he got out the back door, they wouldn't have been at all inclined to think of him as lucky for *escaping from the guards*. No one would think, "How lucky it is that they didn't see him or catch him!" After all, that an invisible person managed to dodge creatures who couldn't see him is not surprising at all. In fact, invisible people can nearly always go where they want without being detected, unless a dragon or Bombadil or a Black Rider is about. Bilbo may have been very lucky to find the ring. But given that he has found the ring, his avoiding the guards isn't a matter of luck.

How did Bilbo manage to squeeze through the tiny crack in the goblins' back door? Again, we might naturally point to luck as the answer. This way of talking may suggest that luck is a kind of cause, a talismanic force that sometimes makes things happen in the world. Imagine that Bilbo were to find a magic ring that, like the Felix Felicis potion in the Harry Potter stories, brings one good luck. Whenever you're in a jam, you simply put on the ring and it helps you in some way by intervening in the natural order. In Bilbo's case, the power of luck might have magically enlarged the opening, for example. Yet Bilbo squeezed himself through the door; there was no magical "luck" at all!

An Aristotelian riddle is lurking here. While we do see Bilbo as lucky, we don't seem to have room for luck in our explanation of his escape. Luck seems to disappear if we try to explain exactly what happened; it adds nothing to the causal account. Yet even though most of us don't seriously believe in magic lucky rings (or potions or whatever), we nonetheless talk about luck fairly often, and surely all this talk about luck isn't just nonsense.

Aristotle's second insight solves this riddle by describing luck as something that's present when causal factors *coincide*, so it's no surprise that we speak of luck and coincidence in the same breath. Aristotle meant something a bit deeper than we do, however. His idea was that luck isn't an *additional* causal factor to the factors that already explain how a particular effect is brought about. Luck isn't a kind of magic. Rather, luck is to be found where two perfectly ordinary causal factors coincide in some unexpected way.

At first, Bilbo's luck seems good, for the back door hasn't been closed all the way even though the goblins had caught a glimpse of him. People often leave doors half closed. Bilbo's apparent good luck here is that a goblin left the door somewhat ajar at just the right time, and when we'd expect him to have closed it because of all the commotion going in the caves. What a lucky coincidence for Bilbo!

However, a few moments later it seems his luck is surprisingly bad, because the crack in the door happens to be just a tad smaller than the width of his body. The cause of his girth is that he's a hobbit—a creature "inclined to be fat in the stomach"—and that he's accustomed to enjoying six meals a day whenever possible. Now two sets of causal factors, one involving goblins and a door and another involving a hobbit and his diet, come together in such a way that something surprising happens. It looks like the crack is a tragically perfect fit for the hobbit to meet his sad end! How often does one encounter an opening just the right size to get stuck in? Bilbo's luck has taken a turn for the worse. As it turns out, though, Bilbo's luck is good after all, for the gap turns out to be just barely big enough for him to fit through when he pushes with all his might. If it had been narrower by even an inch, he would have been out of luck, as we say.

For Aristotle, this kind of coincidence is where luck resides. It's a matter of the relation between causal factors rather than being an independent causal factor itself. We describe someone or something as lucky (or unlucky) when the interplay of causes is unexpected, when what we see is perfectly natural and thus explainable without invoking any magical power of luck, but it's remarkable precisely because we receive a benefit or a harm where we didn't expect one. This is a helpful way to think about luck, and it also shows how nicely Aristotle's first two insights fit together: luck consists of the unexpected coincidence of causes. Luck is not real if we're thinking of it as a kind of magic, but it's perfectly real when understood as a coincidence of causes.

Why doesn't Bilbo want to tell his friends about the ring? There are probably lots of reasons, but Tolkien tells us one of them: "Bilbo was so pleased with their praise that he just chuckled inside and said nothing whatever about the ring." Gandalf and the dwarves praise Bilbo for what they see as "a very clever bit of work."[11] Their effusive praise is based on the belief that Bilbo himself is responsible for his escape. Even if they also think him lucky, they don't deny that his escape (at least as described by Bilbo!) showed ingenuity and some real skill.

Yet as we know, and as Gandalf suspects, the truth is that there's more to the story: Bilbo escaped largely because of the ring. In a sense, then, he doesn't deserve their praise, because they're praising him for something that wasn't up to him. His escape is primarily the result of a remarkably lucky accident: finding a very small ring in a very big and very dark cave. This discovery wasn't due to Bilbo's cleverness. In fact, it wasn't due to Bilbo at all. It was entirely out of his control, which makes it a suitable candidate for luck, according to Aristotle's third insight.

Luck holds sway only when we aren't in control of what's going on. We don't make our own luck, after all. What people usually mean when they say such a thing is that they arrange things so that there's no room for luck to interfere, not that they somehow control luck itself. Gandalf often orchestrates events and usually has the expertise and power to handle whatever comes his way, whereas Bilbo frequently acts out of desperation or on a whim. Gandalf is clever and enjoys telling folks so.[12] Bilbo, in contrast, is lucky mostly because events typically spiral out of his control.

Leaf by Nagel

Contemporary philosopher Thomas Nagel has identified four kinds of luck, three of which can be seen at play in *The Hobbit*.[13] These forms of luck identify important different ways in which something can be out of an agent's control.

Circumstantial luck lies in the circumstances in which we find ourselves. Bilbo finds himself in many lucky circumstances in *The Hobbit*, such as when a fish jumps on his toes, allowing him to guess the correct answer to one of Gollum's tougher riddles.

Constitutive luck has to do with a person's characteristics: position in life, family background, genetic traits, and so on. John Rawls (1921–2002) used the notion of a "natural" lottery—a procedure that's obviously driven by luck—to underscore dramatically how such things are out of our hands.[14] Bilbo is a well-to-do hobbit, with the good name of Baggins and a bit of a Tookish temperament. He didn't choose any of this, nor is any of it under his control. In a real sense, it's simply the luck of the draw.

These first two kinds of luck deal with what a person brings to a given scenario. The third kind, *resultant luck*, has to do with how things actually turn out. We seem to have a certain amount of control over what we decide to do, but we clearly do not control everything that comes of what we do.

We can see all three kinds of luck in the goblin cave episode. It's a matter of constitutive luck that Bilbo is a hobbit and thus small enough to slip through the half-closed cave door. That the cave in which the party spends the night happens to be the goblins' "front porch" is circumstantial luck—bad luck, too, we might think, except that if this hadn't happened, then the train of events leading to Bilbo finding the ring wouldn't have begun. And who knows what awful things might have come to pass in Middle-earth without that pivotal moment? Whether a circumstance is ultimately good or bad may not be immediately obvious. Finally, that Bilbo's discovery of the ring led to the eventual downfall of Sauron, the evil Lord of the Rings, is resultant luck. Bilbo had no control over how Frodo would choose to use the ring.

So who we are, where we find ourselves, and what happens to us and because of us can all be a matter of luck. Like Bilbo, we may be where we are (and who we are) because of a series of events that are largely beyond our control. We may not deserve much credit for whatever "clever work" we've managed to accomplish. For us, too, things could have gone very differently! This is a troubling thought. And like Bilbo, we may be tempted to look away from it and enjoy thinking of ourselves as more in control than we really are. Because if we're not in control, how will that affect our conception of ourselves? Are we more lucky than good?

The Good, the Bad, and the Lucky

Thorin Oakenshield, as we know, has a bit of a temper. He's a proud dwarf who shares with his kind a lust for gold and other treasures. After Smaug's death, he really ought to hear Bard's claim to a share of the hoard ("fair words and true," as Tolkien says).[15] Yet Thorin refuses to acknowledge what is clearly a legitimate claim. Should we see this as revealing that he has a flawed character and that deep down he is greedy and selfish? Or should we see it as an objectionable act that is out of character for Thorin, one he'll later regret, as his deathbed speech ("I would take back my words and deeds at the Gate") might suggest?[16] Or is it some of both, perhaps?

Should our moral evaluations of people and their behavior depend at least partly on luck? Can we blame Thorin for his excessive attachment to gold, given that his dwarfish nature is a matter of constitutive luck and he has the bad circumstantial luck to fall under the spell of dragon-sickness?[17] Should we condemn the goblins for their wicked behavior, given that they had the bad luck to be born goblins rather than hobbits, dwarves, or elves? If morality shouldn't depend too much on luck, and goblins are the big losers in the natural lottery, shouldn't that affect how we think of them? The goblins are a menace, to be sure, but maybe they shouldn't be *blamed* for it.

What about Bilbo? Is he doing the right thing when he takes the Arkenstone from Smaug's hoard? When he first sees it, he's so overcome by its beauty that he puts it in his pocket without telling anyone. At the time, he himself is conflicted about what he's doing. Although he tries to rationalize his action with the thought that he was promised he could pick his share of the treasure, he has "an uncomfortable feeling" that this gem isn't simply part of the treasure to be divvied up.[18]

Bilbo seems to act badly in this secretive acquisition, especially since he knows how much Thorin covets this lost heirloom. Yet it is only because of this act that he is later able to give the Arkenstone to Bard and the Elvenking, a gift that delays the hostilities that threaten to break out among elves, dwarves, and humans. But we might wonder about this act, too, just as Bard does, since it's not clear the stone is Bilbo's to give. Is Bilbo a thief? How we think about the moral importance of resultant luck will have a serious effect on what we make of these two perilous actions of Bilbo's: taking the Arkenstone in secret and then sneaking off to give it to the enemies of his companions.

Each of these actions is fraught with risk. Taking the stone leads to trouble for Bilbo when Thorin sees it as a betrayal. And while delivering the stone to Bard and the Elvenking delays the impending conflict, it could easily have gone otherwise, given how high Thorin's emotions were running. Now, it's one thing if Bilbo had good reason to believe things would turn out as they did. We could then wonder whether the end justifies the means, a moral riddle that's familiar to us all. But when Bilbo took the stone, he didn't even have any of the coming events in mind. He was simply captivated by the dazzling gem. And although he hoped that giving the Arkenstone to Bard and the Elvenking would somehow improve the increasingly dire situation, it was a rather sketchy and unlikely plan.

Did Bilbo do the right thing, simply because it all turned out well, even though this good outcome couldn't reasonably have been predicted? Or did Bilbo do the wrong thing, in spite of the good results to which it led? Surely the latter is a real possibility, isn't it? A person can do something very wrong, yet it may turn out for the best. If we think Bilbo's scheme is dishonest and ill conceived, then we might think that he has done the wrong thing, even if he had good intentions and his actions happen to lead to a desirable outcome. Luck can't make just any action morally acceptable. Thus, morality looks at luck with some unease, it seems, and withholds praise from those who gamble when the stakes are high. But can morality reject luck altogether?

Better to Be Lucky *and* Good

The idea that in some important way morality makes us immune to the pitfalls of luck has a long history. Socrates (ca. 470–399 BCE) famously said in Plato's *The Apology* that "a good man cannot be harmed either in life or in death."[19] Plato (ca. 428–348 BCE) argued that a just person is better off than an unjust person even if the former suffers every kind of misfortune and the latter is as lucky as can be.[20]

Most famously, the German philosopher Immanuel Kant (1724–1804) denied that our moral worth can be influenced by luck at all. He argued, "A good will is not good because of what it effects or accomplishes. . . . Usefulness or fruitlessness can neither add anything to this worth nor take anything away from it."[21] Kant's ideal will is *autonomous*: its goodness depends only on its willing and not on any external factors.

Although all sorts of things can and do happen to people, whether here or in Middle-earth, an agent's will, and thus his or her moral worth, needn't be shaped by them. Luck certainly affects our well-being, but it doesn't have any impact on our value as people. We're glad when we experience good luck, and we rejoice at the good fortune of others, but Kant denied that people deserve our moral *esteem* simply because things happen to go their way. Kant paints a compelling picture, and in many ways it reflects our sense of how things *ought* to be, or how we *wish* they would be.

Yet it can be argued that this picture is misleading. First, the existence of constitutive luck makes it difficult to maintain the Kantian idea that the will isn't also subject to luck. Isn't one's will affected by one's genes, early upbringing, and so on? Although it doesn't surface as much in *The Hobbit* as elsewhere, the ancestry and origin of Tolkien's characters is considerably developed. Their present is rooted in their past. Yet we ignore the significance of all that history if we treat each as a bare rational will that's immune to such factors.

Second, in both Tolkien's world and ours, the will just doesn't seem invulnerable to circumstantial luck. A character's will can be broken or corrupted by the desperation of his circumstances. Think of Thorin or Gollum. Or think of Boromir, Théoden, or Denethor from *The Lord of the Rings*. Some of them, at least, were good men, ruined by events and forces beyond their control. Good men *can* be harmed, not only physically but morally as well. And the lucky results of people's actions *do* affect how we judge them, even if they shouldn't.

Let's face it, we like Bilbo and think highly of him, in spite of his incredible luck. In fact, he's something of a hero, even though an unlikely one. Yet things could so easily have turned out differently if Bilbo's good luck had turned bad. What if a leaky barrel had led to a drowned dwarf or two—or thirteen? What if Bilbo's clumsy attempt to steal from the trolls had caused the deaths of half of the party? What if Bilbo had tripped in his flight from Smaug and been burned up by the dragon's fiery breath?

We cannot deny the presence of luck in Bilbo's adventure.[22] But we also cannot deny that he deserves the praise we want to give him. As it turns out, we do praise and blame people for things that aren't entirely under their control, and that means we should acknowledge that morality is vulnerable to luck after all. Even though some of the elves, men, dwarves, and hobbits in Tolkien's tale may have been better or luckier than others, each deserves a share of the dragon's treasure.

NOTES

1. J. R. R. Tolkien, *The Hobbit: or, There and Back Again* (New York: Del Rey/Ballantine Books, 2001), 212.

2. Ibid., 43.

3. Ibid., 55.

4. Ibid., 78.

5. Ibid., 79.

6. Ibid., 153.

7. Ibid., 155.

8. Ibid., 178.

9. Aristotle, *Physics*, trans. Robin Waterfield (Oxford, UK: Oxford University Press, 1999), 42.

10. Tolkien, *The Hobbit*, 93.

11. Ibid.

12. Ibid., 95.

13. Thomas Nagel, "Moral Luck," in *Mortal Questions* (Cambridge, UK: Cambridge University Press, 1979), 28–38.

14. John Rawls, *A Theory of Justice* (Cambridge, MA: Harvard University Press, 1971), 72–75.

15. Tolkien, *The Hobbit*, 265.

16. Ibid., 290.

17. In Tolkien's works, dragon-sickness is a spell or a curse that produces a powerful lust for treasure on which a dragon has long brooded. Thorin succumbs to the sickness until he heroically breaks free of its influence after the Battle of Five Armies. For more on dragon-sickness in *The Hobbit* and Tolkien's other writings, see John D. Rateliff, *The History of* The Hobbit (Boston: Houghton Mifflin, 2007), 2:595–600.

18. Tolkien, *The Hobbit*, 237.

19. Plato, "The Apology," in *Five Dialogues*, trans. G. M. A. Grube (Indianapolis, IN: Hackett, 1981), 44.

20. Plato, "The Republic," in *Five Dialogues*.

21. Immanuel Kant, *Groundwork of the Metaphysics of Morals*, trans. Mary Gregor (Cambridge, UK: Cambridge University Press, 1998), 8. As is the case with most philosophers, the interpretation of Kant is a tricky business. Kant's defenders would undoubtedly (and fairly) point out that his views are more complicated and sophisticated than we're able to acknowledge in such a brief encounter with his thought.

22. In the closing scene of *The Hobbit*, however, Gandalf signals that Bilbo has not merely been lucky. The idea that what appears to be a matter of luck may be the workings of a hidden providence is even more pronounced in *The Lord of the Rings*. See chapter 15 in this book for a discussion of luck and providence.

THE CONSOLATION OF BILBO

Providence and Free Will in Middle-Earth

Grant Sterling

When I was a kid, I had a rabbit's foot that was supposed to bring me good luck. It didn't work very well, which shouldn't be surprising because it obviously didn't bring the rabbit very good luck, either. But even a genuinely lucky rabbit's foot wouldn't be nearly as good as simply being born lucky.

There's one thing everyone agrees on about Bilbo: he is lucky. His luck is mentioned repeatedly in *The Hobbit*. Not only does Tolkien point out Bilbo's great luck in his role as narrator, numerous characters do so as well: Thorin believes Bilbo is "possessed of good luck far exceeding the usual allowance," Gandalf says to the hobbit that he "began to wonder if even your luck would see you through," and Bilbo himself speaks of trusting his luck more than he used to, calling himself "Luckwearer" in his cagey conversation with Smaug (that being the best way to talk to dragons, it is said).[1]

Furthermore, many of Bilbo's adventures take very lucky turns. He arrives in Rivendell during exactly the right moon phase for reading the moon-letters on the map. As Bilbo and his companions flee from the goblins of the Misty Mountains, the moon is out, giving them light to see. Bilbo chooses to help the dwarves escape from the Elvenking's prisons by way of the river, which was the only good way through Mirkwood to Esgaroth, although he didn't know it. He arrives on Smaug's doorstep just before Durin's Day, the day when the magical keyhole can be revealed, which comes only once in several years. Over and over things turn out just right to allow the members of the party to survive and continue on the quest to a successful conclusion. In many of these cases, the intrepid adventurers are just plain lucky.

What Has It Got in Its Pocketses?

The central moment of the entire story is when Bilbo, lost in the darkness of the goblin tunnels under the Misty Mountains, "crawled along for a good way, till suddenly his hand met what felt like a tiny ring of cold metal lying on the floor of the tunnel. It was a turning point in his career, but he did not know it."[2] On this event, everything else turns. Without the ring, Bilbo cannot escape from the goblins or the spiders, cannot rescue his companions from the elves, and cannot sneak up on Smaug to spot the unprotected patch on his underbelly. This was indeed a turning point in his life! Of course, we discover in *The Lord of the Rings* that this ring is none other than the One Ring, so this event is equally crucial to the entire plot of that great work. (We might say the discovery of the Ring was a turning point in Tolkien's life, as well.) But even here, in *The Hobbit*, where the ring functions only to allow Bilbo to become invisible at will, the quest would have ended in disaster were it not for Bilbo finding the ring.

Indeed, the dwarves begin to respect him soon after this, finding that "he has some wits, as well as luck and a magic ring—and all three are very useful possessions."[3] Luck is not the only thing at work, apparently, a point Gandalf also stresses. By the time the wizard has learned of the ring's true nature, near the beginning of *The Lord of the Rings*, he says, "I can put it no plainer than by saying that Bilbo was *meant* to find the Ring, and *not* by its maker."[4] If Bilbo was *meant* to find the Ring, if some power was at work behind the scenes to arrange this outcome, then the greatest episode of "luck" in Bilbo's life turns out not to be luck at all.

If Gandalf was right, Bilbo was meant to find the One Ring. But who intended and arranged this result? We are told that it was not the Ring's maker, the Dark Lord Sauron. But if not Sauron, then who? It was certainly not Bilbo himself or Gandalf. It could only be someone with the power to bring about such an apparent coincidence as part of a greater scheme of things.

The obvious answer is that Bilbo's discovery of the One Ring is a manifestation of the hand of God—"Eru Ilúvatar," as He is called in Tolkien's Middle-earth. Indeed, Tolkien explicitly says as much in his letters.[5] It was Eru who meant for Bilbo to find the Ring and later meant for it to pass on to Frodo for the great quest in *The Lord of the Rings*.

But now we face a problem. Eru apparently arranged for the Ring to slip from Gollum's finger as he was throttling a goblin-imp. This was done in order to allow Bilbo to find the Ring, as he was *meant* to do. But this providential plan can work only if Eru can foresee that Bilbo will indeed be in that exact tunnel on that day.

So divine providence requires divine foreknowledge. Eru must be able to reliably see future events in a way that allows Him to manipulate the present to get the results He means to produce.

But how is that possible? Bilbo's presence in that tunnel that day was the result of many individual choices by many people. Even leaving aside choices distant in time (such as the dwarves agreeing to allow Gandalf's burglar to come along in the first place), Bilbo had to choose to follow Gandalf away from the Great Goblin's lair. Gandalf had to make the rescue. Dori had to agree to carry Bilbo on his back. Gollum had to choose to twist the neck of "the nasty young squeaker." Thorin, the other dwarves, and the goblins all had to make certain choices at certain times in order to put Bilbo in that spot.

But if Eru knew in advance that all these choices would be made, then it seems that the choices were dictated in advance, and that means they couldn't have been free. If Eru knew that Bilbo was going to be in that exact spot in that tunnel long before he was even headed in that direction (which He must have known, since He arranged for the Ring to slip off Gollum's finger some hours before), then Gollum was obviously not free to choose whether to kill the goblin-imp, and Bilbo was not free to choose to flee, Gandalf wasn't free to choose whether to rescue his friends by showering sparks on the goblins, and so forth.[6]

The Problem of Divine Foreknowledge

For philosophers, the apparent conflict between God's (or Eru's) prior knowledge of what will happen and the freedom of creatures to make their own choices is called the problem of divine foreknowledge. Briefly, the problem is this:

1. God knows everything. He *knows* what's going to happen; He doesn't just make an estimate of what will probably happen, in the way that you or I might do.
2. If God knows everything, He must know what I will do tomorrow (or at any future time).
3. If God knows what I will do tomorrow, then my actions are predetermined—I cannot act in any way other than the one God foresees. (If I did, then God

would have been mistaken, which is impossible, according to the first statement.)
4. If my actions are predetermined, then I have no free will.
5. If I have no free will, I cannot be responsible for anything I do, since I couldn't have done otherwise.

Philosophers have struggled with this problem ever since the notion of an omniscient (all-knowing) God has been around. It seems that those who believe in God have to abandon the idea that He knows the future or else abandon the notion that we have free will, which means they have to give up on the idea of moral responsibility.

Some philosophers have tried the first strategy, attempting to resolve this problem by denying that God knows everything. *Process theologians* like Alfred North Whitehead (1861–1947) and Charles Hartshorne (1897–2000) and *open theists* like Clark Pinnock (1937–2010) argue that since the future hasn't happened, there is nothing about it for God to know.[7] You can know something only if it's true, and there are no truths about the future since the future is still open. God is still all-knowing, however, because being all-knowing means you know all *truths*, and in this view that doesn't entail a knowledge of the future. Thus the notion of free will is retained.

Whether such a strategy can work for other modern theologians confronted with the problem of divine foreknowledge is unclear. Certainly it gives rise to many problems. For example, most religious believers accept the existence of genuine foreknowledge in the case of prophecy, and it is unclear how real prophecy (as opposed to probabilistic estimation) can exist under the open theist scheme. It also seems to conflict with characteristics that many theologians believe God possesses, such as immutability. God's knowledge would change as the future becomes the present, but immutability suggests that God does not change at all.

Whatever may be the case in that theological context, this strategy won't work for Middle-earth theologians, because Eru's knowledge extends to the future. In one of his late but little-read tales, "Ósanwe-kenta" ("Inquiry into the Communication of Thought"), Tolkien contrasts Eru's genuine foreknowledge with the predictive powers of those who cannot see the future. A mind other than Eru's "can learn of the future only from another mind which has seen it. But that means only from Eru ultimately, or mediately from some mind that has seen in Eru some part of His purpose."[8] Thus, Tolkien has not left open the option of denying divine foreknowledge.

In any case, open theism seems to undermine the basis of divine providence, and it was Eru's providential intervention that gave us this headache in the first place. If Eru cannot have foreknowledge because the future is open, then He cannot arrange for Bilbo to find the Ring, and the unfolding of the divine plan cannot function in the way it appears to do.

So we'll have to look for another solution. Some philosophers have tried to solve the problem by denying that if our actions are predetermined, we have no free will. They have claimed that free will is compatible with our actions being predetermined (a theory quite cleverly called *compatibilism*). Others have denied that the lack of free will would relieve us of moral responsibility, holding that even if we don't have free will, it doesn't matter, because moral responsibility is still possible. Philosophers like David Hume (1711–1776) have defended such views, along with several contemporary thinkers such as Harry Frankfurt and Daniel Dennett.[9]

It is highly questionable whether either strategy can work. Critics argue that nothing that can reasonably be called free will can apply to beings whose actions are unalterably determined centuries before they are even born.[10] Nor is it clear how we can be morally responsible for actions that are completely predetermined.

Freedom and the Music

Whatever philosophers may claim about the real world, Tolkien will not attempt to solve the problem of divine foreknowledge by denying the existence of a kind of free will that encompasses real options for acting in *The Hobbit*. Indeed, Tolkien says that human beings have "the gift of freedom," which is "a virtue to shape their life, amid the powers and chances of the world, beyond the Music of the Ainur, which is as fate to all things else."[11]

But what exactly is "the Music of the Ainur, which is as fate to all things else"? Tolkien is referring to his fictional version of the creation story, which can be found in "Ainulindalë: The Music of the Ainur" in *The Silmarillion*. In this story, the Ainur (angelic beings) perform a cosmic symphony that contains in it the future story of the world, which Eru then brings into being. As a result of this, events in history have been prefigured in this divine harmony, so the choices of the Ainur in how to play their symphony serve as a kind of fate for the world—except for humans, who have a free will that allows them to act in a way unencumbered by the dictation of the Music.[12]

Not only are we told that humans (and hobbits) have free will generally, we are also told that Bilbo in particular has free will; for instance, he could have chosen to stay home and not accompany the dwarves at all. In Tolkien's story "The Quest for Erebor," Frodo recounts a conversation he had with Gandalf many years after Bilbo found the Ring.

In this conversation, Gandalf echoes his comments from *The Lord of the Rings*, saying, "In that far distant time I said to a small and frightened hobbit: Bilbo was *meant* to find the Ring, and *not* by its maker, and you therefore were *meant* to bear it. And I might have added: and I was *meant* to guide you both to those points." Frodo responds, "I understand you a little better now, Gandalf, than I did before. Though I suppose that, whether *meant* or not, Bilbo might have refused to leave home, and so might I. You could not compel us."[13]

So for Tolkien, it is clear that Eru really can see the future and make plans according to his foreknowledge, and at the same time Bilbo (like the other people who are part of those plans) has the freedom to choose how to behave. Thus once again we face the problem that Eru can fully know the future even when people have free will. How is that possible?

Tolkien's Boethian Solution

The seeds of another possible solution to the problem of divine foreknowledge were planted by the Roman philosopher Boethius (ca. 480–524 CE) in his classic work *The Consolation of Philosophy*, written while he was in prison awaiting execution on an unjust charge.[14] Boethius argued that human beings possess only a tiny fraction of their being, or their existence, at any one time, since their past has already gone and their future has not yet come. God, he thought, must not be the same way—God has infinite being, so He must have all of his reality at once, not parceled out over time.

But this must mean that God is outside time, not subject to change. We humans live for years, aging and changing each day. We have a past, a present, and a future. God, Boethius held, is not like one of us, and the difference is not just a matter of length of time; instead, time does not apply to God at all. He has no "past, present, and future," but rather only an eternal unchanging "now."[15]

How does Boethius's claim that God is outside time help with the problem of divine foreknowledge? Suppose that Bilbo knows that Bard the Bowman is eating his supper because he is watching him do so. His knowledge of Bard's actions in no way calls into question Bard's free will—knowledge of a *present* event gives rise to no philosophical dilemmas about freedom. But if God is outside time, as Boethius thought, then God can see the future—only from God's perspective, it isn't in the future, it is happening *now*. God doesn't literally have *fore*knowledge at all.

Imagine that you had a film version of Peter Jackson's movie *The Hobbit* unrolled in front of you. You could glance simultaneously at scenes at the beginning of the film and at the end. That, roughly speaking, is how Boethius understood God's view of the universe. Because God is eternal and exists outside time, He can view in one timeless glance events taking place millennia apart, seeing them as though they were all happening at the same moment.

All of this is well and good for Boethius, you might say, but what does it have to do with Tolkien? In fact, there are clear indications that this was Tolkien's own solution to the problem of divine foreknowledge, both in the real world of today and in the fictional Middle-earth of *The Hobbit*.

There are suggestions that Tolkien adopted the Boethian solution in many different places. For example, let's return to the Music of the Ainur. This Music, we are told, is playing in the Timeless Halls. When some of the Ainur (including the Valar, the great archangels such as Elbereth, to whom the elves sing) choose to enter the new world that Eru has created, it is said that "they had entered at the beginning of Time."[16]

Perhaps the most direct discussion of this issue is in "Ósanwe-kenta." This story focuses on the question of how thoughts are transmitted in Middle-earth, with Tolkien using an elvish lore master, Pengolodh of Gondolin, as the putative author. According to the lore master, "the Valar entered into Eä [the physical universe] and Time of free will, and they are now in Time, so long as it endures. They can perceive nothing outside Time, save by memory of their existence before it began: they can recall the Song and the Vision. They are, of course, open to Eru, but they cannot of their own will 'see' any part of His mind."[17]

Notice that it is clear that there are things that are outside time, that beings like the Valar who are in time cannot see those things, and by implication Eru's mind is one of them.

Later in the story, Tolkien offers the following comment on the lore master's point about the Valar's ability to know the future:

> Pengolodh here elaborates . . . this matter of "foresight." No mind, he asserts, knows what is not in it . . . no part of the "future" is there, for the mind cannot see it or have seen it: that is, a mind placed in time. Such a mind can learn of the future only from another mind which has seen it. But that means only from Eru ultimately, or mediately from some mind that has seen in Eru some part of His purpose (such as the Ainur who are now the Valar in Eä). An Incarnate can thus only know anything of the future, by instruction derived from the Valar, or by a revelation coming direct from Eru.[18]

The direct and flowing writing style Tolkien used in his novels is rarely in evidence in his philosophical writings, and this is no exception. But while the reader may be forgiven for thinking that the details of this passage are quite obscure, this much at least seems clear: Tolkien held that no mind that exists in time can see the future. This means that the only way to know the future is to learn of it from a mind that has seen it (and hence must be outside time), and this means that ultimately all knowledge of the future comes from Eru.

Minds that are inside time (whether those of the mighty Valar, ordinary hobbits like Bilbo, or local bookies) may be able to predict the future more or less accurately by deducing it from their evidence, but this is not true foreknowledge at all. Only Eru's timeless mind can see the future directly. And Eru's ability to timelessly see the future as it happens may give us a way to escape from the problem of divine foreknowledge. It is because Eru views all things in a timeless present that He can manifest His providential plan in the lives of the inhabitants of Middle-earth.

Does the Boethian approach really solve the problem? Like everything else in philosophy, that's a controversial matter.

Some wonder whether the notion makes sense or is compatible with other characteristics that God is thought to possess. Others think that timeless knowledge presents the same problems as foreknowledge, since it seems equally "fixed."[19] But even some critics acknowledge that the notion of timelessness is so foreign to our ordinary way of thinking that it is difficult to be certain that such objections cannot be resolved.[20] In any event, it seems clear that Tolkien thought the Boethian solution worked and that it applied to Middle-earth.

And so we return to the beginning. Bilbo's "adventures and escapes," we see, were not brought about by "mere luck" for Bilbo's "sole benefit" but were arranged by Eru for the benefit of all. Real prophecies come from minds inspired by this timeless God with knowledge of what is to come. But perhaps Bilbo *is* truly lucky after all—lucky to have been chosen to play such a great part in a providential plan. We are told that "he remained very happy to the end of his days, and those were extraordinarily long."[21] No rabbit's foot could give anyone better luck than that.

NOTES

1. J. R. R. Tolkien, *The Hobbit: or, There and Back Again* (New York: Del Rey/Ballantine Books, 2001), 212, 223, 289. An early draft of chapter 13 of *The Hobbit* speaks of Bilbo's "proven and astonishing luck." John D. Rateliff, *The History of* The Hobbit (Boston: Houghton Mifflin, 2007), 2:578.

2. Tolkien, *The Hobbit*, 68.

3. Ibid., 166.

4. J. R. R. Tolkien, *The Lord of the Rings: The Fellowship of the Ring* (New York: Del Rey/Ballantine Books, 2001), 88.

5. Humphrey Carpenter, ed., *The Letters of J. R. R. Tolkien* (Boston: Houghton Mifflin, 1981), 201, 253.

6. An excellent sampling of passages from Tolkien's writings regarding these issues can be found in Christina Scull and Wayne Hammond, *The J. R. R. Tolkien Companion and Guide: Reader's Guide* (New York: Houghton Mifflin, 2006), 324–33. Scull and Hammond do not attempt a definitive explanation of how free will and providence or fate can be reconciled.

7. Alfred North Whitehead, *Process and Reality* (New York: Free Press, 1979); Charles Hartshorne, *Omnipotence and Other Theological Mistakes* (Albany: State University of

New York Press, 1984); and Clark Pinnock, *The Openness of God* (Downer's Grove, IL: InterVarsity Press, 1994).

8. J. R. R. Tolkien, "Ósanwe-kenta" [Inquiry into the Communication of Thought], *Vinyar Tengwar* 39 (July 1998): 31. *Vinyar Tengwar* is published by the Elvish Linguistic Fellowship and is available at http://www.elvish.org/.

9. David Hume, *Enquiries Concerning Human Understanding and Concerning the Principles of Morals*, ed. L. A. Selby-Bigge and P. H. Nidditch (Oxford: Clarendon Press, 1975), 80–103; Harry Frankfurt, *The Importance of What We Care About* (Cambridge, UK: Cambridge University Press, 1988); and Daniel Dennett, *Elbow Room: The Varieties of Free Will Worth Wanting* (Cambridge, MA: MIT Press, 1984).

10. Peter van Inwagen, *An Essay on Free Will* (Oxford, UK: Oxford University Press, 1983).

11. J. R. R. Tolkien, *The Silmarillion*, ed. Christopher Tolkien (Boston: Houghton Mifflin, 1977), 41, 42.

12. Exactly to what degree the actions of other beings (such as elves and dwarves) are predetermined is unclear. The Ainur themselves, however, make choices about how to perform the Music, and so to some extent their later actions are simply the reflections of premade free choices of their own.

13. J. R. R. Tolkien, "The Quest of Erebor," in *The Annotated Hobbit*, ed. Douglas A. Anderson (New York: Houghton Mifflin, 2002), 369.

14. Kathleen Dubs also argues for a Boethian interpretation of Tolkien's works, although her claim that it would have appealed to him as a non-Christian approach seems clearly mistaken. Kathleen E. Dubs, "Providence, Fate and Chance: Boethian Philosophy in *The Lord of the Rings*," in *Tolkien and the Invention of Myth*, ed. Jane Chance (Lexington: University Press of Kentucky, 2004), 133–44.

15. Boethius, *The Consolation of Philosophy*, trans. V. E. Watts (London: Penguin Books, 1981), 165.

16. Tolkien, *The Silmarillion*, 20. Tolkien's close friend, C. S. Lewis, also adopted the Boethian view, and he referred to it in *The Screwtape Letters* (New York: Macmillan, 1961), 136–40.

17. Tolkien, "Ósanwe-kenta," 24.

18. Ibid., 31.

19. Linda Zagzebski, *The Dilemma of Freedom and Foreknowledge* (New York: Oxford University Press, 1991), 60.

20. Linda Zagzebski, "Foreknowledge and Free Will," in *Stanford Encyclopedia of Philosophy*, Stanford University, http://www.plato.stanford.edu/entries/free-will-foreknowledge/. This article also serves as an excellent introduction to other approaches to solving the problem. Note also that even if the Boethian solution explains how divine foreknowledge and free will can be compatible, more is needed to explain divine providence, since providence requires God acting in advance of a person's choices. But such issues are beyond the scope of this chapter.

21. Tolkien, *The Hobbit*, 304.

OUT OF THE FRYING PAN

Courage and Decision Making in Wilderland

Jamie Carlin Watson

Early in *The Hobbit,* Thorin and Company are making their way through the wilderness and hit a rough patch. One of their ponies, the one with most of their supplies, falls into a river. Stuck in the rain, cold, and hungry, they notice a light in the distance and begin to reason about whether to pursue it. The discussion goes as follows:

> Some said they could but go and see, and anything was better than little supper, less breakfast, and wet clothes all the night.
>
> Others said: "These parts are none too well known, and are too near the mountains. Travelers seldom come this way now. The old maps are no use: things have changed for the worse and the road is unguarded. They have seldom even heard of the king round here, and the

less inquisitive you are as you go along, the less trouble you are likely to find." Some said: "After all there are fourteen of us." . . . Then the rain began to pour down worse than ever, and Oin and Gloin began to fight.

That settled it.[1]

The decision was risky. Was it *too* risky? Almost every decision we make involves uncertainty and risk: Is this airplane safe? Should I take my money out of the stock market? Is this guy with his turn signal on really going to turn? Is the barista going to get my coffee right? Few of us, however, undertake risks on par with those of Bilbo.

Bilbo is unusual because he's a hobbit who has a taste for adventure. All adventures require taking risks, and adventurers are usually applauded for their abilities to overcome danger and endure hardship, especially when it's for a noble goal. But the best adventurers, it would seem, are those who are the best at calculating risks. If they are careless, they won't be adventurers for very long. If they are too cautious, they will not achieve their noble goals.

In *The Hobbit*, Bilbo and his companions take great risks for what appear to be worthy goals, and they are widely regarded as heroes (at least among nonhobbits). But are Bilbo's decisions well calculated and courageous, or are they careless and rash? Few of us put our lives in danger without an extremely good reason; of course, some of us can't imagine it even then. So how could we know, objectively, whether someone is acting cowardly, courageously, or rashly?

Philosophers can tell us a lot about the principles of good reasoning. Some reasoning is purely formal, as in symbolic logic or abstract mathematics. But most is very practical, as in deciding which political candidate to vote for or which used car to buy. Economists and psychologists have given us some clues about what features of our circumstances are relevant to making good decisions. By introducing us to a few reasoning strategies and showing us how to take careful note of these features, philosophers can help us make the best possible decisions, even in the midst of uncertainty.

Moral reasoning is a unique type of reasoning, distinct from purely formal logic or mathematics. Moral reasoning is practical because it aims at a particular outcome; namely, the *right* thing to do. In his discussion of moral virtue, Aristotle (384–322 BCE) identified two vices, cowardice and foolishness, and distinguished them from their corresponding virtue, courage.[2]

Most of us would agree that by the end of *The Hobbit*, Bilbo is courageous. Many would also agree that Thorin is sometimes rash. Our intuitions diverge when it comes to judging extreme sports enthusiasts, like rock climbers or BASE jumpers, but most of us at least agree about what is at stake in these cases: their lives! When we compare the goals to what is at stake in any given adventure, a question naturally arises: Are the goals worth the risks?

Using Bilbo's adventures, I will explain two ways to determine whether an act is reasonable: expected utility theory and conditional probability. We'll use these to assess how well Bilbo reasons in the midst of a variety of uncertain outcomes. Then we'll see how the results can be judged according to Aristotle's view of courage. Maybe other hobbits are right that he's foolish; maybe not. And perhaps you'll pick up some decision-making tools to pack on your next adventure.

Riddles, Dilemmas, and Luck, Oh My!

To see why reasoning in the midst of uncertainty is so difficult, consider the case of riddles. When Bilbo stumbles into Gollum's lair, he finds himself trapped in a game of riddles with his life at stake. Riddles are difficult to solve because they require you to select a specific answer from a potentially infinite set of information using only a vague set of clues.

For instance, the second riddle that Gollum poses to Bilbo goes as follows:

Voiceless it cries,
Wingless flutters,
Toothless bites,
Mouthless mutters.[3]

There would seem to be a great many things that could match this description: time, age, love, a creaky screen door, an upset stomach, a drop in the stock market—well, the last one might be stretching it. But, of course, the point of a riddle is to find something that *best* fits the clue and, more important, what the riddler *thinks* best fits. In this case, Bilbo had luckily heard something rather like this riddle before, and he fortunately gave the answer Gollum had in mind: wind.

Unfortunately, there is often no way to pare down the possible answers to a riddle to a manageable set. Some riddles require the solver to have information that might not be available to him or her. Just imagine if someone were giving Bilbo a riddle about Facebook. When Gollum gives Bilbo a riddle about fish, we are told that "it was a poser for poor Bilbo, who never had anything to do with water if he could help it."[4] The only reason Bilbo comes up with the right answer is that a fish actually jumps out of the water onto his toes. Lucky for Bilbo!

Unfortunately, life, like riddles, often gives us vague clues about how we should act. And to make good decisions, we need more information than is provided in riddles. We don't need to have all relevant information in making important decisions, but sometimes we need a little help. There are at least two things that make reasoning easier: background information and decision procedures.

Background information consists of contextual facts relevant to our decision. Before we repeal a law that drivers must wear seat belts, we need to know the likely consequences of not wearing a seat belt. We need to consult auto crash statistics to see whether wearing a seat belt really reduces the risk of serious injury or death. We need to see if other states have repealed seat belt laws and, if so, what have been the results. Of course, all the information will be statistical, and the inferences from these statistics for the future of our society won't be absolutely certain. We won't know for sure what will happen, but we'll have a better idea of what might happen if we repeal the law.

Unfortunately, philosophers usually can't provide much background information.[5] For that, you'll need to turn to experts in the relevant field. Decision procedures, on the other hand, are right up philosophers' alley.[6]

Decision procedures are reasoning strategies that help us draw the most likely conclusion from the background information we have. There are many different decision procedures, and which one you need will depend on the information you want. The procedures are pretty straightforward when your information is certain, as in math or logic. But when your information is incomplete or depends on other events, the procedures get more complex. Decisions facing adventurers like Bilbo are almost always made in the midst of uncertainty about the consequences of the available decisions.

A classic example of reasoning in the midst of uncertainty is called the "prisoner's dilemma." Hobbits are, of course, well known for being stealthy thieves if they wish to be. Imagine you are a hobbit, and suppose you and a partner in thievery are caught by the police and are questioned in separate rooms. Your captors present you with two options: You can either rat out your accomplice or refuse to talk. Unfortunately, you learn that in this case, the consequences of each option depend on which choice your partner makes. If you choose to rat and he refuses, you will go free and your partner will get ten years in Lockholes (the holes used as jails by Sharkey's men in *Lord of the Rings*). Similarly, if he confesses and you refuse, he will go free and you will get ten years. If you both confess, however, you'll both go to Lockholes for five years. If you both refuse and your case goes to trial, you'll both go to Lockholes for two years. To evaluate these options more clearly, we can represent it with the following model:

| | | **Accomplice** | |
		Confess	Refuse
You	Confess	5, 5	0, 10
	Refuse	10, 0	2, 2

In this decision schema, there is no way to be *sure* how your accomplice will choose. You know that if you both hold out against the questioning, you can get away with only two years in Lockholes. But you are faced with the deplorable possibility that your partner will rat you out (not very admirable for a hobbit) and you'll have to spend *ten* years in Lockholes while he goes free. Without being able to talk to your accomplice, how do you determine the best course of action?

One of the oldest and best-known tools for reasoning in the midst of uncertainty is called *expected utility theory*. The basic idea is this: when you know the likelihood of the outcomes of each choice in a decision and you know how much you value each outcome, some simple math will tell you which decision is in your best interests.[7] A "decision tree" is the most intuitive way to use expected utility theory, and it works for many simple decision problems. We'll start off applying it to our prisoner's dilemma, and then we'll see how Bilbo could put it to good use.

If I am facing the prisoner's dilemma, I have to make the decision based on what the consequences will be *for me*. Recognizing this allows me to focus on the relevant information. I have two options (see the figure on page 224). For each option, there is a fifty-fifty chance that my partner will either confess or refuse.

If I confess and he confesses, I'll get five years in Lockholes. If I confess and he refuses, I'll get zero years in Lockholes, and so on.

To find out which option is best for me, all I need to do is multiply the likelihood of the outcome (if I have a fifty-fifty shot, that's a 50 percent likelihood) by how much I value the consequences (in this case, I value the least number of years in prison). I then add the results for each potential consequence.

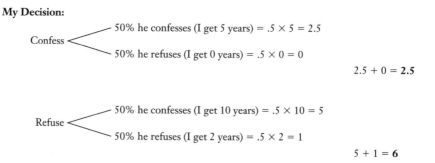

My Decision:

Confess
- 50% he confesses (I get 5 years) = .5 × 5 = 2.5
- 50% he refuses (I get 0 years) = .5 × 0 = 0

2.5 + 0 = **2.5**

Refuse
- 50% he confesses (I get 10 years) = .5 × 10 = 5
- 50% he refuses (I get 2 years) = .5 × 2 = 1

5 + 1 = **6**

The answers are the average number of years I would have to spend in Lockholes for each decision. Since I want the fewest number of years possible, it is in my best interest to confess.

By the Light of the Trolls: Expected Utility Theory

Now, how could all of this help our travelers in *The Hobbit*? Recall the dilemma that Thorin and Company face when they see the light in the wilderness. Should they investigate the light or stay behind, cold and wet? We all know how the story turns out: they decide to follow the light, then they get caught and almost eaten by trolls. It is only because Gandalf returns that the group avoids becoming the trolls' supper. Let's see whether expected utility theory would have led them to the same fate.

First, we'll construct a decision tree (see the figure on page 225). What are the chances that the travelers will run into trouble if they go toward the light? Expected utility is easiest to calculate from an agreed-on set of values, and this is easiest from a single person's perspective. (Who knows what you value better than you?)[8] So let's focus on Bilbo.

Bilbo must decide how likely it is that he will run into trouble if he goes toward the light. Even if we don't know the exact percentage, they agree that they are at greater risk by going rather than by staying, so whatever percentage we give to trouble for option 1, it will be greater than whatever we give it for option 2. For now, let's set it at 50 percent for option 1 and 10 percent for option 2. Later on, we'll see how changing these affects the outcome.

What are the other possible outcomes for each option? For option 1, the other possibility is that they will find a dry and warm place to sleep and will get something to eat. Since we are giving them a 50 percent chance of finding trouble, the chance that they'll find food and shelter is also 50 percent. For option 2, the alternative is a 90 percent chance that they will remain wet, cold, and hungry.

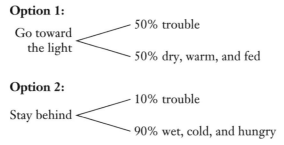

Option 1:
Go toward the light
- 50% trouble
- 50% dry, warm, and fed

Option 2:
Stay behind
- 10% trouble
- 90% wet, cold, and hungry

Now we need to assess the costs and benefits that Bilbo places on each outcome, also called the value of each outcome. This is the most difficult step: you have to assign numbers to the outcomes *according to how much you like or dislike each potential result*. This depends entirely on you, and you can assign whatever numbers you think are appropriate, as long as you keep in mind that positive numbers are benefits and negative numbers are costs. This is much easier with cases involving money or time, where it's easy to assign numerical values.

For instance, imagine that Gaffer Gamgee (Samwise's dad from *The Lord of the Rings*) opens an inn to sell his famous ale. If he sells a pint for twenty-five cents per glass and it costs him fifteen cents per glass to make it, then his cost-benefit analysis (benefit minus cost), or expected value, is ten cents.

Now consider that it takes him eight hours at the bar to sell five pints. His expected value is fifty cents. But there's an additional cost: his time, which, we hope, he values at more than six cents per hour (expected value divided by number of hours). But how does he know how much he values his time? That's a judgment call. Many people are happy making eight dollars an hour until they are offered a new job and are making twelve dollars an hour. Suddenly they can't imagine ever working for eight dollars an hour again.

Let's say that Bilbo values trouble at -100 (he's a hobbit, after all) and being dry, warm, and fed at $+20$. Let's also say that he values being wet, cold, and hungry at -20. You might feel a bit uneasy about assigning numbers to intuitive values. In these cases, where values are assigned blindly, expected utility can still work. We just need to assign a fairly large gap between what we value and what we don't. Now let's try our calculation:

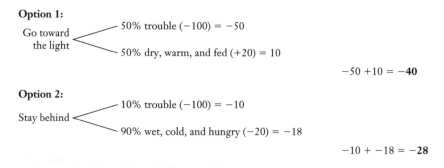

Option 1:
Go toward the light
50% trouble $(-100) = -50$
50% dry, warm, and fed $(+20) = 10$

$-50 + 10 = \mathbf{-40}$

Option 2:
Stay behind
10% trouble $(-100) = -10$
90% wet, cold, and hungry $(-20) = -18$

$-10 + -18 = \mathbf{-28}$

In this calculation, even though staying behind is bad, going toward the light is *worse*.

You've probably already noticed a potential problem here. In the prisoner's dilemma, the numerical values (the likelihood of confessing or refusing and the number of years in Lockholes for each decision) were available up front. It was easy to apply expected utility theory and get a clear answer to the problem. Bilbo, however, has to *guess* the possible outcomes *and* their likelihoods and then attach numbers that he thinks capture how much he values the outcomes. Changing either the probability or the value just a little would lead to a completely different result. If, for option 1, we estimate the probability of trouble to be lower than 50 percent or the benefits of being warm and fed to be greater than 20 percent, the decision goes the other way, and similarly for option 2. This shows that *our starting information must be as accurate as possible*.

Unfortunately, there were no philosophers in Middle-earth to give assistance. What can Bilbo do with variables too vague to calculate? There are several alternatives, but an especially helpful approach is to simplify the problem.[9] With a focus on a narrower range of outcomes, Bilbo's decision would be easier to make. Rather than focusing on warmth, shelter, cold, hunger, and trouble all at the same time, he could focus on a single outcome, perhaps one so significant that it overshadows the other concerns—for instance, trouble.

If the chances of trouble are higher in the decision to go toward the light than in staying behind, and the chances of achieving the ultimate goal (getting the dwarves' treasure back) are not affected much on either decision, the group should probably suffer a little rain and cold rather than pursue unnecessary risk. It is easy to see that the chances of running into trouble are higher for option 1 than for option 2, whether we use real numbers or abstractions.

Simplifying utility calculations can greatly increase your ability to maximize the expected value of an action. If, for Bilbo, trouble is really the central worry about going toward the light, he and the group should have decided differently. Hindsight is, of course, twenty-twenty, and we now see that it was only by luck that they all survived the ill-mannered trolls.

Playing Hide-and-Seek with the
Wood-Elves: Conditional Probability

Sometimes we want to know more than the probability that something will happen; we want to know the likelihood that something will happen given that something else has already happened. This is called *conditional probability*. Conditional probability tells us the chances of event *x* occurring, given that (or, on the condition that) event *y* has occurred.[10]

For instance, if I start to draw a card from a standard deck of playing cards (minus the joker), what are the chances that I will draw a king given that I've already drawn a king? Since we already know all the relevant background information, the conditional probability of this event is easy to determine. We know there are fifty-two cards in a normal deck, and we know there are four kings. So, whereas the probability of drawing a king is 4/52, or 7.7 percent, the probability of drawing a king given that I've already drawn a king is 3/51, or 5.9 percent.

The most interesting feature of conditional probability is that it doesn't matter whether the events are connected. If the events are connected, as they were when we didn't replace the king, they are "dependent." When they are not connected, they are "independent." In the case of drawing kings from a deck, we assumed that we didn't put the first king back. But what if we had? In that case, the probability of drawing a king the second time wouldn't be any different from drawing a king the first time.[11]

What use might our weary travelers make of conditional probability? Primarily, it would help them avoid an error in reasoning about the connectedness of events. Recall their second encounter with lights in a forest at night. The Company has been given strict warnings from both Beorn and Gandalf to stay on the path through Mirkwood. But hunger, thirst, and rain make them vulnerable to the first temptation: lights like torches under the trees.

Bombur, having been asleep for several days because of the magic of the enchanted river, awakens from dreams of feasting to the revelation that the group is, once again, wet and hungry. When the travelers begin to see lights in the woods, Bombur exclaims, "It looks as if my dreams were coming true."[12] At this point, they might have hesitated, recalling that the last time they went toward lights in an unfamiliar forest, they were captured by trolls. They might assume that because they ran into trouble following one set of lights, they will run into trouble following another set. Or perhaps this new set of lights should be safer, since the odds of having bad luck with lights twice in a row must be slim. If they made their decision on either of these grounds, they would commit versions of what is known as the "gambler's fallacy."

A fallacy is an error in reasoning. The gambler's fallacy involves assuming that there must be a connection between two independent—that is, causally unrelated—events. For instance, the probability of a two-sided penny landing on heads when flipped is 50 percent. What is the probability that it will land on heads given that it landed on heads on the previous flip? It's still 50 percent. What about after landing on heads a hundred times? It's still 50 percent. This is because each flip is *independent* of every other. The mistake of treating independent conditions as related is often called the gambler's fallacy because gamblers sometimes assume that if their luck has been poor all night, it *must* turn around soon. Alternatively, a gambler on a winning streak might stick around just a little longer, reasoning (to his or her dismay), "I'll win just one more round, and then I'll quit."

Fortunately, our frustrated travelers don't make this mistake. They hesitate because they have been warned very strongly by Beorn and Gandalf not to stray from the path. Their actual reasoning is quite consistent with expected utility informed by conditional probability. Option 1, to follow the lights, is dangerous. Thorin notes, "A feast would be no good, if we never got back alive from it." But option 2, staying on the path, is no better.

Bombur responds, "But without a feast we shan't remain alive much longer anyway."[13] Both options involve grave risk, but the prospects are better in option 1 than option 2. Therefore, they agree to send spies to check out the lights. Conditional probability is extremely useful when events are connected, and understanding how it works is useful in avoiding fallacies.

To Boldly Go—but Not Too Boldly

What does reasoning in the midst of uncertainty have to do with courage? As we all know, some decisions reveal one's character. Aristotle held that our character is made up of various psychological states, which develop over time in response to certain passions or emotions, such as fear or anger.[14] A state of character is virtuous when it is an appropriate response to a passion. We can respond to passions in ways that are virtuous or not virtuous. Aristotle called a culpable or faulty state of character a "vice." There are two kinds of vices. If an act falls short of virtue, it is a vice of "defect." If an act exceeds what is required for virtue, it is a vice of "excess." A virtue is a "mean," the intermediate point between two vices.

Aristotle explained that courage is the virtuous mean between the defect of cowardice and the excess of rashness. The passion to which courage is a response is fear. Aristotle argued that it is not the fearless person who is courageous, but the one who acts appropriately in the face of fear, especially the fear of death.[15] He wrote:

> The coward, the rash man, and the brave man, then, are concerned with the same objects but are differently disposed towards them; for the first two exceed and fall short, while the third holds the middle, which is the right, position; and rash men are precipitate, and wish for dangers beforehand but draw back when they are in them, while brave men are keen in the moment of action, but quiet beforehand.[16]

Although he admitted that "what is terrible is not the same for all men," so that the sorts of actions that count as courageous will differ from person to person to some degree, Aristotle argued that the brave person is concerned primarily with the most terrible thing, death, and specifically a noble death.[17]

Bilbo and company face death on numerous occasions in *The Hobbit*. Does Bilbo exhibit an appropriate response to the possibility of dying? Does he meet Aristotle's conditions for courage? One way to find out is to see whether Bilbo acts on the best reasons available given uncertain outcomes. If he pursues danger when the risk is unreasonable, he is rash. If he runs away when the risk is reasonable, he is cowardly.

Bilbo clearly experiences fear. He shrieks like a teakettle and shakes like melting jelly when he first learns of the dwarves' dangerous quest. He was "very much alarmed" when faced with the prospect of swiping the trolls' roast mutton.[18] His head swam and he closed his eyes when he was carried high aloft by an eagle.[19] And many times he wished he were back home in his safe and comfortable underground hobbit-hole.

In addition, Bilbo doesn't go boldly into situations that demand caution. If anything, he cowers until he absolutely has to act. When preparing to leave Beorn's home, Bilbo asks Gandalf if they really have to go through Mirkwood Forest. Gandalf explains that all other paths are far worse. It is thus fear of the alternatives that puts them on the least dangerous of paths. In the depths of the Lonely Mountain, under pressure about which course to take, Bilbo explains very simply, "Personally I have no hopes at all, and wish I was safe back at home."[20]

Moreover, Bilbo's decisions are, on the whole, consistent with the best reasons available. We've seen that he and the group should have left the light of the trolls alone, since there was much less chance of trouble by suffering through the night. And we know he wouldn't have risked spying on Smaug had "he known more about dragons and their wily ways."[21] But, of course, he didn't have that information.

We've also seen that it was reasonable for Bilbo and his companions to follow the light of the Wood-elves despite the fact that it led them into the clutches of the spiders. In addition, Bilbo risks his life to save his companions from the spiders, from the confinement of the Wood-elves, and in the battle with the goblins in the Misty Mountains. In each case, he could have used Gollum's ring, become invisible, and escaped danger. But he valued the lives of his companions and the defeat of the goblins as noble goals and worth the risk of death.

Most important, Tolkien gives us an extra glimpse of what the hobbit is really made of when Bilbo is walking alone into the depths of the Lonely Mountain and he begins to sense the presence of Smaug:

> It was at this point that Bilbo stopped. Going on from there was the bravest thing he ever did. The tremendous things that happened afterwards were as nothing compared to it. He fought the real battle in the tunnel alone, before he ever saw the vast danger that lay in wait.[22]

So in these situations Bilbo does meet the classical standards for courageous action. But can we say he is a courageous person, that he possesses the virtue of courage? According to Aristotle, it's not always easy to tell.

Aristotle would probably agree that Bilbo has acted courageously in the few situations we've discussed. But there may be other times when he acts rashly or cowardly. What should we say of someone's character when he or she acts inconsistently, as most of us do?

Aristotle argued that our character is built over time. To possess a virtue, one must practice it. Lifting weights at the gym one time is good exercise, but it doesn't make you strong. To become strong, you must lift weights lots of times over many years. Taking a couple of weeks off will set you back in your progress. For Aristotle, the same is true for our moral "muscles." To become virtuous, we must flex against the temptation to act badly. The more we act virtuously in the face of moral resistance, the closer we will come to being virtuous.

So instead of saying simply that Bilbo is courageous, we can say that he has acted courageously and is developing the virtue of courage. A still greater temptation awaits Bilbo in *The Lord of the Rings*, and once again he will find himself having lost much "more than spoons."[23]

NOTES

1. J. R. R. Tolkien, *The Hobbit: or, There and Back Again* (New York: Del Rey/Ballantine Books, 2001), 33.

2. Aristotle, *Nicomachean Ethics*, trans. W. D. Ross, in *The Basic Works of Aristotle*, ed. Richard McKeon (New York: Random House, 2001).

3. Tolkien, *The Hobbit*, 74.

4. Ibid., 76.

5. Philosophers do, however, regularly criticize faulty data-gathering techniques.

6. Philosophers who work on problems with reasoning are typically concerned with one of two fields. They study either epistemology, which is the study of knowledge and reasons for belief or action, or logic, which is the study of all kinds of reasoning. Many mathematicians and economists also work in reasoning-related fields, like decision theory and game theory. Philosophers benefit greatly from their interactions with experts in these fields.

7. This can also make you a Yahtzee master! For a more involved introduction to expected utility theory, see Ian Hacking, *An Introduction to Probability and Inductive Logic* (Cambridge, UK: Cambridge University Press, 2001).

8. Companies and organizations can use expected utility as long as the group values the same outcomes—for instance, greater profit margin or reducing overhead. In our case, Bilbo might value the creature comforts of home more than he fears trouble. But since he is the son of Belladonna Took, probably not.

9. One alternative is to employ the basic idea of expected utility but to use abstractions rather than real numbers: positive (+), negative (−), and zero (0). (For more on qualitative reasoning, see Simon Parsons, *Qualitative Methods for Reasoning under Uncertainty* ([Cambridge, MA: MIT Press, 2001]). If we judge both outcomes of a decision to be positive, the overall decision is a positive one and probably a safe bet. If both are negative, the decision is negative and probably a poor choice. There is a set of differential equations that makes this approach useful even for complicated decision procedures, but for our simple case, our formula for expected utility will yield the same results. Unfortunately, this method won't help our bedraggled company. Even though we know option 2 is bad, option 1 is unknown. This is because we don't know whether (−) and (+) cancel each other out or whether one is greater than the other. We are in no position to compare results.

10. Conditional probability: $P(B/A) = (P(A) \times P(B)) / P(A)$.

11. To speak precisely about probability, we need a couple of symbols. Let P stand for "the probability that," and let /stand for "given that." So "(K_2/K_1)" should be read: "I draw a king given that I've already drawn a king." Our conditional probability ("The probability that I will draw a king given that I have already drawn a king") now looks like this: $P(K_2/K_1)$. Inserting our figures into our formula from note 10, we can see the difference:

Keeping the first king:	**Putting the first king back:**
$P(K_1) = 4/52$	$P(K_1) = 4/52$
$P(K_2) = 3/51$ (since we kept K_1 out)	$P(K_2) = 4/52$ (since we put K_1 back in the deck)
Therefore: $P(K_2/K_1) =$	Therefore: $P(K_2/K_1) =$
$\dfrac{3/51 \times 4/52}{4/52} = 3/51$ (or 5.9%)	$\dfrac{4/52 \times 4/52}{4/52} = 4/52$ (or 7.7%)

12. Tolkien, *The Hobbit*, 151.

13. Ibid.

14. States of character are "the things in virtue of which we stand well or badly with reference to the passions." Aristotle, *Nicomachean Ethics*, II.5, 1105b25.

15. Someone who has no fear "would be a sort of madman or insensible person." Ibid., III.7, 1115b.

16. Ibid., III.7, 1116a.

17. Ibid., III.6, 1115a.

18. Tolkien, *The Hobbit*, 35.

19. Ibid., 108.

20. Ibid., 221.

21. Ibid.

22. Ibid., 214–15.

23. Ibid., 301.

THERE AND BACK AGAIN

A Song of Innocence and Experience

Joe Kraus

I recently read *The Hobbit* aloud to my sons, then ages six and eight, but I'm not sure that we heard the same book. It's true that the three of us made our way together from the Shire through Mirkwood to the Lonely Mountain, but my experience was different from theirs. I was reading the book for something like the eighth time, but it was new to them.

When they were learning about hobbit-holes, I knew that Bilbo was going to leave for his adventure right away. When they practiced calling roll for all thirteen of the dwarves, I knew that Thorin, Fili, and Kili weren't going to make it. And when they cheered Bilbo's eventual return, I knew it was only a temporary end; I knew from *The Lord of the Rings* that Bilbo's "precious" represented an evil so powerful that it would drain him, leaving him so wounded that he could find healing only by retiring to Rivendell and ultimately by leaving Middle-earth.

While they were going through a story I assured them was worth listening to, I was revisiting the prequel to a larger story, one small chapter in the whole elaborate history of Tolkien's Middle-earth. I wanted to share the book with them because I hoped they'd enjoy it. There was no way I could tell them how different the book looks to someone who knows that else-where in the saga, Morgoth torments the children of Húrin, the Witch-king slaughters the people of Arnor in their homes, or the destruction of the One Ring carries with it the melan-choly of the final passing of the elves.

In other words, *The Hobbit* works in two different and con-flicting ways, depending on how much experience you bring to reading it. To someone who knows nothing about Tolkien's world, it's the best introduction because it assumes no familiarity with the other work and because it echoes a fairy-tale adventure formula. To readers who know their Tolkien already, it offers the opposite appeal. At that point, the challenge is to recover the simple joy of what can seem like a children's story and reconcile it with the darker, heavier work of *The Lord of the Rings* and tales of the Elder Days. That is, it calls on experienced readers to try to return to a state of comparative innocence; it calls on us to go back to the beginning with full awareness of the end.

Consider, for instance, the half promise near the beginning of *The Hobbit*: "This is a story of how a Baggins had an adven-ture, and found himself doing and saying things altogether unexpected. He may have lost the neighbours' respect, but he gained—well you will see whether he gained anything in the end."[1] Read in an innocent light, the break in the sentence seems to promise an old "Once upon a time" sort of tale, imply-ing that we should just sit back and enjoy a rollicking story.

Read in line with what we come to know of Bilbo, however—that the Ring begins to consume him and that "a Baggins" is the subject of a terrifying manhunt throughout

The Lord of the Rings—the break is more ominous. It seems to question whether Bilbo did in fact gain anything in the end. His adventures cost him his innocence and perhaps led him to a darker and more troubled life than the one he would have known if he had simply shut the door on those dwarves while he still had the chance.

Put into a philosophical context, then, one of the questions that *The Hobbit* poses is how to understand innocence in light of later experience. The book's subtitle is *There and Back Again*, but it's worth asking whether Bilbo—at least the Bilbo who worried so much about having clean plates on the morning of the unexpected party—ever really does return from his adventures. In terms of the common good, Bilbo does the right thing.

In terms of himself, though, Bilbo's decision to venture off costs him much of the happiness he knew. He makes a choice on the morning that he sets off with the dwarves, and for all the eventual good it brings to his innocent and sometimes dislikable neighbors, it brings him enough personal disaster that we ought to question whether his stories and treasure are sufficient compensation. In other words, Bilbo trades his innocence for all of his later experiences, but that's a one-way bargain. He can't know the terms to which he is agreeing before he makes the exchange, and he can't undo it once he's begun.

There but Not Quite Back Again

The English Romantic poets of the late eighteenth and early nineteenth centuries believed that we cannot truly understand what we've experienced until we reflect on it in light of the innocence it has cost us. William Wordsworth (1770–1850) argued that true poetry was the product of "emotion recollected in tranquility." As he wrote in the Preface to *Lyrical Ballads*—basically the White Album of the Romantic movement, since it produced many of the era's "greatest hits"— poetry is not so much experience as recalling experience.

That recollection can be restorative—it can return us to the original experience—or it can lead us to a sense of our own distance from who we were.

Wordsworth felt so strongly about the process that he proposed almost a recipe for writing poetry, urging would-be poets to try to re-experience the things that moved them until they could write about them. He wrote, "The emotion is contemplated till, by a species of reaction, the tranquility gradually disappears, and an emotion, kindred to that which was before the subject of contemplation, is gradually produced, and does itself actually exist in the mind."[2]

It may take a bit to untangle all of that, but the gist of it is that Wordsworth and his Romantic contemporaries were interested in how they had changed as a consequence of what they'd gone through. Some of their poetry took them back, allowing them to feel again what they had felt in their youth. Much of it, though, measured the loss they felt in growing from the boys they were into the men they became. More often than not, melancholy won out over celebration, and they failed at the hope of returning to a state of relative innocence. They often asked, in other words, whether growing up isn't a kind of wound from which they could not recover.

Consider, for example, "Lines Written in Early Spring," one of the *Lyrical Ballads*, in which Wordsworth revisited a stream outside the village of Alford. Reflecting on how the place had changed in the decades since he had been there as a child, the poet contrasted his experience of nature with the things he had learned:

> To her fair works did Nature link
> The human soul that through me ran;
> And much it grieved my heart to think
> What man has made of man.[3]

That is, the joy he felt alongside the stream was something pure, something that Nature had made clear to him as a child.

At the same time, he realized that in the course of living his life, he had allowed himself to forget that childhood certainty. In becoming a man, he had made of himself something different, something that struck him as less than what he had been. He had paid a price for growing up, and while it might have been too late to do anything about it, he had at least written the poem as a means of recovering some of what he had lost.

If such Romantic poetry seems a bit far afield of the Shire, it's worth pointing out that many critics see Tolkien as something of a Romantic himself. Like Wordsworth, he favors the idea that we discover our real selves in nature rather than in the midst of others; this idea is particularly clear in the way that Bilbo finds his inner Took only after he enters the wilderness.

Also like the Romantics, Tolkien has a particular interest in the culture of the "folk": the songs, fairy tales, and legends that uneducated communities preserve. In fact, he claims on a few occasions that he began the entire Middle-earth project in order to create a world within which he could present his various invented languages, to create an imaginary folk culture that could serve as the home to the creations he'd dreamed up. In some ways, then, his whole project is an effort to recover a lost, more innocent, sense of the capacity for wonder.

Bilbo himself proves a kind of Romantic figure. Throughout *The Hobbit*, as he ventures from one place to another, he appreciates the splendors he sees, and he finds a way to listen to his own inner voice. Toward the end, when he recognizes that Thorin's greed has compromised not just himself but the entire network of elves, men, and dwarves, he determines to act when others are paralyzed. He asks himself, not others, what the right thing to do is, and then he does it.

In that light, Bilbo's politically sophisticated maneuver is largely a product of the innocence that he has preserved. As Thorin says in his dying conversation, "There is more in you of good than you know, child of the kindly West. Some courage and some wisdom, blended in measure. If more of us valued food and cheer and song above hoarded gold, it would be a merrier world."[4]

Although Thorin clearly intends those words as a compliment, they reflect a strange ambivalence. Referring to Bilbo as a child underscores that he is *un*sophisticated, someone essentially unaware of the forces he has manipulated to happy but perhaps accidental success. And in suggesting that Bilbo shouldn't value hoarded gold, Thorin essentially apologizes for involving Bilbo in the first place. It was, after all, a promise of one-fourteenth of the profits that Thorin originally used to persuade the hobbit to join their Company.

At the end, then, too late to do anything other than praise it, Thorin sees in Bilbo a capacity for simple, childish joys that he suppressed in himself. Even aware of the great victory he has won for his clan of dwarves, Thorin sees virtues in Bilbo that make him question whether it would have been better if he'd never begun the adventure at all.

Seen in that light, the opening pages of *The Fellowship of the Ring* operate, in part, to show the extent of the Ring's evil. When we meet Bilbo again, he has grown tired of the world that so delighted him. The Shire seems small, his old friends seem petty, and he has determined that only another adventure will bring him happiness. He has, in other words, come to value what happened to him more than the experiences of his present-day world.

Most chilling is that he finds himself unable to let go of the Ring. He clings to it, preferring the golden thing to the love he feels for Gandalf and Frodo, and only when he inadvertently calls it his "precious"—a term that Gandalf has to remind him was originally Gollum's—does he sense the extent of his own falling away from himself.

Complicating that situation is the fact that according to Tolkien, we are supposed to understand Bilbo as the essential author of his own story. Although *The Hobbit* is told in the third person, Tolkien invents a history for the text itself, one that begins with Bilbo writing most of what becomes the Red Book of Westmarch, the basis for the eventual version that we have.[5] As part of that, we learn that Bilbo also wrote many of the songs from *The Hobbit* and *The Lord of the Rings* and that he is an accomplished enough writer that Aragorn himself works with him on his compositions.

By the time we meet him again at Elrond's house in *The Fellowship of the Ring*, Bilbo isn't merely someone with a Romantic sensibility; he's actually a parody of a failed Romantic poet who has given in to melancholy and nostalgia. Bilbo is so consumed by the business of recording his past that he regularly excuses himself from the elves' merrymaking to remain alone with pen and manuscript. He is changed, in some ways clearly for the worse, as a result of his experiences.[6]

Some Who Wander Are Lost, or Growing Up Is Hard to Do

William Blake (1757–1827), one of Wordsworth's contemporaries, came closer than any of the other Romantic poets to describing a philosophy of experience. For him, there were two essential states: the innocence of a child and the experience of an adult. Although that contrast may seem unremarkable, consider that it crosses two more common contrasts: childishness with adulthood and innocence with guilt.

Blake wasn't saying that all adults were guilty—and as a father, I can assure you that not all children are innocent—but he combined the two in order to highlight the price we pay for our experiences. It isn't necessarily the case that we turn bad as we grow up, but growing up costs us a state that gave us a more natural relation to the world. That is, innocence has its own kind of wisdom, and we cannot be aware of its power until it's too late, until we gain enough experience to look back on a condition now closed to us.

Blake explored the two conditions in two of his most famous works, sets of poems he called *Songs of Innocence* and *Songs of Experience*. If you've studied poetry at all, it's likely that you've come across some of them. He asked in "The Lamb," for instance, "Little Lamb, who made thee?"[7] This concern becomes more complicated in "The Tyger": "Tyger! Tyger! burning bright / In the forests of the night, / What immortal hand or eye / Could frame thy fearful symmetry?"[8] Each question asks the same thing: "Where do you come from?" In the case of the lamb, however, a creature compared to Christ in its innocence, the poet didn't expect an answer. It's a way of talking almost to a baby, a poetic version of "Who gave you those pretty little eyes?"

The Tyger is something else, however, a dangerous creature capable of hurting others, a creature that ought to cause terror as we look at it. Whether the poem is supposed to be about tigers as we know them or about some dream of a more sinister and demonic creature isn't clear. What we do know, however, is that we cannot so easily escape the question of where it comes from. This is nothing like baby talk; it's a serious inquiry into the nature of evil. The poet later asked, "Did he who made the Lamb make thee?" and the implications are troubling.[9] If the answer is yes, if the same divine power that shaped the innocent lamb made the dangerous Tyger, then that power is not so loving and providential as we'd like. If the answer is no, if some other power could create such a thing, then there is a fearful capacity for evil at work in the universe.

The crucial difference between the two sets of poems, *Songs of Innocence* and *Songs of Experience*, comes not in their subject matter but in their perspective. The first set consists of the poems of a child discovering the world and trying to name it. The second set consists of the meditations of a philosopher, the troubling questions that came to the poet as he grew and saw more of the world.

Blake eventually published the two sets together as a single collection, and part of the experience of reading the poems is to get a sense of how each set contrasts and complements the other. *Songs of Innocence* has a beautiful simplicity to it, but it takes on its more substantial power only in light of the darker perspective of *Songs of Experience*. The early poems contain a perpetual wisdom that only experience makes clear: that there is a joy in the world around us, a joy that we lose as a price of exploring what lies beyond that which we can immediately discover.

Blake is relevant for thinking about Tolkien because at least some critics see him as one of Tolkien's inspirations.[10] Although it isn't clear from the shorter poems, Blake used his longer narrative poems to invent a whole universe of symbols and characters representing questions about the nature of human experience in a world much larger than ourselves. He wrote about strange, angelic and demonic types of figures named Thel, Urizen, Orc, and Ahania, and he produced lavishly illustrated editions of his own work, helping to move forward the science of lithography as he did so.

Blake stopped short of inventing his own languages, but the scope of his project—not to mention its religious overtones—makes it appear to some readers as an inspiration for Tolkien's own lifelong project. I'm not saying that the Tyger was the model for Smaug, but they do have a great deal in common. Each is a creature that threatens innocents, and its very existence calls on us to ask how it's possible for evil to exist side by side with goodness. What immortal hand or eye could give us both the comforts of Eden (or the Shire) and the terrors of World War II (or Sauron)?

Such questions come through more clearly in Tolkien's later work, but we can see him starting to raise them in *The Hobbit*. Consider, for instance, the way he introduces Elrond. "In those days of our tale there were still some people who had both elves and heroes of the North for their ancestors, and Elrond the master of the house was their chief."[11] That is, he tries to let us see Elrond as both a figure in Bilbo's fairy tale and a representative of the deeper and darker histories that he and his son Christopher eventually pulled together as *The Silmarillion*. That brief introduction, the first published reference to Elrond, seems a peculiar compromise. It's more than any first-time reader of Tolkien can likely grasp, yet it is also vague and unilluminating to anyone who's read *The Lord of the Rings* with much care.

Tolkien's dilemma in describing Elrond's first appearance is telling. From Tolkien's other writings, we learn that Elrond is over sixty-five hundred years old, that his great-great-grandmother was Melian, a divine being of the race of the Maiar, and that his father, Eärendil, is what we know as the planet Venus. We can't appreciate who this remarkable being is without having a sense of the scope of the Elder Tales, but we can't enter the Elder Tales without first experiencing the charm of *The Hobbit* and developing the interest necessary for reading on.

We cannot, in other words, appreciate Elrond the first time we meet him. By the time we have the experience necessary to get a sense of his importance to the wider Middle-earth story, however, we've lost the innocent perspective—innocent in Blake's sense of the term—to which the description appealed. We cannot be both "there" and "back" at the same time.

Striving to Be Original, Again and Again

The most famous of the American Romantics, Ralph Waldo Emerson (1803–1882), began his work with an almost ecstatic optimism about the possibility of discovering a new sense of self in nature. In several of his early essays and lectures, he proposed what I like to call the Declaration of Intellectual Independence through his insistence that nineteenth-century Americans could discover an "original relation to the universe" if they cast aside what they'd been taught, relied on their own intuitive wisdom, and declared themselves free of all expectations.[12]

Emerson had no patience for the melancholy that sometimes afflicted the English Romantics. He called on people to forget what they thought they knew and to trust in the power of fresh experience to shape them into something original, something worthy at the artistic and intellectual level of the political freedom that the American Revolution had won two generations earlier.

In the relative innocence of his early years as the leading U.S. philosopher and poet, Emerson often seemed willing to risk everything he knew in one intellectual experiment after another. His essays are notoriously difficult, but most of them follow a similar path: they deal with a particular contemporary topic and then gradually find their way to his usual theme. It's easy to get lost in individual sentences from Emerson's work, but they almost all point to the same insistent claim: that the self sits at the center of the universe and that we have the potential to discover a radical new self if only we grant ourselves the freedom.

In one of the weirdest images in literature, at the end of the first chapter of his book *Nature*, Emerson declares, "In the woods, we return to reason and faith. There I feel that nothing can befall me in life,—no disgrace, no calamity, (leaving me my eyes) which nature cannot repair. Standing on the bare ground,—my head bathed by the blithe air, and uplifted into infinite space,—all mean egotism vanishes. I become a transparent eyeball; I am nothing; I see all."[13]

At one level, at least, Emerson is trying to describe a sense of innocence different from Blake's. Rather than understanding it as something that we necessarily lose as we age, he sees it as something that we can strive to grasp even as adults. We pay a price for such grasping, though, and that price is the certainty that experience gives to most of us. We force ourselves to become, in at least one dimension, childlike again; we willingly set aside what we think we know for the chance of something dramatically new. The image is arresting and troubling. It doesn't easily resolve itself into a clear claim, yet it remains a famous and often quoted description. If you want originality, there it is.

The transparent eyeball as a liberating image has implications for Bilbo, of course, since that is more or less what he becomes whenever he slips the Ring onto his finger. Once he is someone who can see others and not be seen himself, he discovers parts of the world he'd never seen before. The first time he wears the Ring, he finds he has the opportunity to stab Gollum in the back, yet in one of the great moments of grace in Tolkien's work, he resists the temptation.

The text says, "A sudden understanding, a pity mixed with horror, welled up in Bilbo's heart: a glimpse of endless stone, cold fish, sneaking and whispering."[14] In his first, most innocent encounter with the Ring, his invisibility gives him a glimpse into another's humanity. The power to see and not be seen—the power to be, by Emerson's lights, innocent in the face of what he confronts—liberates him and allows him to show mercy in a way that, as the end of *The Lord of the Rings* shows, proves essential to Sauron's downfall.

In that light, it's troubling to consider that in *The Lord of the Rings*, the image of the transparent eyeball belongs not to a hobbit but to Sauron himself. That awful unblinking eye, the original intellect that used the Ring to create a new and more powerful self capable of governing all of Middle-earth, is evil incarnate, but it is also an emblem of experience, of the certainty that comes from ages of scheming toward a single goal.

Sauron boasts of his power to see everyone at all times, and that terrifies on two levels. First, he claims to know what you are doing. Second, he claims to know who you are. His knowledge of you, his ability to guess when you are most vulnerable to the suggestion of the Ring or to the allure of power, threatens to define you. Sauron counts on his ability to inflame your desire for wealth, power, and control, and his Ring most easily commands those who already share his desires. For others, it takes longer, but the poison is more sinister; it eats away at the innocent sense of self of a Frodo or a Bilbo, replacing that childish virtue with Sauron's own desire. As we come to see, the great drama that Frodo endures is the internal one that pits his innocence against the Ring's determination to awaken his inner tyrant.

In *The Hobbit*, Bilbo has no consciousness of the potential for evil in the Ring; when we reread the book after *The Lord of the Rings*, however, it's hard not to see it. The Bilbo who dances the spiders away is a comical and funny fellow, but with more experience of Tolkien—with the knowledge that Bilbo will one day feel thin and stretched as he almost enters the shadow world—it's hard not to see him as we might see the young Marie Curie. For all of his pluck, and for all of her elegant inventiveness, they're playing with something radioactive, something that is exacting a price from them deeper and darker than their innocence can comprehend.

Back Again to the Beginning

When he chose *There and Back Again* for his subtitle, Tolkien was almost certainly aware of its echoing the Greek word *nostos*, usually translated as "homecoming." The Greeks saw a return home as a cause for celebration, and their word comes to us in English as the root of "nostalgia." We can see in that a darker ambiguity, however. That is, the problem of nostalgia is that it celebrates what *was* over what *is*. It's one form of melancholy, one price that we often pay for venturing away in the first place.

The Bilbo who spends his days scribbling at Elrond's house is so overcome with nostalgia that, ironically, he cannot see, in at least one crucial way, that he has never returned to the home he left. His experiences—mostly the burden of carrying the Ring in the decades after his adventures with the dwarves—have transformed him. They have sapped him of the childish wisdom that Thorin recognized in him, the innocence that let him, for at least the duration of *The Hobbit*, imagine that he could return.

Soon after my sons and I finished reading *The Hobbit*, Richie, the older one, began demanding that we move on to *The Lord of the Rings*. I was happy to give it a shot, and we managed to get all the way through Moria, to not long after Gandalf's fall and the Company's meeting Galadriel. At that point, though, Max, my younger son, said he'd had enough. When we pressed him for why, he gave varying reasons: it was boring, he was losing track of the different characters, he was scared of what it meant for Gandalf to die, and he sensed that some still more frightening things were coming. Richie and I tried to keep him interested, dragging him through a chapter or two, but he eventually refused to travel with us.

I like to think that Max recognized part of what *The Hobbit* has to tell us. There are rewards for leaving one's home and then returning to it, but there is a heavy price to pay as well. I like to think that Max, saddened by the deaths of Thorin, Fili, and Kili at the end of the prequel, sensed that reading *The Lord of the Rings* would call on him to experience more deaths, more terror, and a greater sense of the profound evil that the Ring represents.

I don't claim that my six-year-old had the sense to intuit one of Tolkien's subtler insights. Instead, I mean that Tolkien seems at least partly to have understood one of the truths that most of us know when we are six and then somehow forget. Our first homes satisfy us because they preserve us in all our childish sensibilities. When we leave them, we risk our innocence; we trade something we can never recover for an uncertainty.

We who have left childhood behind, we who have read what comes after *The Hobbit*, should perhaps listen to the six-year-olds who know in some ineffable way that there is no returning to childhood. We should perhaps consider that even though Bilbo "remained very happy to the very end of his days,"[15] he might have been even happier if—assuming Gandalf found someone else to fight dragons—he'd remained in his comfortable home, leaving the experience of adventure to someone else.

NOTES

1. J. R. R. Tolkien, *The Hobbit: or, There and Back Again* (New York: Del Rey/Ballantine Books, 2001), 2.

2. William Wordsworth, "Preface to *Lyrical Ballads*, with Pastoral and Other Poems," in *Selected Poems*, ed. John O. Hayden (London: Penguin Books, 1994), 450.

3. Ibid., 61.

4. Tolkien, *The Hobbit*, 290.

5. There is, in fact, a strange moment during the Council of Elrond in *The Lord of the Rings* when Gandalf has to explain that Bilbo is now relating the true story of how he got the Ring from Gollum. Those of us who have read *The Hobbit* as it stands in all of the editions available over the last fifty years end up hearing the story that we have always heard. In the first edition of *The Hobbit*, however, the story was somewhat different, a fact that Gandalf accounts for in his claim that Bilbo initially lied.

6. For ways in which Bilbo becomes ennobled as a result of his experiences, see chapter 1 in this volume.

7. William Blake, *Poetry and Prose of William Blake*, ed. David V. Erdman (New York: Doubleday, 1970), 8.

8. Ibid., 24.

9. Ibid., 8.

10. For discussions of possible connections between Tolkien and Blake, see Robley Evans, *J. R. R. Tolkien* (New York: Warner Books, 1972), 25–26, 45–46; and Randall Helms, *Tolkien's World* (Boston: Houghton Mifflin, 1974), 57–59, 69–72. According to his diary, Tolkien first read Blake's prophetic books in early 1919 and was astonished at some of the similarities between Blake's imaginative creations and his own. Christina Scull and Wayne G. Hammond, *The J. R. R. Tolkien Companion and Guide: Chronology* (Boston: Houghton Mifflin, 2006), 107–108.

11. Tolkien, *The Hobbit*, 51.

12. Ralph Waldo Emerson, "Nature," in *The Complete Essays and Other Writings of Ralph Waldo Emerson*, ed. Brooks Atkinson (New York: Modern Library, 1950), 3.

13. Ibid., 6.

14. Tolkien, *The Hobbit*, 87.

15. Ibid., 304.

CONTRIBUTORS

Our Most Excellent and Audacious Contributors

Gregory Bassham is a professor and the chair of the Philosophy Department at King's College (Pennsylvania), where he specializes in the philosophy of law and critical thinking. He edited *The Ultimate Harry Potter and Philosophy* (2010), coedited The Lord of the Rings *and Philosophy* (2003) and The Chronicles of Narnia *and Philosophy* (2005), and is coauthor of *Critical Thinking: A Student's Introduction* (2010). Wheels, engines, and explosions have always delighted him.

Michael C. Brannigan is the George and Jane Pfaff–Endowed Chair in Ethics and Moral Values at the College of Saint Rose in Albany, New York. He also has a joint appointment with the Alden March Bioethics Institute at Albany Medical College. His specializations are ethics, medical ethics, Asian philosophy, and intercultural studies. He has written numerous articles, and his books include *The Pulse of Wisdom: The Philosophies of India, China, and Japan* (1999), *Striking a Balance: A Primer on Traditional Asian Values* (2009), *Healthcare Ethics in a Diverse Society* (2001, coauthored), *Ethical Issues in Human Cloning* (2000, edited), *Cross-Cultural Biotechnology* (2004), and *Ethics across Cultures* (2004). For fun, he plays piano, ocean-kayaks, and practices martial arts. As with Balin, a little beer would suit him better.

Eric Bronson is a visiting professor in the Humanities Department at York University in Toronto. He edited The Girl with the Dragon Tattoo *and Philosophy* (2011), *Poker and Philosophy* (2006), and *Baseball and Philosophy* (2004), and coedited The Lord of the Rings *and Philosophy* (2003). He is currently writing a Gollum-inspired cookbook for "things more slimy than fish."

Laura Garcia is a scholar in residence in the Boston College Philosophy Department, where she specializes in the philosophy of religion and metaphysics. She also writes on sex, marriage, and personalist feminism, taking the radical view that the three are compatible and mutually reinforcing. Laura enjoys reading, writing, slinking, and nosing about.

Tom Grimwood teaches at Lancaster University and the Open University and is an honorary research fellow at the University of Cumbria. His research focuses on the relationship between interpretation, ambiguity, and ethics, and he has written about this on a range of areas including medieval anorexia, Friedrich Nietzsche, Simone de Beauvoir, and *Lost*; with articles in journals such as the *British Journal for the History of Philosophy*, *Angelaki*, and the *Journal for Cultural Research*. While usually found sitting at his desk, he does always keep a "detachable party hood" nearby in case of adventure.

Randall M. Jensen is a professor of philosophy at Northwestern College in Orange City, Iowa. His philosophical interests include ethics, ancient Greek philosophy, and the philosophy of religion. He has written several chapters connecting philosophy and popular culture, including essays in Battlestar Galactica *and Philosophy*, Batman *and Philosophy*, and The Office *and Philosophy*. He regularly teaches a course on the writings of J. R. R. Tolkien and C. S. Lewis. He's convinced that Gandalf's interrogation of Bilbo's sincerely offered "Good morning!" demonstrates that the wizard is a true philosopher.

David Kyle Johnson is an assistant professor of philosophy at King's College (Pennsylvania). His philosophical specializations include the philosophy of religion, logic, and metaphysics. He edited *Heroes and Philosophy: Buy the Book, Save the World* (2009), *Introducing Philosophy through Pop Culture* (2010, with William Irwin), and Inception *and Philosophy: Because It's Never Just a Dream* (2011). He has also contributed to books on *South Park, Family Guy, The Office, Battlestar Galactica*, Quentin Tarantino, Johnny Cash, *Batman, The Colbert Report, Doctor Who*, and Christmas. Kyle has taught many classes that focus on the relevance of philosophy to pop culture, including a course devoted to *South Park* and another devoted to *Star Trek*. He is not a member of the White Council, but he does do consulting work for it from time to time. The other members usually don't listen.

Amy Kind, whose specialty is philosophy of mind, teaches at Claremont McKenna College (California). Her research has appeared in journals such as *Philosophy and Phenomenological Research, Philosophical Studies*, and the *Philosophical Quarterly*, and she has also previously written on philosophy and pop culture topics such as *Battlestar Galactica, Star Trek*, Harry Potter, and *Angel*. She was recently pleased to learn from the Hobbit Name Generator that her hobbit name is Azaelia Broadbelt of Buckland.

Dennis Knepp teaches philosophy and religious studies east of the misty Cascade Mountains at Big Bend Community College in Moses Lake, Washington. His previous essays have appeared in Twilight *and Philosophy*, Alice in Wonderland *and Philosophy*, and The Girl in the Dragon Tattoo *and Philosophy*.

He hopes this book explains what a burrahobbit is and whether yer can cook 'em.

Joe Kraus is an associate professor of English and theater at the University of Scranton (Pennsylvania), where he teaches American literature and creative writing and directs the honors program. He is coauthor of *An Accidental Anarchist* (2000), and his work has appeared, among other places, in the *American Scholar*, *Callaloo*, *Riverteeth*, the *Centennial Review*, *Moment*, and other volumes of the Popular Culture and Philosophy series. On occasion, and for no apparent purpose, he interrupts his lectures with the shout "Dawn take you all!"

Craig Lindahl-Urben earned a BA in philosophy at Reed College in Portland, Oregon, and has spent many years in the computer industry, both as owner of a computer software company and as an executive for large computer companies. He was formerly the publisher and editor in chief of a weekly newspaper but always wanted to live in the Last Homely House if he couldn't persuade Bombadil to take him on as an apprentice.

Anna Minore is an assistant professor of theology at King's College (Pennsylvania). She has a PhD in theology and spirituality from Catholic University of America and an MA in the history of religion from Syracuse University (New York). She has taught courses in world religions, the spirituality of the body, and female mystics. Gollum gave her nightmares as a child, and she is happy to render him a hungry ghost as an adult.

David L. O'Hara is an associate professor of philosophy and classics at Augustana College (South Dakota). He is coauthor of *From Homer to Harry Potter: A Handbook of Myth and Fantasy* (2006) and *Narnia and the Fields of Arbol: The Environmental Vision of C. S. Lewis* (2008). A lover of games and sports, he plays on his faculty dodgeball, kickball, and golf(imbul) teams. He hates leaving home without a pocket handkerchief.

Grant Sterling is an associate professor of philosophy at Eastern Illinois University, specializing in ethics and medieval philosophy. He is the author of *Ethical Intuitionism and Its Critics* and is currently coauthoring *What Is Judicial Activism?* He teaches a class on the philosophical ideas in Tolkien and has presented papers and published essays on the subject. He loves maps, runes, letters, and cunning handwriting, although his own writing is thin and spidery.

W. Christopher Stewart is a professor of philosophy at Houghton College, which is situated in a rural hamlet in western New York, where there is not much noise and there is plenty of green. Although he is passionate about the history and philosophy of science and owns a car, he shares Tolkien's disdain for both electric street lamps and "the noise, stench, ruthlessness, and extravagance of the internal-combustion engine."

Charles Taliaferro, a professor of philosophy at St. Olaf College (Minnesota), is the author or editor of fourteen books, including *The Image in Mind*, coauthored with the American painter Jil Evans, and has contributed to other volumes on philosophy and popular culture. Although Taliaferro has never slain an actual dragon, out of an overactive imagination and an admiration for Bard the Bowman he once built a twenty-five-foot-long dragon out of wood and cloth that he then battled (successfully) in an effort to save a small town in North America.

Philip Tallon is an affiliate professor of philosophy and religion at Asbury Theological Seminary (Kentucky). He is the author of *The Poetics of Evil* (2011) and coeditor of *The Philosophy of Sherlock Holmes* (forthcoming). He recently celebrated his eleventy-first birthday.

Jamie Carlin Watson is an assistant professor of philosophy and the chairman of the Department of Religion and

Philosophy at Young Harris College (Georgia). He is coauthor (with Robert Arp) of *Philosophy Demystified* (2011), *What's Good on TV: Understanding Ethics through Television* (2011), and *Critical Thinking: An Introduction to Reasoning Well* (2011), and he has contributed to a variety of popular culture and philosophy compilations, including "The Beast in Me: Evil in Cash's Christian Worldview," in *Johnny Cash and Philosophy*, and "For *L'Amore*: Love and Friendship in *The Office*," in The Office *and Philosophy*. Jamie hopes that one of his wanderings will end with gold and a dragon, although he knows he's probably too risk averse for that.

INDEX

The Moon Letters